PRAISE FOR CATHY GLASS

'Poignant and revealing ... real-life stories such as these have helped to move and inspire a generation' *Sunday Mirror*

'A true tale of hope' *OK!* Magazine

'Heartbreaking' *Mirror*

'A life-affirming read ... that proves sometimes a little hope is all you need' *Heat* Magazine

'A hugely touching and emotional true tale' *Star* Magazine

'Foster carers rarely get the praise they deserve, but Cathy Glass's book should change all that' *First* Magazine

'Cannot fail to move those who read it' *Adoption-net*

'Once again, Cathy Glass has blown me away with a poignant story' The Writing Garnet, book blogger

'Brilliant book. I'd expect nothing less from Cathy ... I cried, of course' Goodreads review

'... gripping page-turner from start to finish ... emotive and heart-wrenching ...' Kate Hall, book blogger

'… another great read … no complex narrative, just pure storytelling …'   5* Kindle review

'Filled with compassion and love'   Victoria Goldman,
Lovereading

'Never disappoints and brings a tear to my eye'   Hannah,
book blogger

'Simply yet eloquently told … Cathy's years of fostering experience shine a beam of light across the pages'
Liz Robinson,
Lovereading

'Amazing writing from an incredible lady'
5* Amazon review

'Wonderfully written book'   5* Kindle review

'A captivating insight into the life of a foster carer'
Victoria Goldman,
Lovereading

'I have read all Cathy Glass's books and none disappoint'
5* Amazon review

'Great job, Cathy Glass. Keep doing what you do and I'll keep reading'   Goodreads review

Where Has Mummy Gone?

ALSO BY CATHY GLASS

CATHY GLASS

Where Has Mummy Gone?

A young girl
and a mother who
no longer knows her

HARPER
element

Certain details in this story, including names, places and dates, have been changed to protect the family's privacy.

HarperElement
An imprint of HarperCollins*Publishers*
1 London Bridge Street
London SE1 9GF

www.harpercollins.co.uk

First published by HarperElement 2018

9

A catalogue record of this book is available from the British Library

ISBN 978-0-00-830546-8

Printed and bound in Great Britain by
CPI Group (UK) Ltd, Croydon

MIX
Paper from
responsible sources
FSC™ C007454

ACKNOWLEDGEMENTS

A big thank you to my family; my editors, Carolyn and Holly; my literary agent, Andrew; my UK publishers HarperCollins, and my overseas publishers, who are now too numerous to list by name. Last, but definitely not least, a big thank you to my readers for your unfailing support and kind words. They are much appreciated.

CHAPTER ONE

FAMILIAR?

I was sure I'd heard it all before …

The child I was being asked to foster had been badly neglected for years by her single mother, who was an intravenous drug user and alcohol dependent. The social services were going to court later that morning to bring the child into care. Melody was eight years of age and had been sleeping on an old stained mattress on the floor of a damp, cold basement flat with her mother, and they were about to be evicted. She hadn't been attending school, and despite the social services putting in support, there was never any food in the cupboards and she and her mother were often hungry, cold and dirty.

'She is also very angry,' Jill, my supervising social worker from the agency I fostered for, continued over the phone. The referral from the social services had come through her.

'The mother is angry?' I asked.

'Yes, and Melody – her child – is too. She tried to kick and thump the social worker when she visited yesterday and threw something at her when she began talking to her mother. The social worker will take a police officer with her when she removes Melody, assuming the care order is granted.'

'Is there any doubt?'

'There shouldn't be, but you never can tell. It will depend on the judge. The case is in court shortly, so it's likely to be early afternoon before they are with you.'

'All right.' Forcibly removing a child from their home wasn't a good start, but if the parent wasn't cooperating there was no alternative. The mother had been given plenty of opportunities to sort out her life and parent her daughter properly but had repeatedly failed.

'Amanda, the mother, can't control Melody,' Jill said. 'She's failed to put in place any boundaries and Melody can easily become angry. One social worker described her as feral.'

One of the reasons I had been asked to foster Melody was because I had years of fostering experience, much of it working with children with challenging behaviour, and I knew why Melody was angry. Even though she had been living in appalling conditions and had not been looked after, she was being taken away from the mother she knew and loved.

'She's very loyal and protective of her mother,' Jill continued, 'and won't hear any criticism of her. They both hate social workers. Melody does as she likes and is very much the one in control.' Again, this wasn't unusual for a child who'd had to raise herself.

'And her father?' I asked. Knowledge of the family helps the foster carer.

'They don't live together. It's unclear if Melody sees him at all. He's also an intravenous drug user. Both parents have served prison sentences for drug dealing.' Which again I'd heard before. 'Melody has four older half-siblings, different fathers. All those children were taken into care and then adopted years ago.'

'Why leave it so long to bring Melody into care?' I asked, almost sure of the answer.

'Her mother, Amanda, is very good at evading the social services,' Jill said. 'She has been moving flats regularly and doesn't answer the door when a social worker visits, or she gets someone else to say they don't live there. The social worker only got access yesterday because the main door was open. It's a multiple-occupancy house and their room is in the basement. The room was freezing, and Melody and her mother were watching television in bed with their coats on.'

'Dear me,' I sighed.

'Amanda has been funding her drug habit from prostitution. If she's brought the clients back to her room, there is a possibility Melody has witnessed her mother with them, and might even have been sexually abused herself. So be vigilant for any disclosures she may make. Oh yes, and she has nits,' Jill added. This was common for children coming into care.

'I assume Melody won't be returning home?'

'Highly unlikely. The social services intend to apply for a Full Care Order, so she will remain in care.' Sad though this was, in cases like these there really was no alternative. It was too early to say if Melody would have the chance of being adopted, but aged eight and with behavioural problems it was unlikely.

'So, Cathy,' Jill said, rounding off, 'that's it really. Neave, the social worker, will phone once she's left court, then she and a colleague will take a police officer to collect Melody from home and come to you. I'll try to be with you when she is placed.'

'Thank you.' Jill, as my supervising social worker, offered support and made sure I had all the information I needed and the correct placement forms were signed when a child was placed.

'See you later then,' she said, and we said goodbye.

Yes, it was a depressingly familiar story, which I was sure I'd heard before about many children brought into care. As it turned out, I couldn't have been more wrong. There was another side to Melody's story, which at this point no one knew.

CHAPTER TWO

SAFE AND HAPPY

Even after many years of fostering I'm still slightly anxious before a new child arrives, wondering if they will like us and what I will be able to do to help them. Now I had the added concern of Melody's angry and challenging behaviour. But by lunchtime I'd given her bedroom a final check, cleaned, hoovered and tidied all the communal areas in the house (I might not have another chance for a while), then I tried to concentrate on the part-time administration work I did mainly from home. As a single parent – my husband having run off with another woman some years before – the admin work plus the small allowance I received from fostering helped to make ends meet. I'd have fostered anyway, even without the allowance. I enjoyed it, and it had become a way of life.

My three children – Adrian, aged sixteen, Lucy, fourteen, and Paula, twelve – were at school, so they'd have a surprise when they arrived home to find Melody here, although it wouldn't be a huge one. Adrian and Paula had grown up with fostering and knew children could arrive at very short notice. Lucy had been in foster care herself before I'd adopted her, so was only too familiar with the way the system worked. (I tell Lucy's story in my book *Will You Love Me?*)

I had a sandwich lunch as I worked and it was nearly two o'clock before the front doorbell rang, signalling Melody's arrival. I felt my pulse step up a beat as I left the paperwork on the table in the front room and went to answer the door. A female social worker I took to be Neave stood on one side of Melody and a male social worker was on the other, as if escorting her.

'Hello, you must be Melody,' I said with a smile. 'Come in. I'm Cathy.'

Melody glared at me but didn't move. 'This is the foster carer I told you about,' Neave said, and touched Melody's arm to encourage her to move forward.

'Get your hands off me!' Melody snapped, angrily shrugging her off, but she did come in.

'I'm Neave, and this is my colleague Jim,' Neave said as they too came in.

Jim shook my hand. I guessed both social workers were in their early forties, and were dressed smartly in dark colours, having come straight from court.

'Shall I take your coats?' I offered, but Neave was already halfway down the hall, looking to see which room she should go in. 'Straight ahead!' I called. Jim took off his coat and also his shoes, which he paired with ours beneath the hall stand.

'Would you like to take off your coat and shoes?' I asked Melody, who was still standing beside us and hadn't followed her social worker into the living room. She looked at me as though I was completely barmy, probably having never taken off her shoes and coat as part of the routine for entering her home. 'We usually do,' I added.

Melody was of average height and build, but her pale skin was grubby. There were dark rings under her eyes from lack of sleep and her brown, shoulder-length hair was unwashed and matted. I already knew she had nits and I would treat those later. Her zip-up anorak was filthy, a long rip down one sleeve showed the white lining and the zipper was undone and hanging off. Beneath her jacket she was wearing a badly stained jumper and short skirt. The skirt and ankle socks she wore were more suitable for summer than winter; her legs must have been freezing. Her filthy plastic trainers had holes in the ends where her toes poked through. Not for the first time since I'd started fostering, I felt greatly saddened that in our reasonably affluent society a child could still appear in this state.

'Are you going to take off your coat and shoes?' Jim now asked.

'No!' Melody said, and headed down the hall.

'That told us,' I said quietly to Jim. He smiled. Foster carers and social workers have to maintain a sense of humour in order to survive the suffering and sadness we see each day. I'd ease Melody into our way of doing things as we went along.

'Would anyone like a drink?' I asked as Jim and I entered the living room.

'Coffee, please,' Neave said from the sofa. 'Milk, no sugar.'

'And for me too, please, if it's not too much trouble,' Jim added.

'And what about you?' I asked Melody, who'd sat next to Neave.

'No. I don't want anything from you.' She scowled.

'OK, maybe later. There's a box of games you might like to look at,' I said, pointing to the toy box of age-appropriate games I'd put out ready. 'There's some children's books on the shelves,' I added.

'Not looking,' she said. Folding her arms defiantly across her chest, she glared at Neave. 'I want to go home. Take me back, now!'

'You know I can't do that,' Neave said. 'I explained in the car what was happening.'

'I don't care what you said. It's not your decision. It's up to me and I want to go home!'

'That's not possible,' Neave said evenly. 'You're staying with Cathy and her family for now, and she is going to look after you very well. You'll do lots of nice things and you'll see your mother soon.'

'I want to see Mum now!' Melody's anger flared and for a moment I thought she was going to hit Neave. Neave thought so too, for she moved further up the sofa. 'My mum needs me!' Melody said with slightly less aggression. Many children come into care believing that their parents won't be able to manage without them, and part of my role is to take away the inappropriate responsibility they've had at home and encourage them to be children.

I made my way towards the kitchen to make the coffee but as I left the living room the front doorbell rang. 'That'll be Jill,' I said, and went to answer it.

'Sorry I'm late,' she said. 'I've come straight from placing another child. Are they here?'

'Yes, just arrived. They're in the living room. I'm about to make coffee. Would you like one?'

'Oh yes, please,' she said gratefully. 'Have you got a biscuit too? I haven't had time for lunch.'

'I could make you a sandwich?' I offered.

'No, a biscuit is fine.'

Jill went into the living room and introduced herself, while

I set about making the coffee. I could hear Jill talking to Melody in a reassuring voice, telling her she would be happy with me, that I'd look after her and there was nothing for her to worry about. Jill was a highly experienced social worker and I greatly valued her input, support and advice.

I took the tray carrying the drinks and a plate of biscuits into the living room and set it on the coffee table. 'Are you sure you wouldn't like a drink?' I asked Melody as I handed out the mugs of coffee.

'No, but I'll have a biscuit.' Standing, she grabbed a handful of biscuits and returned to the sofa to eat them.

'Are you hungry?' Neave asked her as they quickly vanished.

'No,' she snarled.

'I'll make her something to keep her going until dinner once we've finished,' I reassured Neave.

I passed the plate of biscuits to the adults and then put the empty plate on the tray. For a few moments there was quiet as they sipped their coffee and ate the biscuits. I thought Jill wasn't the only one who hadn't had time for lunch. Neave set her half-empty mug on the coffee table and took a wodge of papers from her briefcase. When a child is placed there are formalities that need to be completed, and Neave handed Jill and me a copy each of the Essential Information Form Part 1. This contained the basic information I needed about the child I was fostering, and I began to look through it, as did Jill, while Neave finished her coffee. Much of the information I already knew from Jill. It included Melody's full name, most recent home address, date of birth and her parents' names, and in the box for other family members was printed *Four half-siblings, all adopted*, but not their names.

Melody's ethnicity was given as white British and her first language English. The box for religion showed *None*, and her legal status showed *Interim Care Order*. There were no special dietary requirements and Melody had no known allergies. Her school's name and address were shown with a comment in the box saying she'd only been there since September. It was January now, so she'd joined four months previously.

'Melody changed school last term then?' I asked Neave.

'Yes, with the most recent move,' she replied. 'She's had a lot of changes of school, with long gaps in between when she didn't attend at all. Now she's in care she'll have more stability in her life. She's very behind with her school work.'

'I hate school. I'm not going,' Melody said, her face setting.

'All children have to go to school,' Jill said gently.

'I don't!' Melody snapped.

'You do, love,' I said. 'All the children in this house go to school and tomorrow we'll buy you a nice new school uniform.' Not a bribe, but an incentive.

'I was going to mention her clothing,' Neave said. 'I'm afraid she just has what she is wearing. Her mother said she has other clothes, but they needed washing.'

'Not a problem,' I said. 'We'll use my emergency supply until we can go shopping and buy her new clothes. The school usually sells the uniform, so we can get that tomorrow morning when we go in.'

'That'll be nice, won't it?' Jill said encouragingly, turning to Melody. 'Lots of new clothes.'

Melody scowled, but not quite so forcibly. All children like new things, especially when they haven't had any before.

Jill and I returned to the Essential Information Form. The next line was about special educational needs – *Melody requires classroom support* was printed in the box. The next question asked if the child had any challenging behaviour and printed in the box was *Melody has challenging behaviour. She can be angry*. The next box about contact arrangements was empty.

'Contact?' Jill queried.

'I'll confirm the contact arrangements when I've spoken to the Family Centre to check availability,' Neave said. 'Melody will have supervised contact with her mother at the Family Centre – I'm anticipating on Monday, Wednesday and Friday, four till five-thirty. You'll be able to take and collect her?' Neave asked me. It's expected that foster carers take children to and from contact, school and any appointments they may have.

'Yes,' I said, and made a note of the days and times in my diary.

'I want to see my mum now!' Melody demanded, having finished the biscuits.

'You've just seen her,' Neave said, 'and you'll see her again tomorrow – Wednesday.'

'That's not long,' Jill said positively.

'I want to see my mum at home!'

'The Family Centre is like a home,' I said. 'It's got sofas to sit on and lots of games to play with. I've taken children before and they always have a good time.'

Melody threw me a withering look and I returned my attention to the form, as did Jill.

'Sibling contact with her half-brothers and sisters?' Jill asked Neave.

'No, there is no contact.'

'And the care plan is long-term foster care then?' Jill said.

'Yes,' Neave confirmed.

We had come to the end of the form and I placed my copy in my fostering folder.

'I'll need to arrange a LAC review,' Neave now said. 'I'll let you know as soon as I have the details.' LAC stands for 'Looked After Child', and all children in care have regular reviews to make sure everything is being done as it should to help them. The first review is usually held within the first four weeks of a child coming into care.

Toscha, our very old, docile and lovable cat sauntered out from behind the sofa where she'd been sleeping next to the radiator.

'A cat!' Melody cried in horror.

'Don't you like cats?' Jim asked her.

'No, they're horrible. They have fleas that bite you.' She began scratching her legs and I saw she had a lot of old insect bites.

'Toscha doesn't have fleas,' I said.

'My mum says all cats have fleas.'

'I treat Toscha with flea drops so she doesn't ever get them,' I explained.

'Do you have cats at home?' Jill asked.

'They come in when we open the door.'

'There's always a lot of stray cats around the entrance to the house and inside the communal hallway,' Neave said. 'I don't expect anyone treats them.'

'Try not to scratch,' I said. 'You'll make them worse. I'll put some antiseptic ointment on after your bath tonight.'

'I don't have baths,' Melody said firmly. 'It's too cold.' I'd heard similar before from other children I'd fostered who'd come from homes where they couldn't afford heating and hot water.

'It's warm here,' I reassured her. 'The central heating is always on in winter and there's plenty of hot water.'

Melody looked bewildered.

'It's bound to seem a bit strange at first,' Jill said, 'but Cathy is here to look after you. If you need anything or have any questions, ask her or one of her children. You'll meet them later.' Jill knew, as I did, that despite Melody's bravado, as an eight-year-old child away from her mother, she must be feeling pretty scared and anxious.

'Shall we look round the house now?' Neave said to Jim. 'Then we need to get back to the office.'

It's usual for the foster carer to show the social worker and child around when they first arrive, so we all stood. I began with the room we were in, which looked out over the garden. 'As you can see, we have some swings at the bottom of the garden,' I said to Melody. 'And there are bikes and other outdoor play things in the shed. You can play out there when the weather is good.'

'And there are parks close by,' Jill told her. 'Cathy takes all the children she fosters to the park and other nice places, like the zoo and activity centres.'

Melody looked at us blankly. Giving her a reassuring smile, I led the way out of the living room and into our kitchen-cum-dining room. 'This is where we eat,' I said, pointing to the table. Toscha had followed us out and I saw Melody eyeing her carefully as she wandered over to her empty food bowl in a recess of the kitchen. 'It's not her dinner time yet,' I said to Melody, trying to put her at ease.

'Cats are always hungry,' Jim added.

Melody looked suspiciously at Toscha and gave her leg another good scratch. 'Honestly, love, she hasn't got fleas,' I said. I then led the way down the hall and into the front room. 'This is a quiet room, if anyone wants to be alone,' I explained. It held the computer, sound system, shelves of books, a cabinet with a lockable drawer where I kept important documents, and a small table and four chairs. It was sometimes used for homework and studying, and if anyone wanted their own space.

'Thank you,' Neave said and we headed out.

We went upstairs, where I suggested we look at Melody's room first. 'It's not my room,' she said grumpily.

'It'll feel more comfortable once you have your things in here,' I said as we entered. I told all the children this when I showed them round, for while the room was clean and tidy with a wardrobe, shelves, drawers and freshly laundered bed linen, it lacked any personalization that makes a room feel lived in and homely. Then I realized my mistake. Melody hadn't come with any possessions. 'Will her mother be sending some of her belongings?' I now asked Neave and Jim.

'There isn't much,' Neave replied. 'They moved around so often that what they did have got ditched or left behind along the way. I'll ask Amanda tomorrow.'

'Have you got a special doll or teddy bear you would like from home?' Jill asked Melody. A treasured item such as this helps a child to settle. Most children would have at least one favourite toy, but Melody just shrugged.

'Perhaps one you sleep with?' I suggested.

'No, I sleep with my mum,' she said. That Melody didn't have one special toy was another indication of the very basic

14

existence she'd lived with her mother. 'I've got a ball,' she added as an afterthought.

'Would you like me to ask your mother for it?' Neave asked her.

'Don't know where it is,' she said disinterestedly, so I changed my approach.

'You can choose some posters to put on the walls of your bedroom when we go shopping at the weekend,' I said brightly. 'And I'm sure I have a spare teddy bear here if you'd like one to keep you company.' I always have a few handy.

'Don't mind,' she said, which I took as a yes.

I showed them where the toilet and bathroom were, and then led them in and out of my children's bedrooms, mentioning as we went that all our bedrooms, including Melody's, were private, and that we didn't go into each other's rooms unless we were asked to, and we always knocked first.

'That's the same in a lot of homes,' Jill told Melody, who was looking rather nonplussed. Having spent most of her life living in a single room with her mother in multi-occupancy houses, this was probably all very new to her.

Lastly, I opened the door to my bedroom so they could see in. 'This is where I sleep,' I told Melody. 'If you need me during the night, call out and I'll come to you.'

'Do you leave a nightlight on in the landing?' Neave asked.

'Yes, and there's a dimmer switch in Melody's bedroom so we can set it to low if she wants a light on at night.'

We returned downstairs, where Neave confirmed she'd ask Melody's mother to take any toys and clothes of Melody's to contact tomorrow so they could be passed on to me, then she and Jim said goodbye and I saw them out. Jill stayed for another five minutes to make sure Melody had settled and then left. As soon as the front door closed, Melody asked, 'When can I go home?'

'What did Neave tell you?' I asked gently.

'That I had to live with you for now.'

'That's right. Try not to worry, you'll see your mother tomorrow and again on Friday. Then every Monday, Wednesday and Friday. That's three times a week.' But what Neave wouldn't have told Melody at this stage – and neither would I – was that, as it was likely she would be remaining in long-term care, the level of contact would gradually be reduced. Then at the end of the year when the final court hearing had been heard and the judge confirmed the social services' care plan, Melody would probably see her mother only a couple of times a year for a few hours. Sad though this was, it was done to allow the child to bond with their carer and have a chance of a better life in the future. I should probably also say that when children come out of care at eighteen they invariably go back to their birth families – not always, but often.

'I want to go home. My mum needs me,' Melody said.

'I understand, but try not to worry. Your mother is an adult and can look after herself, and Neave will make sure she's all right.'

'No, she won't,' Melody said.

Best keep Melody occupied, I thought. 'Adrian, Lucy and Paula will be home from school in about half an hour,' I said. 'So we have time to treat your hair and give you a bath before I have to start making dinner.'

'Treat my hair?' she queried.

'Yes, with nit lotion.' I always kept a bottle in the bathroom cabinet, as so many children who come into care have head lice.

'How do you know I have nits?' Melody asked, seeming surprised I knew. 'My mum said if I didn't scratch no one would know.'

'Your social worker told me,' I said. 'It must be very uncomfortable for you.'

'It bleeding well is,' she said, and jabbing both hands into her matted hair, she gave her scalp a good scratch. 'Aah, that feels so much better!' she sighed, relieved.

'Good, but we don't swear. Come on, let's get the nit lotion on and you won't have to scratch.'

'Is not swearing another of your rules?' she asked as she followed me upstairs. 'Like knocking on bedroom doors.'

'Yes, I suppose it is.'

'Do you have many rules here?'

'No, just a few to keep everyone safe and happy.'

'I'll tell my mum. She needs rules to make me safe and happy, then she can have me back.'

I smiled sadly, for of course it was far too late for that. Amanda had had her chance, and Melody wouldn't be going back.

CHAPTER THREE

MUMMY NEEDS ME

'I can smell nit lotion!' my daughter Lucy cried from the hall as she let herself in the front door.

'We're in here!' I called. I was in the kitchen peeling vegetables for dinner, and Melody was sitting at the table colouring in while the head-lice lotion took effect. I'd given her a bath – her first in months, she told me – and she was now dressed in clean clothes from the spares I kept. The lotion had a dreadfully pungent smell and needed to be left on for an hour, but I knew from using it on other children that it was very effective.

'This is Melody,' I said, introducing her to Lucy.

'Hi, how are you? Don't look so grumpy, you'll be fine here.' Having been neglected herself before coming to me as a foster child, Lucy could relate in a special way to the children we fostered. She had an easy manner with them and most of the children formed an attachment to her before they did me.

'I'm not grumpy,' Melody said. 'I don't like this stuff on my hair. My mum never put it on.'

'That's why you had head lice. That will kill the little buggers.'

'Lucy,' I admonished, 'I've just told Melody not to swear.'

'Ooops,' Lucy said, and theatrically clamped her hand over her mouth. 'Sorry.' And for the first time I saw Melody smile. 'Nice picture,' Lucy said, going over and admiring Melody's colouring in. Then to me she added, 'I'm going to my room now, Mum.'

'Fine, love. Did you have a good day at school?'

'I guess.'

'I want to go with you,' Melody said, clearly finding Lucy's company far more interesting than mine.

'Not until the lotion is washed off. It'll make my room smell.'

I glanced at the clock. 'Only fifteen more minutes,' I said.

'That's not fair,' Melody moaned. 'I want to go with you now.'

'I'm flattered,' Lucy said. 'But you can't until you've had your hair washed. See you later.' Throwing her a smile, she left the room.

When I think back to how Lucy was when she first arrived, I feel so proud of all she's achieved. I'm proud of Adrian and Paula too, of course, but Lucy had a shocking start to life and could so easily have gone off the rails. She had a lot of catching up to do, but she didn't let her past hold her back. Her self-confidence has developed immeasurably; she is happy, has a good circle of friends, eats well and is achieving at school. I couldn't love her more if she'd been born to me, and I feel very lucky that I have three wonderful children and am allowed to foster more.

No sooner had Lucy disappeared upstairs than Paula came home. She had a different nature to Lucy and was quieter, more placid and could easily let things worry her.

'Hi, Paula,' I called. 'Come and meet Melody.'

'Hello,' Paula said, coming in.

'Are you Lucy's sister?' Melody asked.

'Yes.'

'You got any more sisters?'

'No.' Paula smiled.

'Good day?' I asked her as I always ask my children when they first come home.

'Yes, but I've got tons of homework. I'm going to start it now before dinner.'

'OK, love. I'm nearly finished here, then I'll wash Melody's hair, so we'll eat around six o'clock.'

Paula poured herself a glass of water and, giving Melody a small smile, left.

'Where's she gone?' Melody asked.

'In the front room to start her homework,' I said.

'Can I go?'

'No, she needs quiet to concentrate. You will see her at dinner when we'll all eat together.' I put the chicken casserole in the oven. 'Now, let's wash your hair, then you can see Lucy.'

Melody didn't object, probably because she knew she'd only spend time with Lucy once her hair was washed. We went to the bathroom where I thoroughly washed her hair. As I was rinsing it I heard my son Adrian arrive home. 'Hi, Mum!' he called from the hall. At sixteen, he was now six feet tall, although of course to me he'd always be my little boy.

'I'm in the bathroom, washing Melody's hair!' I called down.

'OK. I'll say hi to her later.' I heard him go through to the kitchen. When he came home from school he always fixed himself a drink and a snack to see him through to dinner.

'You got any more kids?' Melody asked, head over the bath as I continued to rinse her hair.

'No, that's it. Just the four of you.'

'I'm not your kid,' came her sharp retort.

'OK, but while you're living with me I'll look after you as if you are.' There was no reply.

With her hair thoroughly washed, rinsed and nit-free, I towel dried it and then brushed out the knots. She complained throughout that I was pulling, although I was as gentle as I could be. I then dried it with the hair dryer and it shone. It looked quite a few shades lighter now all the grease and grime had been removed. I don't think it could have been washed for many months.

'Can I go into Lucy's room?' Melody asked as soon as I'd finished.

'Yes, but don't forget to knock on her door first.'

She dashed around the landing and banged hard on Lucy's door – not so much a knock, more a hammering.

'Hell! Open the door. Don't break it down!' Lucy's voice came from inside.

'Can I come in?' Melody yelled.

'Yes! If you've had your hair washed.'

'I have!'

She disappeared into Lucy's room and that was the last I saw of her until I called everyone for dinner. Lucy knew that while Melody was with her she should leave her bedroom door open as part of our safer-caring policy, and to call me if there was a problem. All foster carers have a safer-caring policy and follow similar guidelines to keep all family members feeling safe. One of them is not to leave a foster child in a room with someone with the door closed. Leaving the door open means I and others can hear what is going on, and the child can come out easily whenever they want. There's no knowing what a closed door might mean to an abused child, and Adrian knew that any girl we fostered wasn't to go into his room at all, for his own protection. Sadly, many foster families have unfounded allegations made against them and they are very difficult to disprove.

Once dinner was ready I called everyone to the table and showed Melody where to sit. For us, it was a lively, chatty occasion as usual, when we shared our news as we ate. It's often the only time we all sit down together during the week and it's a pleasant focal point for us. Indeed, foster carers are expected to eat at least one meal a day together, as it bonds the family. At weekends we sometimes had breakfast together too. But Melody stared at us overawed as she ate.

Like many children who come from disadvantaged backgrounds, she wasn't used to sitting at a table or using a knife and fork, having relied largely on snacks. She struggled to use the cutlery I'd set, so I quietly slipped her a dessertspoon to help with the casserole. She ate ravenously, all the while keeping a watchful eye on us. I'd seen the same vigilant awareness – a heightened state of alert – before in children I'd fostered who'd had to fend for themselves. They constantly watch those around them for any sign of danger. Children who've been nurtured and protected don't do this, as experience has taught them that those they know can be trusted. It would take time for Melody to trust us.

I served rice pudding for dessert. It was a winter favourite of ours and despite Melody's initial reluctance to try it, saying it looked like sick, she ate it all, and then asked for seconds. 'Can I take some for my mum?' she said as she finished the second bowl. 'I think she'd like it.' My heart went out to her.

'Yes, I'll put some in a plastic box and we can take it to contact tomorrow.'

'Will it be cold?' she asked.

'Yes, but she can warm it up at the Family Centre. There's a kitchen there with a cooker and a microwave.'

'I'll take her some of that casserole too,' Melody added.

'I'm afraid that's all gone. Next time I make it I'll do extra so she can have some. But please don't worry about your mum. I'm sure she'll have something to eat.'

Melody looked at me as if she was about to say something but changed her mind. Hopefully when she saw her mother she'd be reassured that she was managing without her.

After dinner, which I thought had gone well, Adrian, Paula and Lucy helped me clear the table, then disappeared off to do their homework. I was assuming that once Melody started going to school regularly she too would have some homework, but there wasn't even a school bag tonight. I suggested we play a game together and I opened the toy cupboard in the kitchen-diner, but she said she wanted to watch television like she did at home with her mother. In the living room I switched the television channel to one with an age-appropriate programme, told her I'd be in the kitchen if she needed me and, taking the remote with me (so she couldn't change channels to something less appropriate), set about doing the washing up. If my children have homework then they are excused from washing the dinner things.

* * *

First nights can be very difficult for a new child. Apart from suddenly finding themselves in a strange home and living with people they've only just met, the carer's routine is likely to be very different from any the child has been used to. At 7.30, when the television programme Melody was watching had ended, I told her it was bedtime, which didn't go down well. 'What's the time?' she demanded, unable to read the time for herself.

'Half past seven. Plenty late enough. You have school tomorrow.' Indeed, it was only because she'd already had her bath and hair wash that she'd stayed up this late. Tomorrow she'd be going up around seven o'clock so that she was in bed and hopefully settled by eight o'clock. Children of her age need nine to eleven hours sleep a night.

'At home I stay up with my mum. We go to sleep together. Sometimes she's asleep before me.'

'Is she?' I asked lightly. 'What do you do when she's asleep?' Clearly Melody wouldn't be supervised if her mother was asleep.

'Watch television. You can see the television from our mattress on the floor.' She stopped, having realized she'd probably said too much. 'Don't tell the social worker I told you that.'

'I think she already knows,' I said. 'Now, come on up to bed.' I stood and began towards the living-room door. 'You can say goodnight to Lucy, Adrian and Paula. They're in their bedrooms.'

This seemed to clinch it and without further protest Melody came upstairs with me. I took her to the bathroom first, where I supervised her brushing her teeth with the new toothbrush and paste I'd provided. Like all foster carers, I keep spares of essential items. We went along the landing where Melody knocked first on Lucy's bedroom door. 'I'm going to bed!' she called.

Lucy came out to say goodnight and gave Melody a big hug, which was nice. Then we went to Paula's room. She too came out and said, 'Goodnight. See you tomorrow.' Then Adrian came to his door. 'Goodnight. I hope you'll be happy here,' he said. Melody hadn't seen much of him, only at dinner. He had exams in the spring, so it was important he studied. She'd see more of him at the weekend.

She used the toilet, then we went into her bedroom. I'd found a new teddy bear that Adrian had won at a fair and didn't want, so I'd propped it on her bed. I asked her if she wanted her curtains open or closed at night and she said a little open. It's details like this that help a child settle in a strange room, so I drew the curtains, leaving a gap in the middle. As I turned I saw she was about to climb into bed with her clothes on.

'Melody, there are some pyjamas for you, love.' I picked them up from where I'd left them on her bed. 'You can wear these until we have time to buy you some new ones. They're clean.' I'd taken them from my selection of spares and was pretty sure they were the right size, as she was average build for an eight-year-old.

She paused and looked a bit confused. 'I keep my clothes on at night at home because it's so bleeding cold.'

'Well, it's not cold here, love, and remember we don't swear.'

'OK. It's all so different here.'

'I know, you'll soon get used to it.' But I was saddened to hear yet another example of the impoverished life Melody and her mother had led. No one should have to keep their clothes on to keep them warm at night.

I always give the child I'm fostering privacy whenever possible. Melody was of an age when she could dress and undress herself, so I waited on the landing while she changed into her pyjamas, as I had done when she'd had a bath. Once she was ready I went into her bedroom, thinking how nice it would be for her to climb into a comfortable, warm bed rather than the old mattress on a cold floor she'd been used to, but she didn't get in. 'I can't go to bed here,' she said anxiously. 'My mum needs me.'

'You'll see her tomorrow,' I reassured her. 'Please try not to worry. She'll be fine. I expect she'll be going to bed soon too.' Clearly I didn't know what Melody's mother was doing, but it wouldn't help Melody to keep fretting about her.

'She's no good by herself,' Melody said, still not getting in. 'She needs me to tell her what to do.'

'Melody, love, I know you're missing your mother and she will be missing you, but she's an adult. She can take care of herself.'

'No, you don't understand,' Melody blurted, her anger and concern rising. 'She forgets things. I have to be there to tell her what she needs and where things are.'

I paused. 'Is that when she's been drinking or taking drugs?' I asked gently. Aware that her mother had a history of drug and alcohol abuse, this seemed the most likely explanation. Of course she would be 'forgetful' if she was under the influence of a substance.

'Sometimes, but not always,' Melody replied and then stopped, again realizing she'd probably said too much. Many children I've fostered have been warned by their parents not to disclose their home life to their foster carer or social worker. It can be very confusing for the child. Before saying anything, they have to sift through all the information they carry and work out what they can or can't say. 'Mum can remember some things, but other times she needs my help,' Melody said carefully, and then she teared up.

'Oh, love, don't upset yourself. Come here.' I put my arms around her and she allowed me to hold her close. 'I do understand how you feel, honestly I do. I've looked after children before who've felt just as you do. They worry about their parents, and that they won't be able to cope without them. Then, when they start seeing them regularly at contact, they find they're managing fine without them. Your mother will be missing you, but believe me she can look after herself.'

How those words would come back to haunt me.

CHAPTER FOUR

SCHOOL

Melody finally went to sleep shortly before nine o'clock, cuddling the teddy bear I'd given to her and with me sitting on her bed, stroking her forehead. Bless her. I felt so sorry for her. I was sure she was a good kid who was badly missing her mother. Yes, she was feisty, streetwise, could become angry at times and would need firm boundaries, but I felt positive that once she'd settled I could help her to a better life, which is what fostering is all about. Because it was unlikely Melody could return to her mother, the social services would try to find a suitable relative to look after her as the first option. They are called kinship carers and are considered the next best option if a child can't be looked after by their own parents. If there wasn't a suitable relative then she would be matched with a long-term foster carer, and if that happened it was possible I might be considered, but that was all in the future.

Once I was sure Melody was in a deep sleep, I moved quietly away from her bed and, turning the light down low, came out of her bedroom. I left the door ajar so I could easily hear her if she was restless in the night. I checked that Paula, Lucy and Adrian were taking turns in the bathroom. Even at their ages they still needed the occasional reminder to make sure they were in bed at a reasonable time. Some evenings, as with this evening, they were mostly in their bedrooms, doing their homework or relaxing, but at other times, especially at the weekends, they would all be downstairs in the living room, talking, playing a board game or watching television. I felt it was easier for a new child to relax and settle in if my family carried on as normal. I'd see them later before they went to bed, but now I went downstairs to write up my log notes.

All foster carers in the UK are required to keep a daily record of the child or children they are looking after. This includes appointments, the child's health and wellbeing, education, significant events and any disclosures the child may make about their past. As well as charting the child's progress, it can act as an aide-mémoire for the foster carer if asked about a specific day. When the child leaves, this record is placed on file at the social services. I wrote objectively and, where appropriate, verbatim about Melody's arrival and her first day with us – about a page, which I secured in my fostering folder and returned to the lockable drawer in the front room.

I checked on Melody – she was fast asleep – and then as Adrian, Lucy and Paula came downstairs I spent some time talking to them before they went to bed. By 10.30 p.m. everyone was asleep and I put Toscha in her bed for the night and went up myself, again checking on Melody before I got into bed.

I never sleep well when there is a new child in the house. I'm half listening out in case they wake, frightened, not knowing where they are and in need of reassurance. But despite my restlessness and looking in on Melody three times, she slept very well, and I had to wake her at 7 a.m. to get ready for school.

'Not going,' she said as I opened her bedroom curtains to let in some light. 'I need to go home and get my mum up.'

'Melody, your mother will be able to get herself up, love. You'll see her later at the Family Centre. Now get dressed, please. I want to go into school early today so I can buy you a new school uniform.' She reluctantly clambered out of bed. 'You can wear these for now,' I said, handing her the fresh clothes I'd taken from my store.

'Not more clean clothes!' she sighed. 'You must like washing.'

I smiled. She could be so quaint and old-fashioned with her remarks — an old head on young shoulders — but then of course she'd had to grow up quickly and take care of herself, living with her mother.

'The washing machine does it,' I said.

'My mum and me had to go to the launderette.'

'Yes, many people do that.' I left her to get dressed.

Melody wasn't used to a routine or having to leave the house on time to go to school, because she'd hardly ever gone to school, so I had to chivvy her along. She didn't even know the name of her school, let alone where it was. I explained it was on the other side of town — about a thirty-minute drive in the traffic. Adrian, Lucy and Paula were of an age where they went to school by themselves, meeting friends along the way. Melody saw them briefly at breakfast and passed them on the landing and in the hall as we all got ready to leave. We left first, calling 'goodbye' and 'see you later' as we went.

'What's the time?' Melody asked, bleary-eyed despite a wash, as we stepped outside into the cold morning air.

'Eight o'clock. I can teach you the time if you like.'

'Why?'

'So you're not late.'

Having never had to be anywhere regularly, punctuality must have been a bit of an alien concept to her. She shrugged and climbed into the back of the car, and I showed her how to fasten her seatbelt, closed her car door and got into the driver's seat.

'My mum knows the time,' Melody said as I pulled away.

'Good. Adults usually do.'

'She's still late, though, and misses things. It takes ages for her to wake and get up.' Which was doubtless a result of her substance misuse.

'What time we got to be in school?' Melody asked after a moment.

'School starts at eight-fifty, but it's good to be there at least five minutes early. Today I'm hoping to arrive by eight-thirty so we can sort out your uniform.'

'My mum went to the school a few times,' she said as I drove.

'Good.'

'What time am I seeing her?'

'Four o'clock until five-thirty,' I said, glancing at her in the rear-view mirror. 'That's an hour and a half. School ends at three-twenty, so I'll collect you and drive straight to the Family Centre.' I'd checked the location of the school and knew where it was in relation to the Family Centre. 'Morning playtime will be around eleven o'clock and you'll have lunch between about twelve and one o'clock,' I added, trying to give her a sense of the day. Time is a difficult concept for children, but by Melody's age most children are able to read the time.

'So am I having my dinner at school like I did when I was with my mum?' she asked.

'Yes, you have school dinners,' I confirmed.

'I like school dinners, they're free.'

While Melody had been living with her mother she was on benefits and would have been entitled to free school meals. Now she was in care I would pay for her school dinners and any other expenses; for example, her school uniform, outings, clubs, hobbies and so on – that's what the fostering allowance is for.

I arrived at the school just before 8.30 a.m. and parked in a side road.

'Why are we stopping here?' Melody asked, peering through her side window.

'That's your school there,' I said, pointing to the building on our left. It was a two-storey brick building surrounded by a tall wire-netting fence but it was clearly visible from the road.

'Oh yeah, I remember now,' she said.

'Melody, when was the last time you were here?' I asked, turning slightly in my seat to look at her.

'I dunno.' She shrugged.

I got out, went round to the pavement and opened her door, which was child-locked. She clambered out and we made our way towards the main entrance. As we entered the playground we passed some children playing and others were slowly joining them.

'I remember coming here before Christmas,' Melody said. 'They had a Christmas tree.'

'Was that the last time you were here?' It was the third week in January now.

'Think so,' she replied. 'It's all a bit of a haze.'

We went through the main door into the reception area. Behind a low counter on my right was a small open-plan office where two ladies worked at desks. One came over and I introduced myself, explaining I was Melody's foster carer.

'News to me,' she said. 'Let me try to get hold of Mrs Farnham, our deputy head, she might know what's going on.' She turned her back and picked up a phone on the desk behind her. I threw Melody a reassuring smile. It wasn't the best start to the school day. Usually when I take a child into school the staff know the child well and are genuinely pleased to see them. This school secretary appeared very distant and not to have recognized Melody, or been aware she was in foster care. That relied on the social worker notifying the school. Melody looked around at the walls displaying the children's artwork as we waited.

'Yes, they're here now,' I heard the secretary say on the phone. Then, 'All right. I'll tell her.' She set down the phone and returned to the counter. 'Mrs Farnham is coming down now to see you. Take a seat.' She nodded to the row of four chairs against the far wall. Melody and I sat down as another parent came in to talk to the secretary.

A couple of minutes later the door to our right, which led from the school, opened and a woman came through it and walked straight to us.

'Nice to see you again, Melody,' she said with a very welcoming smile. Then to me, 'I'm Mrs Farnham, the Deputy Head.'

'Cathy Glass, Melody's foster carer,' I said, standing.

'Lovely to meet you. Melody's social worker phoned me late yesterday afternoon, so I haven't had a chance to update the staff. Shall we go somewhere more private to talk? The Head's office is free – I'm covering for her this week.'

I was relieved that someone knew what was going on. Melody and I followed Mrs Farnham through the door, up a short flight of stairs and into a large comfortable office overlooking the playground. The room was carpeted, with framed prints on the walls, a desk and filing cabinets at one end and a small sofa and two easy chairs at the other.

'Do sit down,' she said. Melody and I settled on the sofa as Mrs Farnham took one of the easy chairs. 'How are you?' she asked Melody, who was eyeing her cautiously. 'We haven't seen much of you in school.' Which I thought was a tactful way of putting it. It is a legal requirement in the UK, as it is in most countries, for children to attend school and the parent(s) can be prosecuted if their child doesn't attend.

'I'm all right,' Melody said quietly, a little overawed at being in the Head's office.

'Melody tells me she thinks the last time she was in school was before Christmas,' I said.

'She's right. I looked it up. Seventeenth of December, so exactly a month ago.'

'She'll be coming in every day from now on,' I said.

Melody gave a small sigh and Mrs Farnham threw me a knowing look. 'Melody joined our school in September, having moved into the area during the summer holidays, but she only ever attended a couple of days a week during the whole of the autumn term. Melody has a lot of catching up to do,' Mrs Farnham added, as much for Melody's benefit as mine. 'She'll have classroom support from a lovely teaching assistant, Miss May.'

'I'll help Melody at home,' I said. 'I have three secondary-school-aged children of my own and they have homework to do most nights.'

'Excellent.' I guessed Mrs Farnham to be in her late thirties, and her warm, child-friendly manner was combined with a quiet efficiency. Clearly the children in the school were her priority, but I sensed she could be firm when necessary, as any good teacher needs to be. 'Melody is in Miss Langford's class,' she said. 'She'll introduce herself to you at the end of school. You'll be collecting Melody?'

'Yes, and bringing her in.'

'Good. We gave her a school uniform from our quality seconds when she first started.'

'She hasn't brought it with her, or anything else,' I said, 'so I'll buy her a new school uniform today if possible.'

'Yes, of course. We stock most items here. Aren't you lucky?' she said, looking at Melody, who managed a subdued nod. 'In fact, why don't I ask our welfare lady, Mrs Holby, to sort out Melody's uniform now so we can have a chat? Do you remember Mrs Holby?' she asked Melody. 'She gave you a uniform when you first arrived.'

Melody nodded uncertainly.

'I'll take you to her now and then you can come back here in your new uniform to say goodbye to Cathy.'

'Thank you,' I said. 'That is helpful. I'd like her to have a spare set of the uniform and the PE kit. Also, if your school has its own logoed book bag and PE bag, I'd like her to have those and anything else she needs.'

'You've done this before,' Mrs Farnham said with a smile as she stood.

'Quite a few times,' I admitted.

Melody looked a bit apprehensive as she left with Mrs Farnham. Unused to school and certainly never having had a complete new school uniform before, I guessed she was a bit overwhelmed, but Mrs Farnham was lovely. I sat back in the chair as the distant sounds of children laughing and shouting in the playground drifted in and occasional footsteps passed outside the door. A few minutes later Mrs Farnham returned. 'Mrs Holby will bring Melody back here once they've finished, then you can settle up the bill at the office on the way out.'

'Thank you.'

'So how has Melody been with you?' she asked, returning to her chair. 'We hardly know her, we've seen so little of her.'

'We had a good first night, although she's worrying about her mother, but that's natural. Once she's seen her tonight at contact I think she will be reassured.'

'I raised concerns about Melody with the social services halfway through last term,' Mrs Farnham said. 'On the few occasions she was in school, she arrived late, unwashed and hungry. Miss Langford, her class teacher, went to the address her mother gave us, but a man answered the door and said he'd never heard of her. It was one of those big Victorian houses in Station Road converted into small flats.'

'Yes, that's it. The social worker had a problem getting to see her too.'

Mrs Farnham nodded. 'We met Melody's mother in September when she first brought Melody to school, but that was the only time. Melody appears to have had very little schooling or parenting. Why wasn't she taken into care sooner?'

'I'm not sure exactly, but they moved around a lot, which means they could have evaded the social services.'

'Melody will be staying with you now?' Mrs Farnham asked.

'Yes, until the final court hearing when the judge will make a decision on where she should live permanently.'

'We'll obviously do all we can to help her catch up with her schoolwork. We tested her when she first arrived last September and her results showed she was working at reception level, so about four years behind what she should be.'

'Oh dear. That is a long way behind.'

'We'll test her again, but I doubt she's improved much because she's hardly been in school. Have you met her mother?'

'Not yet. I should this evening at contact.'

'She's got a reputation for being very volatile. Other parents have seen her outside the school causing a scene. On one occasion, when she was rushing Melody to school late, she attacked a driver who didn't immediately stop to let her cross the road. She swore at him and kicked his car. He called the police, but she'd disappeared by the time they arrived. Another time – I think it was in October – she screamed at a parent because her daughter wouldn't play with Melody.'

'Does Melody have any friends?' I asked.

'Not really. She wasn't in school often enough to make friends. Also, when she did come she was grubby and had head lice, so the other children didn't want to play with her. Hopefully that will change now. She looks so much cleaner already.'

'I gave her a good bath last night and treated her hair.'

'It shows,' Mrs Farnham said. 'There's a couple of other children in the school I have concerns about who could do with a good wash. And if head lice aren't treated, they quickly spread through the class.'

A bell suddenly rang outside, signalling the start of school. At the same time a knock sounded on the door. 'Come in!' Mrs Farnham called. Melody came in dressed in a new school uniform, followed by a woman I took to be the welfare assistant, Mrs Holby. 'Don't you look smart!' Mrs Farnham exclaimed. Melody smiled proudly.

'I'll buy her some school shoes today,' I said, glancing at the torn plastic trainers, which seemed even more noticeable now.

'She'll need some plimsolls for PE too,' Mrs Farnham said. 'We don't stock them here.'

'This is Mrs Holby, our lovely welfare assistant,' she said, introducing her to me. 'It's time for lessons, so if you would like to go with her to the office, I'll take Melody to her class.'

'Thanks again,' I said, standing. I said goodbye to Melody, told her to have a good day and that I'd meet her in the playground at the end of school. She went with Mrs Farnham while I accompanied Mrs Holby to the office, where I settled the bill for the uniform. She also gave me a school prospectus, which included term dates, and a form for my contact details, which I filled in there. I thanked Mrs Holby again and made my way out of the school. The playground was empty now, with all the children in their classrooms for the start of lessons. Outside the gates a few parents stood chatting in a small group.

Mrs Farnham had said that Melody's mother, Amanda, had a reputation for being volatile and aggressive. Aware she would know it was highly likely that I had brought Melody to school, I kept a watchful eye out as I made my way to my car. I'd had impromptu meetings before with the parents of children I'd fostered. Sometimes they were friendly and just wanted a glimpse of – or a few words with – their child, but at other times they'd vented their anger at me for having their child taken into care. I didn't know what Amanda looked like, but I couldn't see anyone watching or following me and I made it safely to my car. As it happened, it was later that day that Amanda found the opportunity to turn her anger on me.

CHAPTER FIVE

AMANDA

I drove straight from Melody's school into town, where I bought her a set of casual clothes, underwear, tights, socks, pyjamas, some posters for her bedroom and a pair of school shoes. The shoes size was a guesstimate; I knew the size of her trainers and went up one size. I could change them if necessary. If by Saturday none of Melody's belongings had arrived from home, I'd take her shopping to choose more clothes, including a warm winter coat – she was wearing one from my spares today. It's preferable for a child in care to have at least some of their clothes from home, as they are comfortingly familiar, but from what her social worker Neave had said it wasn't likely, so we couldn't wait for them indefinitely.

When I arrived home there was a message from Jill on my answerphone asking how Melody had been on her first night. I returned her call and updated her, including that Melody was missing her mother, but had slept well, had eaten a good dinner and breakfast and was now in school. Jill said she'd let Neave know and to phone her if there were any problems. I had a late lunch, filled the washing machine, cleared up the kitchen, which I hadn't had time to do after breakfast, then

Blu-Tacked Melody's posters to her bedroom wall. Down-stairs again, I made a cottage pie for dinner and then it was time to collect Melody from school. I placed a note prominently on the side in the kitchen:

> Dear Adrian, Lucy and Paula, hope you've had a good day.
> Would someone please put the cottage pie that is in the
> fridge in the oven at 5 p.m. at 180°C and keep an eye on it?
> I should be back from contact at 6 p.m. See you later.
> Love Mum xx.

I had told them at breakfast I was going to contact, but I was pretty certain no one had been awake enough to hear me.

The bag containing Melody's shoes was ready in the hall to take with me. She would try them on in the car and, if they fitted, wear them for contact so she looked smart. I liked the children I fostered to look well turned out when they saw their parents, as it was a special occasion, just like when we visited my parents. I then remembered the stay-fresh plastic box containing the rice pudding in the fridge. I hesitated. Melody hadn't mentioned it again and it seemed rather an odd thing to take to contact, but on the other hand she had wanted to give it to her mother, so I took it with me.

I drove to the school and parked in the same side road I had that morning and then waited in the playground with the other parents and carers for school to end. It was a cold, bright day with the low, wintry sun giving little warmth, but it was a pleasant change from the previous days of overcast grey skies. The bell rang from inside the building, signalling the end of school, and a few minutes later the classes began to file out one at a time, led by their teacher. I looked at the sea of faces

– I hadn't met Melody's teacher yet so didn't know who I was looking for. Melody must have spotted me, because suddenly through the milling crowd of children she appeared, coming towards me with her teacher.

'Hello, I'm Miss Langford, Melody's class teacher,' she said with a warm smile.

'Cathy Glass, Melody's foster carer.'

'The Deputy said you'd be here to collect her. So pleased to meet you. Our class's teaching assistant, Miss May, has been working with Melody today. She's done some nice work and there is a reading book and some literacy homework in Melody's book bag. We like the children to read a little every evening. Miss May had to leave early today but is looking forward to meeting you tomorrow.'

'Thank you.'

Young and fashionably dressed, Miss Langford came across as a very enthusiastic teacher.

'Please let me know if there is anything I can do to help Melody,' she said. 'She's a lovely child. A delight to teach.'

'Excellent,' I said, although I was pretty certain she said this about all the children she taught.

I usually ask to meet privately with the teacher of a new child I'm fostering to learn more about how they are doing in school, but as Melody hadn't been in school long and I'd had a good chat with the Deputy this morning, I didn't think I could learn much more.

'They have swimming on Monday afternoons,' she added. 'One-piece swimming costume, please, black or navy, and a regulation white swimming hat.'

'OK,' I said. 'I'll make sure she has it.' I made a mental note to buy those too on Saturday.

AMANDA

'So have a good evening then,' Miss Langford said. 'Melody tells me she is seeing her mother.'

'Yes, that's right. We're going there now.'

'Did you remember the rice pudding?' Melody now asked.

'Yes, I did,' I said, pleased I'd included it. Miss Langford looked at me, puzzled. 'I made rice pudding yesterday evening,' I explained. 'Melody said her mother would like some.'

'Mmm, that sounds nice,' she enthused with a big smile and smacking her lips. 'I love homemade rice pudding.'

'Well, the next time I make it I'll bring some in for you too,' I joked.

She laughed and we said goodbye.

I opened Melody's car door, gave her the new shoes and then waited on the pavement as she tried them on. They fitted, just. 'Can't I have trainers?' she asked.

'Not for school, but we can buy you some for casual wear at the weekend.'

'OK. They're nice,' she said. 'What shall I do with my old trainers?'

'Put them in the bag your shoes were in for now.' As worn out as they were, I'd be keeping them, together with the clothes Melody had been wearing when she'd arrived. They were the property of her mother and would be offered back to her. If she told her social worker she didn't want them then I could dispose of them, but not until then. Sometimes all parents have left of their children are photographs, their old clothes and toys, and faded memories.

I checked Melody's seatbelt was fastened and gave her the box of rice pudding to hold. Then, with her looking very smart in her new school uniform, shoes and coat from my

43

spares, I began the drive to the Family Centre, chatting to her as we went.

'How was school?' I asked. 'Miss Langford said you'd done some nice work today.'

'I played with someone in the playground.'

'Great. You'll soon make friends.'

'That's what Miss May said.'

'You like Miss May?'

'Yes. She helps me with my work. There's me and two boys sit with her and she helps us do what the teacher says. Cathy, why don't I know as much as the kids on the other tables? You know, the ones that don't sit with Miss May.'

I glanced at her in the rear-view mirror. Children intuit that they are behind their peers. 'Because you haven't been in school much,' I replied honestly.

'Is that why kids go to school? So they know lots of stuff and are clever?' Her question was another indication of just how little schooling she'd had; children of her age usually know why they go to school.

'Yes, and also to make friends and join in activities.'

'I guess I should have gone to school more, but my mum needed me at home.'

I didn't want to demonize her mother, but she had a lot to answer for. 'Your mum is doing fine, so don't worry,' I reassured her. 'I'm sure you'll soon catch up with your school-work, and I'll help you at home.'

'I hope my mum is OK,' she said, fretting again. 'I kept thinking about her at school and I told Miss May. She said my mummy was grown up and would know how to look after herself and I shouldn't worry.' Thank you, Miss May, I thought.

'That's right. I'll be meeting Miss May tomorrow,' I said. 'What else did you do at school?' But Melody didn't answer and was clearly worrying about her mother again. 'We'll soon be at the Family Centre,' I told her. There was no reply.

Five minutes later I parked in one of the bays outside the Family Centre and cut the engine. I'd already explained to Melody what to expect: that there were six rooms in the centre, so other children in care would be seeing their parents too, and a lady called a contact supervisor would be in the room with them making notes. The parent(s) often find this more intrusive than the child(ren), for they know why the contact supervisor is there: to observe them with their child and write a report on each session. These reports go to the social worker and ultimately form part of the judge's decision on whether their child will be allowed home. I sympathize. I think it's an awful position for a parent to be in, but there is little alternative if contact needs to be supervised. Some contact supervisors handle it better than others and are able to do their job while putting the family at ease.

'Is Mummy here?' Melody asked anxiously as I opened her car door to let her out.

'Hopefully,' I said. It was exactly four o'clock and parents usually arrived early.

She clambered out, clutching the box of rice pudding, and we went up the path to the security-locked main door where I pressed the buzzer. The closed-circuit television camera over-head allowed anyone in the office to see who was at the door. After a few moments the door clicked open and we went in. I said hello to the receptionist sitting at her computer behind a low security screen on our right. I knew her from previous visits with other children I'd fostered. I gave Melody's name. 'Is her mother, Amanda, here yet?' I asked.

She glanced at her list. 'No, not yet.'

'Mummy's not here!' Melody cried.

'I am sure she will be soon,' I said. 'I'll sign us in and then we can sit in the waiting room – there are toys and books in there.'

'Why isn't she here?' Melody lamented as I entered our names in the Visitors' Book.

'I don't know, love. Come on through here.'

'I bet she got lost. Mum often gets lost when we have to go somewhere new. She needs me to show her.'

'Your social worker will have told her how to get here,' I said. 'Try not to worry.' The waiting room was empty and we sat on the cushioned bench.

'What if Mum hasn't got the money to come here on the bus?' Melody asked.

'Neave, your social worker, will have checked she has enough money.' Parents of children in care are given all the help they need to get to contact, including bus or taxi fares when appropriate.

'Mum's not good without me,' Melody said again.

I thought she was worrying about her mother far more than most children I'd fostered, and I was hoping that when she saw her she would be reassured that she was coping. I was also hoping Amanda wouldn't be much longer. Her lateness, which was making Melody even more anxious, would be noted by the contact supervisor, who would now be waiting in the allocated room. I knew from experience that we wouldn't be allowed to wait indefinitely and at some point the manager of the Family Centre would make the decision to cancel the contact and I would return home with Melody. It's devastating for the child, but not as bad as waiting until the bitter end and having to accept the parent hasn't come to see them. The child's feelings of rejection at not being able to live with their parents are compounded and they feel even more unloved. Parents of children in care have to make contact a priority, which I'd have thought was obvious, but isn't always, especially if the parents are struggling with drink and drug misuse or have mental health issues.

The minutes ticked by. I tried to distract Melody with books and games, but she just sat there clutching the box of rice pudding, listening for any sign of her mother, and asking me every few minutes what time it was. We heard the security buzzer on the main door go a few times, but it wasn't her mother. Melody wrung her hands and worried something bad had happened to her. Then at 4.30 p.m. the centre's manager came in and said that they'd tried to phone Amanda but there was no reply, and they'd give her until 4.45 and then they'd cancel it, unless she phoned to say she was on her way. This was more generous than usual and it was because it was the first contact. Usually if a parent doesn't phone to say they've been delayed then only thirty minutes are allowed.

'Where's my mum got to?' Melody asked me again after the manger had left. 'Something really, really bad must have happened to her, I know. She needs me, it's my fault.' Her bottom lip trembled and her eyes filled.

'It's not your fault, love,' I said, putting my arm around her shoulders. I wondered if Amanda had any idea of the pain she was causing her child.

Five minutes later we heard the security buzzer sound again and the main door open and close, followed by a thick, chesty cough.

47

'That's my mum!' Melody cried, jumping up from her seat. 'She's here. Mummy!' She ran out of the waiting room. I quickly followed her down the short corridor and into reception, where a woman I assumed to be Amanda was giving her name to the receptionist. 'Mummy! Mummy!' Melody cried and rushed to her.

Amanda turned and for a second seemed to look confused, as if she wasn't sure where she was and who was calling her, then, recognizing her daughter, she opened her arms to receive her.

'Mummy, where've you been? You're late. I was going to have to go home without seeing you!' Melody cried.

'Over my dead body!' Amanda snapped in a threatening tone.

Deathly pale, with a heavily lined face and sunken cheeks, Amanda was stick thin and her jeans and jumper hung on her skeletal frame. Her hair was falling out and her scalp was visible in round bald patches. She looked haggard and aged well beyond her forty-two years. If ever there was an advertisement to deter people from drink and drug abuse, it was her. I'd seen it before in the parents of children I'd fostered and would sadly see it again. She lisped as she spoke and as I went closer I saw her two front teeth were missing.

'Hello Amanda, I'm Cathy, Melody's foster carer,' I said positively. 'Pleased to meet you.'

She'd let go of her daughter and was now trying to understand what the receptionist was telling her, which was to sign the Visitors' Book.

'The Visitors' Book is here,' I said, trying to be helpful and pointing to it.

'Come on, Mummy, you have to write your name,' Melody said. Taking her hand, she led her mother to the book and then gave her the pen beside it to sign. I exchanged a glance with the receptionist, who was looking at her, concerned. Amanda wouldn't be the first parent to arrive at contact under the influence of drink or drugs, although I couldn't smell alcohol and she seemed confused rather than high or drunk. I watched as she made an illegible scrawl in the book, then, setting down the pen, she turned to her daughter.

'Where do we go?' she asked her.

'You're in Yellow Room,' the receptionist said. 'The manager is coming now to show you.' It's usual on the parent's first visit for the manager to show the parent and child around so they know where the toilets, kitchen and rooms are. Six rooms lead off a central play area where the larger toys are kept, and each room takes its name from the colour it is painted.

'How are you?' I asked Amanda, trying to strike up conversation. It's important for the child so see their carer and parent(s) getting along. Amanda looked at me, puzzled, as if she'd forgotten who I was, and I was about to remind her when the manager appeared. It was now time for me to go, as contact had started and this was Amanda's time with her daughter.

'When will contact end?' I asked the manager, as we were starting late

'Five forty-five,' she said.

'See you later then,' I said to Amanda and Melody. There was no reply. I signed out, and as I left they were following the manager down the corridor and into the hub of the building.

It was dark outside now in winter, and cold. I pulled my coat closer around me and returned to my car. I usually try to put the time when a child is with their parent(s) to good use, either by doing some essential grocery shopping or by catching up on some paperwork in a local café, but now I sat in the car thinking about Amanda. I was starting to see why Melody was so worried about her. She appeared incredibly fragile and vulnerable and clearly needed Melody's help – as she'd been telling me. The social services had been aware of the family for a while and support had been put in, so I assumed Neave knew of Amanda's dependency on Melody. But now, having met Amanda, I wondered how the two of them had coped at all. Far from fearing Amanda at that point, I felt sorry for her. No one starts their life wanting to make a complete mess of it and lose their children and die prematurely, which surely must be Amanda's fate.

CHAPTER SIX

THE WAY HOME?

Normally when I collect a child from the Family Centre at the end of contact I sign the Visitors' Book and go through to whichever room they are in, while the parent(s) make the most of their last few minutes with their child. But now as I stepped into reception I saw that Amanda and Melody were already there, together with the manager and another woman I took to be the contact supervisor. For a moment I assumed they'd just finished contact punctually, but then I saw their expressions and knew something was wrong.

'That's her,' Amanda said accusingly, jabbing her finger towards me.

'We've got a few problems we need to clear up,' the manager said, taking a step forward.

'You bet we have!' Amanda snarled. I could see she was chomping at the bit to get at me.

'Amanda is very concerned about Melody's clothes,' the manager said evenly.

'What about her clothes?' I asked, immediately anxious. 'She's wearing her school uniform.'

'I told you, Mum,' Melody said, looking embarrassed.

'Where are the clothes my daughter had on when she was taken off me yesterday?' Amanda snapped at me, her eyes blazing. 'You've stolen them.'

It was ludicrous, but they were all waiting for an answer.

'They're in the wash,' I said.

'How can I be sure she's telling the truth?' Amanda turned to the manager. 'And what about her trainers?' she demanded.

'They're in the car,' I said.

'And her hair!' Amanda said, nudging the manager. 'Tell her.'

'Amanda was worried about what you put on her daughter's hair.'

'It's poison,' Amanda snapped, glaring at me.

'Do you mean the head lice lotion?' I asked. 'If so, it's a standard preparation I bought from the chemist to kill head lice. Apart from that, and shampoo and water, she's had nothing else on her hair.'

'She hasn't got head lice!' Amanda growled.

'We couldn't find any,' the contact supervisor agreed.

'No, because I treated her hair and killed them.' I couldn't believe how ridiculous this was, although they were all looking at me doubtfully. 'Ask her social worker,' I added. 'Neave was aware that Melody had head lice.'

'I told you I kept itching,' Melody said to her mother.

'And where's her jacket?' Amanda now demanded.

'At home,' I said. 'It was badly torn, but I can return it to you if you like. The one she is wearing is a spare I had. I was going to buy her a new winter coat at the weekend. Don't you want me to do that?'

Amanda fell silent and I struggled to hide my annoyance.

The manager should have defused this situation, not turned it into a drama.

'You mentioned her dinner?' the supervisor now prompted Amanda.

'What about her dinner?' I asked. There was silence.

'Can't remember,' Amanda said, and the contact supervisor had the good sense not to remind her.

'Is that all?' I asked curtly.

The manager nodded.

'Say goodbye to your mother then,' I said to Melody, who should never have heard all of this.

I was now expecting a long emotional goodbye, but Amanda suddenly said she had to go to the toilet, and shouting, 'Bye!' she rushed off down the corridor. I said a cool goodbye to the manager and contact supervisor and left with Melody. I was seething inside, more so with the manager and the contact supervisor than I was with Amanda. She was angry and irrational from losing her child and I was an easy target, but the manager and contact supervisor should have known better and calmed her anger instead of pandering to it and making an issue out of everything she'd complained about. Foster carers don't expect gratitude, but a bit of moral support wouldn't go amiss. In bending over backwards to accommodate the parents' wishes, the staff involved in contact sometimes ingratiate themselves with the parents at the carer's expense.

Melody didn't say anything until we were in the car. Then, before I started the engine, she said quietly, 'I'm sorry, Cathy.'

I turned in my seat to look at her. 'What for, love?'

'Mum being horrible to you. She's like that with lots of people. She did it at school.'

'You don't have to apologize,' I said. 'It's not your fault. Your mum is upset because you are in care. It will get easier for her each time she sees you at contact as she gets used to it. Did you have a nice time?'

'I think so. I gave her the rice pudding.'

'Good.' I'd noticed Melody wasn't carrying the stay-fresh box. 'Did she like it?'

'She hasn't eaten it yet. She's going to take it home and have it for her dinner. There's nothing else there.' Hearing that, all my anger evaporated and my heart went out to Amanda again. The picture of that fragile, emaciated woman, aged beyond recognition, who'd lost all her children into care, sitting alone in her cold, damp flat eating rice pudding moved and worried me. I'd telephone Jill in the morning and make sure Neave was aware of just how needy Amanda was, for when a child is taken into care the social services have a duty to help the parents where possible.

When I dished up the cottage pie that evening I set aside a portion with vegetables and gravy for Amanda. Once it had cooled, I'd put it in the freezer to take with us to contact on Friday. Melody had said there was a microwave and kettle in their flat but no cooker or hob, and I knew there was a microwave at the Family Centre. Despite Amanda's rudeness, the woman needed help.

After dinner I left the washing up for later, and as Adrian, Lucy and Paula disappeared off to do their homework I told Melody to fetch her book bag from where she'd left it in the hall. We then sat together at the table and I helped her with her homework – reading, and spellings to learn. She needed a lot of help, but unlike some children I'd fostered who'd come from homes where education wasn't a priority, she had the right attitude and wanted to learn. 'Mum says you can get a good job and earn lots of money if you go to school and pass your exams.' Which was ironic considering her mother hadn't been sending Melody to school, but I didn't comment.

After Melody had finished her homework I began her bath and bedtime routine, finishing with a bedtime story. She was in bed in her new pyjamas at eight o'clock. I find bedtime, when the child is tired, is when they can start fretting and worrying. Far from being reassured by seeing her mother at contact, Melody was even more anxious, as indeed I was. Now I'd met Amanda I had a better understanding and appreciation of Melody's concerns.

'Melody, I don't want you to worry about your mother,' I said. 'Tomorrow I'm going to telephone Jill – you met her – who will speak to Neave and make sure your mother is OK.'

'Mummy is never OK,' Melody lamented. 'She's getting worse. She forgets to eat, get up and get dressed or go where she has to. That's why she was so late.'

'Is she still drinking alcohol or taking drugs?' I asked her gently. 'You know what I mean by drugs?'

'Yes. I don't think so. I haven't seen her do it for a bit. The man upstairs calls her nuts, and says she's done her head in with the stuff she put in her arm, but she can't help it.'

'No, all right.' I looked at her thoughtfully. Neave had said that Amanda had been funding her drug habit from prostitution and had asked if I could find out if she'd brought clients back to their flat, which opened up the possibility that Melody had witnessed her mother with a man or, heaven forbid, had been sexually abused herself. Foster carers can't afford to be squeamish or delicate about these matters and now seemed like a good time to ask. 'Melody, do you know where your mummy got her money from?'

She nodded. 'Benefits. I know because I had to help her get the money out of her bank so we could go shopping for food and pay the bills. Also she had some friends who gave her money.'

'Did you meet any of her friends?'

She shook her head.

'Were they women friends, do you know, or men?'

'Men. She always said "he".'

'Did she ever bring her friends home to your flat?'

'No. She always went out to meet them. She wasn't gone long and I had to stay in the room with the door locked. On the way home she bought me a chocolate bar if she remembered. Most of our money went to the man who owned the places we lived in. Mum said we were ripped off.'

'I understand. So Mummy never brought her men friends back to the places you lived in?'

'No.' Which was a relief.

'Do you know about the private parts of our body?' I asked, taking the opportunity to raise the matter. 'Did your mummy ever tell you?'

'No, but I saw it on television. In the morning there are programmes on for schools and I learnt about how babies are made, and our private parts that only we can touch.'

'Good,' I said. 'So what would you do if someone tried to touch your private parts? Do you know?'

'Scream and run away and tell an adult I trust straight away. That's what they tell the kids at school. It was in a programme called *Staying Safe*.'

'Excellent. And no one has tried to touch your private parts?'

'No! I'd kick him in the balls if he tried.'

I nodded, although I was pretty sure that hadn't been the exact wording used in a programme for school children! I was relieved that Melody didn't appear to have been sexually abused, and I would let Neave know. However, Melody should never have been left repeatedly alone in a flat while Amanda met her clients – she had placed them both in danger: Melody, a young child all by herself, and Amanda working the streets. The majority of prostitutes who work the streets alone do so to fund a drug habit, and they are regularly found abused and beaten.

Once Melody was asleep I spent time with Paula, Lucy and Adrian and then I wrote up my log notes, including the conversation I'd had with Melody. After that I printed Melody's name and class in indelible ink in all her school uniform items as the school requested, and at eleven o'clock I fell into bed. I slept well, as did Melody, and the following morning we continued the routine that would see us through the school weeks for however long Melody was with us. I woke everyone, made breakfast for Melody, Paula and myself while Adrian and Lucy – that much older – prepared whatever they fancied. Then, once ready, Melody and I left first, calling goodbye as we went.

When I returned home after taking Melody to school I telephoned Jill to update her. As my supervising social worker she was my first point of contact and we were on the phone for nearly an hour. I told her about the complaints Amanda had made about me at contact and she agreed they were irrational and felt they wouldn't go any further. I told her what

Melody had said about her mother being very forgetful and gave her examples of how she relied heavily on Melody. I said that according to Melody her mother had never brought her clients home and it seemed she hadn't been sexually abused. Jill said she'd pass all this on to Neave. I said Melody was eating and sleeping well, was in a full school uniform (which is considered important) and was generally settling in well, apart from worrying about her mother.

'That's only to be expected,' Jill said.

'Yes, except having now met Amanda I can see why Melody is so anxious. Amanda is very needy and appears to have relied on Melody far more than I've seen in a parent before. She's very forgetful and I noticed a vagueness about her, like she zones out.'

'Drugs?'

'I don't know. Melody says she's stopped using, but perhaps she's started again.'

'I'll tell Neave. She can run a drugs test if necessary,' Jill said, and winding up the conversation, we said goodbye.

I made a coffee and then returned to the phone and made appointments for Melody to have a check-up at the dentist and optician. I knew from experience that when a child first comes into care this was required. Neave would arrange for Melody to have a medical too.

At the end of school I met Miss May, the teaching assistant who was helping Melody. She accompanied Melody into the playground and to begin with she couldn't get a word in. Melody had so much to tell me. 'We did PE and I wore my new PE kit like everyone else,' Melody enthused excitedly. 'I'm good at PE, Miss May said. This is Miss May who helps me. She sits with me and the other two boys and we've done lots of good work today.'

Miss May laughed. 'We have indeed. Hello, you must be Cathy.'

'Yes, nice to meet you. Thank you for all you're doing to help Melody.'

'You're welcome. She's a delight to work with and works hard, although she has been worrying an awful lot about her mother.'

'I know, her social worker is aware, and I've tried to reassure Melody that her mother can look after herself.'

'Did you speak to my social worker?' Melody now asked, her previous excitement replaced by concern.

'I spoke to Jill and she's going to talk to Neave, so don't you worry.'

'It's such a shame,' Miss May said. 'It's difficult for me to know what to tell her for the best.'

'I think time will help. I've found before that once a child sees their parents doing all right, they let go of some of the responsibility they feel for them. Also, her social worker will talk to her mother about what she can do to reassure Melody at contact.'

'That's good.' She smiled at Melody. 'You see? There's no need for you to keep worrying about Mummy.'

Melody gave a small nod.

I usually work closely with the teaching assistant (TA) of the child I'm fostering. Not only do TAs help the child to learn, but they often give a level of pastoral support, and help the child develop their self-confidence and self-esteem. If a child is struggling at school it can have a knock-on effect on other aspects of their life. I'd taken an immediate liking to Miss May. Short, a little chubby, with a round, open, smiling face, you felt you wanted to hug her. I guessed she was approaching retirement age, but I doubted she would retire. She clearly loved her job, just as the children clearly loved her. As we stood talking I lost count of the number of children who'd gone out of their way to call and wave to her – 'Goodbye, Miss May♪ 'See you tomorrow, Miss May!' and so forth.

As Melody and I went to the car she said, 'Don't tell anyone, but Miss May likes sweets. She keeps a packet in her handbag. She gave me one, and the boys she helps, but no one else in the class.'

'Lucky you,' I said. I was pleased Melody was starting to enjoy school – some children don't.

That evening passed as most school nights do, with dinner, homework, bath and bed. The following day was Friday and Melody had contact again. She woke up worrying about her mother. 'I hope Mum's not late again,' she said anxiously. 'I hope she remembers to come. She might not remember how to get there. I hope she has something to eat.'

'I've got some dinner for her,' I said. 'I saved some of the cottage pie we had on Wednesday. I'll defrost it and bring it with me.' The look of gratitude on Melody's face was heartbreaking. Then it was replaced with yet more anxiety. 'It's Saturday tomorrow, isn't it?'

'Yes.'

'Mum and me go shopping on Saturday to buy food for the weekend. I won't see her again until Monday, so she won't have anything to eat all weekend.'

'Melody, I am sure your mother will buy herself something to eat over the weekend. She's an adult. Please don't worry about her. Now come on, time to get dressed ready for school.'

60

I was about to leave her room when she said, 'Cathy, you said you give us pocket money on Saturday. Can I have mine early?'

'What for?'

'To buy food for my mum.' She wasn't the first child I'd fostered who'd wanted to use their pocket money to help out their parents.

'Love, that money is for you, but as you're so worried I've got a couple of ready meals in the freezer, which your mum can have. I'll bring them with me at the end of school and she can have them at the weekend.'

'Thank you,' Melody said, and threw her arms around me, which made me tear up. Clearly I wouldn't be providing Amanda with all her meals – this was a short-term measure to stop Melody from worrying and to get them both through their first weekend apart. Amanda had her benefit money, and if she really had stopped using drugs she should have enough to buy food.

Later, before I left to collect Melody from school, I added some fruit, crisps and biscuits to the bag I was taking.

Melody needn't have worried about her mother being late for contact, for when we arrived she was already there, and had been for two hours! The receptionist said it wasn't clear why Amanda had arrived so early, but she'd insisted on staying in the waiting room for the whole two hours so she didn't miss Melody. She was now in Yellow Room with the contact supervisor for the start of contact. Melody was of course delighted that her mother was already there. She was sitting on the sofa, looking at a children's book, and the contact supervisor was at a small table at one end, writing.

'Hello, Mummy!' Melody cried, running to her, the bag of food dangling at her side.

Amanda looked up and for a second seemed startled, as if she hadn't been expecting to see Melody or didn't recognize her, but then she stood and hugged her. I said hello to Amanda and then left. I walked to a small local café where I did some paperwork over a cup of tea and a teacake. I returned to collect Melody at 5.30 p.m. and went through to Yellow Room. The door was open and the three of them were putting on their coats. I said hello. Amanda looked in my direction but didn't say anything. Melody was naturally reluctant to leave her mother and kept hugging and kissing her until the contact supervisor said, 'Time to go.' With a final hug and kiss for her mother, Melody came to me and we left.

Outside the centre Melody said, 'Mum liked your cottage pie. She ate it all.'

'Good. She warmed it up in the microwave?'

'Yes, the contact supervisor helped her, as children aren't allowed in the kitchen. She was starving and said it was the first thing she'd had to eat since your rice pudding.'

'But that was Wednesday,' I said, shocked. 'Are you sure?'

'Yes. She ate the crisps and biscuits too. I keep telling you, Mum forgets to eat without me telling her to.'

If Melody was right then it was very worrying and exceeded any adult–child dependency I'd seen before.

'All right. I'll make sure Neave knows.' But shouldn't her social worker have known already? I wondered. Melody and her mother had been known to the social services for some time. Unless of course Melody was exaggerating, perhaps thinking this was the way to get home.

CHAPTER SEVEN

LOST

On Saturday, I took Melody shopping to buy her some more casual clothes, a swimming costume, posters and knick-knacks for her room to make it more personal. Also, a rag doll she spotted and immediately fell in love with, as it reminded her of a doll she'd once owned that had been lost in one of the moves. Lucy and Paula came too and we had some lunch out. Adrian was playing football and then studying in the afternoon. It was a successful day and I could see that Melody was delighted with all the purchases and to have the company, attention and advice of the two older girls, who helped her choose her clothes.

'Are you being spoilt?' Lucy asked her.

Melody looked as though she might have done something wrong.

'It's OK, she's joking,' I said. 'Lucy has everything she needs.'

On Sunday we had a leisurely morning, including a full English breakfast – a first for Melody. In the afternoon I took her to the cinema, leaving the others at home to finish their homework and chill out. I'd learned that young people need their own space sometimes, especially in a family that fosters where there is often a lot going on, including regular visits from social workers, sometimes the child's family, meetings and phone calls, all of which can be disruptive and intrusive to normal family life. Melody was mesmerized by the cartoon film and for the time it lasted she stopped worrying about her mother. However, as soon as it ended and we were on our way home she grew anxious again. 'I hope Mummy has got up.' 'I hope she hasn't got lost.' 'I bet Mummy hasn't eaten.' I reminded her we'd given her ready meals, which only had to be heated in the microwave. 'I hope Mum remembers how to work the microwave,' Melody continued.

'I'm sure she will. You only have to press a couple of buttons.'

Melody looked doubtful.

On Sunday evening I telephoned my parents for a chat as I usually did if we hadn't seen them during the weekend. They were very supportive of my fostering and knew we'd get together once Melody had settled in. The children I'd fostered loved my parents, as of course did Adrian, Paula and Lucy. They were the typical doting grandparents and welcomed all the children we looked after into their hearts and homes.

Too quickly it was Monday again and I was waking my family ready for school. Melody was happy as she was seeing her mother that evening and had a swimming lesson at school. She couldn't wait to wear her new swimming costume and use the new towel she'd chosen when shopping. It had a large picture of Walt Disney's Donald Duck. 'You're quackers!' Adrian joked when she showed it to him, and we all groaned.

Melody and I left the house first as usual and once I'd seen her into school I stopped by the supermarket to top up on some essential groceries. Once home, I telephoned Jill to update her. Foster carers like me who foster for an Independent Fostering Agency (IFA), rather than directly for their Local Authority, usually report to their supervising social worker at their agency first, who then updates the child's social worker. Jill was in the office and began by asking me if we'd had a good weekend. I said we had and told her briefly what we'd done. She wasn't just making conversation; as my supervising social worker she needed to know what I'd arranged for the child to do over the weekend. I then told her what Melody had been saying about her mother not eating or being able to do anything without her being there.

'When Neave placed Melody she didn't say anything about Amanda's total dependency on her daughter,' I said. 'It seems strange she didn't reassure Melody, and it's obviously upsetting her.'

'Perhaps Neave didn't know,' Jill said. 'Parents can hide what they don't want the social worker to see, and Melody could have been covering up for her too. I didn't manage to speak to Neave on Friday – she wasn't in her office – so I'll call her now and see if she is aware. Also, the contact supervisor should have included it in her reports if it is going on at contact.'

'Yes, OK, thank you, Jill.'

It was the afternoon before Jill returned my call. She had a number of issues to cover. 'I've just spoken to Neave. She hasn't been able to see Amanda since Melody came into care so hasn't been able to get any of Melody's belongings. Neave thinks Amanda is avoiding her, and there's a possibility she may be on the move again.'

'I seem to remember that Amanda was being evicted.'

'Yes, that was mentioned. I told Neave what Melody has been saying about her mother and she is going to observe contact on Friday. It will give her a chance to speak to Amanda and watch how she relates to Melody. Neave has received the contact supervisor's report for Wednesday, but not for Friday yet. Apparently the contact supervisor noted that Amanda seemed confused and angry at times. Your name came up, as Amanda kept blaming you for some things, quite irrationally, including stealing her daughter's clothes and putting poison on her hair. A few times she seemed disorientated. When she left the room, to go to the toilet or get a drink, Melody went with her so she could find her way back. At one point she appeared to have forgotten Melody's name. But the contact supervisor also noted that Amanda was loving towards Melody and was able to show her affection appropriately. Neave feels it could be that Amanda's confusion was a result of being in an unfamiliar setting and being flustered by arriving late for contact, or it could be that she's still using. There was no smell of alcohol. She's going to see how it goes at contact this week and then may ask for a drugs test if she feels it's appropriate.'

'OK.'

'She asked if you can tell Melody that she'll be there on Friday observing contact, so it doesn't come as a shock.'

'Yes, I will.'

'Neave also said she'd requested a medical for Melody, so you should receive a letter in the post with details of the appointment before too long. She's given your contact details to the Guardian ad Litem, who will be in touch to arrange to see Melody.' This is standard for a child when they first come into care.

'All right, thanks, Jill.'

That afternoon I prepared dinner for later – pasta, cheese and broccoli bake – and set aside a portion for Amanda. Melody had asked that morning if we could take her mother some dinner. Before I left I wrote a note for Adrian, Paula and Lucy saying what time to put the dish in the oven and the setting. I then drove to Melody's school and waited in the playground for her to come out. She appeared with Miss May and the first thing she asked was, 'Have you remembered Mummy's dinner?'

'Yes, don't worry. It's in the car.'

Miss May said that Melody had had a good day, although she had been rather nervous in the swimming lesson. It seemed it was the first time she'd ever been swimming, so she'd stayed in the shallow end with armbands on. 'She was worried about drowning,' Miss May said. 'She told me her mother never took her swimming because she thought she would drown.' I could see from Miss May's expression that she thought this was an odd thing to tell a child, as did I.

'You won't drown,' I said to Melody. 'But it is important you learn to swim.'

'We make it fun and the children are never asked to do anything they are not comfortable with,' Miss May added.

'I know. I'll reassure her,' I said. 'I guess it was all a bit new today.'

'Yes, we let her spend the lesson walking widths and doing small jumps to get used to the feel of the water.'

I thanked Miss May and we said goodbye. On the way to the car Melody said, 'Lots of the children in my class can swim and go in the deep end without armbands.'

'And you will too one day,' I said brightly.

'Will I?'

'Yes. As well as the swimming lessons at school I could take you swimming at the weekend to help.'

'No. Mummy won't like that,' she said adamantly. 'It will worry her.'

'We'll see. I'll talk to Neave about it,' and I dropped the subject. While I didn't want to worry Amanda or Melody, I would be pursuing the matter, for here was another opportunity Melody had missed out on. Now she was in care (under a court order) the social services had responsibility for her, and usually they felt the child should have access to opportunities like this that they'd previously missed, so I would ask Neave if I could take Melody swimming.

When we arrived at the Family Centre Amanda was in reception signing the Visitors' Book.

'Mummy!' Melody cried, rushing to her. Amanda turned and they hugged, but then Amanda suddenly drew back.

'You've got fleas,' she said.

'No, I haven't,' Melody said, hurt.

'Yes, from their cat.'

'No, I haven't, Mum,' and she looked to me for help.

'She hasn't got fleas, Amanda,' I said, going over. 'Our cat doesn't have fleas. Melody had head lice, but they're all gone now.'

'Really?' Amanda said, apparently truly astonished. 'How did you make them go away? Magic?'

I looked at her. 'With head lice lotion,' I replied. Did she really not remember after all the fuss she'd made last week about me putting 'poison' on her daughter's hair?

'I think I need some of your magic lotion,' she said and

began scratching her arm quite roughly, which can be a sign of drug withdrawal.

'Come on, Mummy,' Melody said, taking her hand. 'Let's go to the room.' I followed them, carrying the box of pasta bake as Melody guided her mother down the corridor. It was my responsibility to see Melody into the room, then I would leave. Amanda didn't appear unsteady on her feet and there was no smell of alcohol, but she was disorientated, and what she'd just said seemed quite bizarre. She kept looking around and into the rooms she passed as if searching for something familiar. I doubted she would have found Yellow Room again without Melody showing her. The centre tries to give families the same room each time for continuity. I said a polite hello to the contact supervisor – the same one as before – and placed the box of pasta bake on the coffee table. 'I hope you like it,' I said to Amanda.

'It's pasta, Mum,' Melody said. 'Your favourite.'

But Amanda just looked blank, so perhaps she'd forgotten I'd brought in food before. I said goodbye to her and Melody, and then left.

I went to the café again where I did some paperwork and read a book over a cup of tea. I was starting to enjoy this quiet time alone – our house was always so busy. I returned to the Family Centre at 5.30 p.m. to collect Melody and went through to Yellow Room. She and her mother were sitting side by side on the sofa with a pencil each and a sheet of paper on a clipboard between them. 'We're playing noughts and crosses,' Melody said.

'Great. That sounds like fun.'

I went over to look. For anyone not familiar with it, it's a simple game for two players who take turns to place a nought or a cross in a three-by-three grid. The player who manages to make three of their marks in a horizontal, vertical or diagonal row wins the game. Another grid is then drawn for the next game. It's a 'fill in' game you play in your spare time for about ten minutes. But their sheet of paper was covered in dozens and dozens of small completed grids. Beside them on the sofa was a stack of similarly covered sheets. 'Have you been playing noughts and crosses all this time?' I asked.

Melody nodded as her pencil hovered over the grid and she tried to decide where to place her cross.

'Come on, your turn.' Amanda nudged her. 'You can't go until we've finished.'

Melody made her cross in a place that would allow her mother to win. Amanda added a nought and yelped with joy. 'Time for another game!' she said, and quickly drew another grid.

I glanced at the contact supervisor. It wasn't for me to say it was time to go. 'One more game and then you need to pack away and say goodbye,' she said.

As I waited I picked up from the coffee table my empty stay-fresh box that had contained the pasta bake.

'Why are you taking that?' Amanda asked, looking up.

'I'll take it home so I can use it again,' I said.

'It's Cathy's,' Melody added.

'Oh, is it?' Amanda said, as though she had forgotten.

The game ended with Amanda winning again and she began to draw another grid for the next game. It was now nearly 5.45. Contact should have ended fifteen minutes ago. 'Time to pack away,' the contact supervisor finally said. Standing, she came over.

'Oh, just when I was winning!' Amanda lamented, like a child might.

'We can play it again next time,' Melody said, and handed the clipboard and pencils to the contact supervisor. She then hugged and kissed her mother goodbye.

'See you Wednesday,' I said. Amanda looked confused. 'Wednesday is the next contact. It's Monday today.'

'Is it?' she asked.

'You should have a letter with the days and times of contact,' the supervisor said.

'She'll have lost it,' Melody said.

I picked up one of the unused sheets of paper from the coffee table and, taking a pen from my bag, wrote down the days and times of the contact. 'Here we go,' I said, passing the sheet to Amanda.

'I hope I don't lose this too,' she laughed. Melody smiled.

With a final goodbye, we left. I felt I had been of some help and Amanda had appeared less resentful towards me.

'You like playing noughts and crosses then?' I said to Melody as we went down the corridor.

'It's OK.' She shrugged. 'Miss May taught me today and I showed Mummy how to play. It was all right to begin with, but then it got boring. I kept playing because Mummy didn't want to stop. So I let her win.'

'But you had a nice time?'

'Yes. Mummy was happy.'

'Good.'

I was pleased they'd had a nice time and Amanda had been happy. It's important for the child to leave contact with a positive feeling.

* * *

On Wednesday, I made a casserole and rice pudding again. I tend to make the children's favourite dishes every week and these were good winter warmers. Melody was sure her mother would like the casserole, and she'd already had some of my rice pudding the week before and enjoyed it. We arrived at contact five minutes early, with Melody carrying the two stay-fresh containers. The receptionist said that Amanda hadn't arrived yet and asked us to sign in and go to the waiting room. Melody immediately grew anxious. 'I bet Mum's got lost again.'

'Melody, we're early, and your mother has been here three times before,' I said. 'I'm sure she won't get lost now. Let's sit down and I'll show you what five minutes is on my watch.' We settled in the waiting room and I explained the time as I was doing at every opportunity so that Melody would learn to tell the time. But as the minutes ticked by I realized this exercise was becoming counterproductive, as I was drawing attention to the fact that her mother was getting later and later. Instead, I picked up a couple of children's storybooks from the table and tried to distract Melody by reading, but without success. The door to the centre periodically opened and closed as other families came or left, and Melody kept going into the corridor to check if it was her mother.

'Where is she? Where has Mummy got to?' she asked, worried, returning again to sit beside me.

At 4.20, when Amanda was twenty minutes late, I left Melody in the waiting room and went to speak to the receptionist. 'Has Amanda phoned in?' I asked.

'No, nothing yet. We have been trying to call her, but she's not answering.'

'How much longer will you give her?'

'I'll have to speak to the manager.'

I returned to the waiting room and the minutes ticked by. At 4.30 the manager appeared. 'I'm sorry, but it seems that your mummy isn't coming today,' she said to Melody. 'We'll give her five more minutes.'

I nodded sombrely. 'She hasn't phoned then?'

She shook her head. Melody looked crestfallen.

It's dreadful for a child to sit waiting for a parent who doesn't show, and the next five minutes were excruciating. Now I was more aware of just how vulnerable and needy Amanda was I shared some of Melody's concerns, although I didn't tell her. I reassured her as best I could and at 4.35, when the manager reappeared and said we should go, it was something of a relief. If Amanda wasn't coming then it was better we left now before Melody became more anxious and upset.

'Mummy hasn't had her dinner,' Melody said as I picked up the boxes. 'Can we leave them here in case she comes, then she can have her dinner later?'

I looked at the manager. 'Is that possible?' I asked, although I knew the centre closed at 6 p.m.

'I'll put them in the fridge,' she said.

'Thank you.' It helped to reassure Melody a little, although whether Amanda would arrive before the centre closed we wouldn't know.

Melody and I left, signing out on the way, but outside she burst into tears. 'Where's my mummy? Where is she? She's lost and all alone.' I put my arm around her and comforted her as best I could.

CHAPTER EIGHT

DIFFICULT

When Melody and I arrived home on that Wednesday Lucy and Paula were downstairs, holding a ruler each, and were surprised to see us home early.

'Mummy didn't come to contact,' Melody said, fighting back fresh tears.

'Oh dear! Did she phone to say why?' Lucy asked, having had experience of similar.

'No,' Melody said, her bottom lip trembling. Paula was looking sad too.

'Could you take Melody to play a game or something while I make a phone call?' I said.

'You can help with my maths homework,' Paula said. 'We're measuring everything in the living room. I have to make a scale drawing.'

Sufficiently intrigued, Melody went with them, which allowed me to phone my fostering agency without being overheard. 'Amanda didn't show for contact,' I told Jill. 'I wondered if you'd heard anything from Neave?'

'No, and I doubt there's anything to be gained by phoning her now. She'd have called if she knew. I'll phone her in the morning. How has Melody taken it?'

'She's upset and worried.'

'The poor dear. Her mother has probably just forgotten – you said she was very forgetful.'

'Yes, I know, thanks, Jill. Speak tomorrow.'

During the evening I reassured Melody a number of times that nothing bad had happened to her mother, and that I'd find out tomorrow from her social worker where she'd got to.

'Will I be able to see Mummy tomorrow, as we missed contact tonight?' she asked.

'I doubt it, love. The Family Centre is usually fully booked, but I can ask, and Friday – your next contact – will come quickly.' It was all I could offer.

Melody took a while to settle that night and I sat with her until she fell asleep with her face pressed against the rag doll we'd bought on our shopping trip on Saturday. She'd named the doll Lizzie after a girl she'd been playing with at school and whom she now viewed as a friend.

The following morning Melody was already awake when I went into her room. I suspected she had been for some time and she'd been dwelling on what had happened. 'If you speak to my social worker, can you tell her to tell Mummy I love her, and to make sure she knows where the Family Centre is, and she has to go on Friday? She might have lost the sheet of paper you gave her, like she did the letter.'

'I'll tell her,' I said.

'And Neave has to tell her which bus to catch.'

'Yes. OK. I'll remember.'

I doubt parents of children in care fully appreciate just how much their children worry when they don't show for contact. It also adds to their feelings of rejection.

'I expect that's what happened,' Melody said, still trying to rationalize her mother not seeing her. 'She lost the letter, then lost the paper you gave her, and didn't know which bus to catch.'

'It's certainly possible,' I said. 'Now come on, up you get, ready for school.' Although how the poor child would ever concentrate on her schoolwork I had no idea.

Melody, Paula and I had porridge for breakfast – Adrian and Lucy had had theirs – and then, calling goodbye, Melody and I left for school. Once I'd seen her into school I returned home, expecting Jill to phone having spoken to Neave. However, when the phone rang mid-morning it was Neave herself. 'I understand Amanda didn't show for contact last night. Do you have any idea where she might be?'

'None.'

'Melody hasn't said anything?'

'No, she thinks she might have got lost. She said to tell you to make sure her mother has the details of the Family Centre and knows which bus to catch. Amanda is very forgetful, you know.'

'Yes, but it seems to be getting worse. I've tried to phone her, but she's not answering. I'm in a meeting soon and I'll visit her flat when I get out. Amanda threatened to commit suicide if I took Melody into care, but she seems to have been coping. I understand from the contact supervisor that they had a good contact on Monday.'

'Yes, they played noughts and crosses.'

'How did Amanda appear then?'

'A bit disorientated and confused, but otherwise all right. She didn't seem depressed.'

'No, that's what the contact supervisor said. Hopefully

Amanda will be home again by the time I visit her, and remember I'll be observing contact on Friday.'

'Yes.'

'Can you update Jill? I don't have time now,' she said.

'I will, and Melody said when you speak to her mother, please tell her she loves her.'

'Sure.'

We said goodbye. I felt very uneasy at what Neave had said about Amanda threatening suicide. I phoned my fostering agency to update Jill. She wasn't in the office, so I left a message with a colleague, paraphrasing what Neave had told me.

I didn't hear anything further from Neave or Jill, so just before I left to collect Melody from school I telephoned Jill again.

'Sorry, Cathy, I've been tied up. I got your message and I've spoken to Neave. She visited Amanda's flat earlier this afternoon but she wasn't there. She spoke to someone in the house who seemed to know her. He said she was hardly there now and thought she may have moved. Neave said that contact will go ahead on Friday.' This seemed reassuring, as it was quite possible Amanda had missed contact because she was in the process of moving. Some parents of children in care lead very chaotic lives, especially when substance abuse is involved. They can disappear for days, even weeks, and then reappear somewhere else. I would need to think carefully about what I told Melody.

When I met her at the end of school it was Miss May I had to reassure first. 'Have you found her?' she asked anxiously. 'Melody said her mother was lost. I do hope she is all right.'

'I'm sure she is,' I said. 'She didn't arrive for contact, but Melody should be seeing her tomorrow as usual.'

'There you go,' she said to Melody, clearly relieved. 'I said she'd be all right.'

Miss May then told me what homework Melody had in her school bag and, wishing each other a pleasant evening, we said goodbye. As Melody and I crossed the playground a girl of a similar age to Melody came up to her. 'Have they found your mummy now?' she asked her quietly.

'Maybe,' Melody said a little sullenly.

I smiled at the girl and she returned to her mother. 'Was that Lizzie?' I asked.

Melody nodded.

'She seems very nice. You could invite her to our house to play one time.'

But Melody's thoughts were on other matters. 'Did you speak to Neave?'

'Yes. She thinks your mummy may have moved, but she will come to contact on Friday.'

'We're always moving,' she sighed. 'She'll get even more lost now!'

Without any evidence to the contrary, Melody, like me, accepted this as a plausible explanation for her mother not going to contact. Once home she watched some children's television until dinner was ready, and then after we'd eaten I helped her with her homework.

'When you cook tomorrow can you do some for Mummy?' she asked me as I took her up to bed.

'Yes, of course. Although I'm not sure what it will be yet.'

'Chicken nuggets and chips is her favourite and mine,' she said.

'OK. We'll have that,' I smiled. I usually cooked proper

meals, so processed food wasn't going to harm anyone once in a while.

The following morning Melody was very happy because she thought she would be seeing her mother and was having her favourite dinner. 'Six nuggets and medium French fries,' she told me in the car as if ordering from a fast-food take-away. I had to laugh.

Having seen Melody into school, I drove to a large super-market on the edge of town to do a big shop for the weekend, as my parents were coming for dinner on Sunday. On return-ing home, I'd just finished putting the cold foods in the freezer and fridge when the phone rang. I answered it in the kitchen, surrounded by the bags I'd yet to unpack. It was Jill, and I knew straight away that something was wrong: she has a habit of saying 'Cathy,' and then pausing, as though steeling herself before continuing. 'Amanda is in hospital.'

'Oh no. What's the matter?' Immediately my thoughts raced through possible scenarios, including her being knocked down, a drug overdose and a suicide attempt.

'She has been sectioned under the Mental Health Act,' Jill said. 'She's been in hospital since Wednesday but wasn't carrying any ID, so the police have only just found out who she is.'

'Wednesday. So is that why she wasn't at contact?'

'It seems she was on her way to the Family Centre but got on the wrong bus. When she realized, she wanted the bus driver to turn the bus around and take her back. The driver thought she was joking to begin with, but then she became aggressive and kept hitting his arm and shouting while he was driving. He parked the bus and called the police. They found her to be very confused and agitated, and arrested her.

They took her to the police station, where her behaviour gave them further cause for concern. They called the duty psychiatrist, who felt she needed hospitalization. Amanda refused to go voluntarily, so she was sectioned under the Mental Health Act.'

'Oh dear. How long will she be in hospital?'

'It's a Section 2, so up to twenty-eight days, although it could be extended if necessary. She's in –' and Jill named a large hospital in the area that had a psychiatric unit. 'Neave said it's not appropriate for Melody to visit her until she is assessed and stabilized.'

'No, I can see that. Do you know how long that is likely to take?'

'Probably about a week. Neave will meet Amanda and the clinician responsible for her towards the end of next week. Best tell Melody that her mother is in hospital without going into details, unless she asks.'

'I will,' I said, worried. 'Poor Amanda.'

'At least she will get the help she needs now,' Jill said. 'Apparently her behaviour has been giving cause for concern for some time.'

'Yes, it was very odd and worrying at times. So Melody will be able to see her once she's assessed and stabilized in a week or so?'

'It's not definite. It will depend on how quickly Amanda responds to the treatment, so don't build up Melody's hopes.'

'No, I won't.'

'Keep her busy over the weekend and phone the agency's out-of-hours service if you need to.'

'I will, thank you.' My fostering agency provided an emergency service twenty-four hours a day, every day of the year.

I replaced the handset with a deep feeling of sadness and concern for Amanda. Here I was in the familiar comfort of my home, looking forward to the weekend, while Amanda was being detained in a psychiatric hospital against her will. While I appreciated it was for her own good and she would get the help she needed, I felt a cold pang of fear. I think most of us at some point in our lives tread a narrow line between being mentally healthy and harbouring strange and irrational thoughts. How easy it would be to slip over that line and lose touch with reality and not be able to make decisions for oneself. I could picture Amanda on the bus, suddenly realizing she was heading the wrong way and then panicking that she would be late for contact. Her response may have been ridiculous, but it had a child-like logic to it: I need to see my daughter, make the bus driver turn the bus around. It saddened me greatly, and the rest of the afternoon I was plagued by worrying thoughts of Amanda. Did she understand why she was in hospital? Did she know her daughter was safe with me? Did she have a change of clothes with her? Was she frightened or heavily sedated? I knew she would be well looked after, but it didn't stop me from worrying. And what would I tell Melody?

When the phone rang shortly before I was due to leave to collect Melody from school I snatched it up, thinking there might be more news about Amanda, but a female voice I didn't recognize said, 'Hello, Cathy Glass?'

'Yes, speaking.'

'This is Nina French, the Guardian for Melody.' It took me a moment to realize who I was talking to.

'Oh, yes, hello. Neave said you would be in contact.'

'Good. You understand my role?'

'Yes.' The Guardian ad Litem (or Guardian) is a social worker appointed by the court in child-care proceedings for the duration of the case. He or she is independent of the social services but has access to all the files. They see all parties in the case and report to the judge on what is in the best interests of the child.

'I'm phoning to introduce myself,' she said, 'and make an appointment to visit you and Melody. I suggest after school, so she doesn't miss any more schooling. I'll be speaking to her teacher and also observing her and her mother at contact.' This was usual for the Guardian, except of course there wouldn't be any contact in the foreseeable future.

'You know Amanda is in hospital?' I asked

'No, I didn't. When was this?'

'Wednesday evening.'

'It would be nice if someone told me,' she said, clearly put out.

'I understand that it's taken a while to find out who Amanda was, as she didn't have any ID on her.'

'Couldn't she tell them?'

'I don't know all the details, but she's been confused and is now sectioned under the Mental Health Act.'

'I'll need to speak to their social worker. Will Melody be seeing her mother while she is in hospital?'

'Not right away.'

'I'll have to get back to you. I was going to make an appointment to visit Melody this week, but that doesn't seem appropriate now. I'll speak to the social worker first. How is Melody settling in?'

'All right really, until now. Obviously she misses her mother and I'm not sure how she will take this news.'

'She doesn't know yet?'

'No, I've only just found out.'

'OK. Thank you for your help. I'll be in touch.'

It was the first time I could ever remember having more up-to-date information than the Guardian ad Litem.

I drove to Melody's school, going through what I would say to minimize the impact of her mother being in hospital. Children in care often show amazing resilience and are true little heroes, but a sick parent is particularly difficult for them to cope with. I'd been in similar situations before with children I'd fostered, and knew how worried they could become. Also, mental health is an especially difficult concept for a child to understand – much easier if their parent has a physical illness like a broken arm or is recovering from an operation.

I parked the car and then waited in my usual spot in the playground for the end of school. Melody, of course, was expecting to see her mother at contact and came out of school smiling. Miss May was with her, but having checked I was in the playground she went to see the mother of a boy she also helped.

'We're going to see Mummy!' Melody cried, elated as she bounced over to me. 'Did you remember the chicken nuggets and chips?'

'Listen, love. I'm afraid I've got some disappointing news. We won't be seeing your mummy tonight.'

'Why not? It's Friday! I'm allowed to see Mummy on a Friday,' she said angrily. Parents close by glanced in our direction.

'Come on, I'll explain.' I offered her my hand but she refused it, and walked beside me as we began across the playground. 'Your mummy is in hospital, being looked after by the doctors and nurses. There's nothing for you to worry about, but you won't be able to see her today.'

'Why not?' she demanded again.

'Because she's not well enough.'

'She's not going to die, is she?' Melody asked, now close to tears. I put my arm around her as we left the playground.

'No, love. Let's get in the car and I'll explain.' I opened the rear door and we slid into the back seat. I looked at her sad and dejected face. 'There are many different types of illness and people get sick for different reasons. Sometimes it's easy to see what is wrong with the person; they may have a rash or a bad cough. But other times it's because of how they feel inside and the things they say and do, or can't do. Your mummy hasn't been coping well lately, and you've been help-ing her a lot.'

'I don't mind,' Melody sniffed.

'I know you don't, and you've been doing a good job of helping her. But sometimes, no matter how much we help a loved one, they have to go into hospital so the doctors and nurses can give them medicine and make them better.'

'Why can't I see Mummy?' she asked again.

'Because the doctor wants to get her a bit better first.'

'How long will that take?'

'I'm not sure exactly. Neave will tell us, but I hope she will be well enough for us to visit in a week or so.'

'We'll visit her in hospital?'

'Yes, I think so.' There were so many unknowns here, I was being careful not to give her false hope as Jill had warned.

'Why can't I see Mummy now?' Melody persisted.

'Because she isn't well enough yet. If you think about how

Mummy has been – getting lost and not remembering things – I think you'll understand. It is important the doctors work out what is wrong and then get her better.'

'And once she's better, we can both go home?'

'That's a nice thought.'

It was one of the most difficult conversations I'd ever had with a child, and I hoped I'd handled it right. Foster carers receive ongoing training to help them foster, but it doesn't prepare us for breaking bad news like this. The carer has to rely on experience, sensitivity and common sense.

'If you have any questions, ask me and I'll do my best to answer,' I said. 'I'll tell you when I hear anything further. We'll go home now, and have a nice weekend. Your mummy is being well looked after.'

'Will we still be having chicken nuggets and chips?' she asked.

'Yes, love.' And she allowed me to give her a hug.

CHAPTER NINE

WHEN CAN I SEE MUMMY?

I kept Melody occupied during the evening, as I would be doing for most of the weekend. I quietly told Paula, Adrian and Lucy what had happened, for clearly we were home earlier than usual and wouldn't be going to contact the following week. Now they were aware, they would be sensitive to what Melody was going through and give her extra attention. Interestingly, Melody didn't keep asking after her mother and worrying about her as she had been doing. I think this was due to her accepting that her mother was safe and being well looked after in hospital. It must have been a huge burden for her – with just the two of them at home and Melody, aged eight, the more responsible. Now that burden had been lifted, although, of course, Melody thought that at some point she and her mother would be returning home. It wasn't for me to tell her otherwise at this stage, and I supposed it could be possible, depending on her mother's diagnosis, but given the history of neglect and Amanda's drug and alcohol addiction, I didn't think it was likely. I knew from experience that as the months went by and all the reports on Amanda and Melody were written the picture would become clearer, and then the judge would make his or her decision at the final court hearing when Melody would be told the outcome, usually by the social worker.

We had chicken nuggets, chips and peas with large helpings of tomato ketchup for dinner, followed by jam roly-poly pudding and custard, which we all enjoyed. Melody stayed up later than usual that evening, as it was the start of the weekend and we didn't have to be up early in the morning for school. Lucy, Paula and I played some games with her, I read her a bedtime story and then she said goodnight and I took her up to bed. I always went up with her and waited on the landing while she washed and changed, then I saw her into bed. It was part of our evening routine. She climbed into bed and cuddled the rag doll. 'I'm calling her Mandy now,' she announced, so I thought perhaps she and Lizzie were no longer friends – children of her age often make and break friendships – but then she added, 'Mummy's friends at school used to call her Mandy when she was little.'

'That's nice. Amanda is sometimes shortened to Mandy. What made you suddenly think of that?' I asked.

'Mummy used to talk about when she was happy as a child before bad things happened to her.'

'I see,' I said, and sat on the edge of the bed.

'She told me it was the bad things that were done to her that made her drink and take drugs to try to forget.'

'That is sad,' I said. 'Did she tell what bad things happened to her?' I hoped the answer was no, but Melody gave a small nod.

'Her step-father did rude things to her that hurt her a lot.'

'Oh, that's dreadful. I am sorry to hear that. No one will hurt your mummy now. She is safe and being well looked after. There will be a special doctor there called a psychiatrist she can talk to.' But surely it hadn't taken all this time for Amanda to get the help she needed? I thought. Child abuse ruins lives if it is not dealt with. Counselling and therapy often help.

'Do you think Mummy is in bed now?' Melody asked, kissing the rag doll.

'I expect so. She is probably snuggled down in a comfortable bed, just as you are.'

'Thinking about me.'

'Yes, of course.'

She smiled and kissed the doll again. 'Night-night, Mummy. I miss you, but you are safe and being looked after by the doctors and nurses.'

'That's right, love.' I said goodnight, kissed her forehead and then, once I was sure she was going to sleep, came out. Interestingly, that evening Melody had been the most relaxed I'd ever seen her, for while she missed her mother she no longer had to constantly worry about her.

Saturday morning Adrian was up, showered and dressed at a reasonable time and left to play football, while the girls and I had a more leisurely morning. The girls stayed in their dressing gowns to have their breakfast and then dressed late morning and set about doing their homework. My parents were coming the following day and I didn't want it left and then done in a hurry after they'd gone. I helped Melody do her homework and then took her to our local park. It was a cold but dry day and she enjoyed playing on the apparatus.

After dinner, with everyone unusually home on a Saturday evening, we got out the Monopoly board and taught Melody how to play the game. She saw a different side to us as the noise level rose and land was won or lost, and piles of Monopoly money rose and fell. It was great fun; she enjoyed herself and so did we. I think it's important for families to play games together sometimes, as it helps bond and unite them. Afterwards Melody confided in Paula that she felt it was OK for her to laugh and play games now her mummy was safe in hospital. It was another revealing comment about the weight of responsibility she'd been carrying. Later, I noted it in my log when I wrote up the day's events.

My parents arrived on Sunday around midday and I introduced them to Melody as Nana and Grandpa, which is how most children we fostered looked upon them. They were kind, with plenty of attention for everyone, and Melody immediately took to them, especially my mother. Melody had never had grandparents of her own, but she talked easily to Nana. She told her about her own mummy and how she came to be in hospital, while Mum listened sympathetically. Melody sat next to her on the sofa before and after dinner and opposite her as we ate. My children were very indulgent of Melody monopolizing Nana's company, but I made sure they had a chance to talk to her, and Grandpa. Adrian always spent time with my father, and since my husband had left some years before in many respects he had become a father figure, providing my children with a good male role model.

We had a truly lovely day and when it was time for my parents to say goodbye Melody came with us to the front door to see them off, hugging and kissing my mother as we all did, and kissing my father's cheek. I think that loving grandparents are invaluable and provide a backbone of love and stability that can see a family through bad times as well as rejoicing in the good. That night we all went to bed with a warm glow, a feeling of peace and wellbeing after their visit, and with our batteries recharged to face whatever the new week would bring.

Monday was the first day of February and the temperature dropped further. Snow was forecast on higher ground, with a possibility of it reaching us later in the week. I received the appointment letter Neave had mentioned for Melody's medical – Thursday at 3.30 p.m. – so I would need to collect her early from school. I'd mention it to Miss May when I saw her later. It was turning into a busy week. Straight after school that day Melody had the dental appointment I'd booked for a check-up, and the following day she had an appointment with the optician. But at least all the medicals would be done by the end of the week and in time for Melody's first review.

I didn't hear anything from Jill or Neave on Monday and the week progressed. Melody needed some fillings, which wasn't good news, but when we saw the optician he said her eyesight was perfect. On Thursday, notice of the review arrived in the post. It was to be held the following Monday at 2.30 p.m. at her school. Sometimes reviews are held in the foster carer's home, a meeting room at the council offices or at the child's school. It depends on a number or factors, including the size of the review, availability of rooms and if the child's parent(s) are attending. Children in care have regular reviews. The child's parent(s), social worker, teacher, foster carer, the foster carer's support social worker and any other adults closely connected with the child meet to ensure that everything is being done to help them and that the care plan (drawn up by the social services) is up to date. Very young children don't usually attend their reviews, but older children are expected to. Given that the review was being held at Melody's school, I assumed she would be attending at least some of it. I wondered if Amanda would be well enough to attend.

Jill telephoned that afternoon, asking if I'd heard anything further from Neave or the Guardian.

'No, and Melody is asking when she will be able to see her mother.'

'Neave was going to make a decision when she'd seen Amanda and the psychiatrist. I haven't heard from her so I've left a message on her voicemail to phone me.'

'Thank you. Can you make sure she knows that Melody has been very patient, but I do think she needs to see her mother before long or she'll start worrying about her again. Despite everything, they were very close.'

'Yes, I'll call you after I've spoken to her. Did you receive your invitation for the review and the review forms?'

'Yes. I'll help Melody fill hers in.'

'I should take them with you to the review; they may not arrive in time if you put them in the post.'

'OK.'

I collected Melody from school early that afternoon and took her to the Health Centre for her medical, where I'd taken children I'd fostered before. Dr Wainwright, the paediatrician, was lovely and immediately put Melody at ease. It was a standard medical examination for looked-after children and the doctor checked her ears, eyesight, throat and mouth, then weighed and measured her, and asked me some questions about her diet and how she was settling in. She pronounced her fit and surprisingly healthy given the neglect she'd suffered prior to coming into care. A copy of the medical report would be sent directly to the social services to go on their file. On the way out I praised Melody. 'We've had a busy week with all these appointments. You've done very well.'

'It's Friday tomorrow, will I see Mummy?'

'I don't think so. I'm waiting to hear from Neave.'

'It's not fair,' she said. 'It's ages since I've seen Mummy.' I agreed.

'I'm sure it won't be too long,' I said. But my reassurance was starting to sound worn.

Melody didn't have much homework that evening, so after dinner I thought it would be a good opportunity to complete her review form. As usual two sets of forms had arrived: one for me as her foster carer to fill in, which I would do later, and one for the child. We sat at the table and I opened Melody's form between us. It was a small, illustrated, child-friendly booklet designed to encourage the child to give their views on being in care. As a foster carer I had a duty to ensure the child received the booklet and to help them fill it in if necessary.

The first question asked: *Do you know why you are in care?* Because Melody was so behind with her reading, I read it out.

'What's the right answer?' she asked, as if it were a school test.

'There isn't a right or wrong answer. They want to know if you understand why you are in care. Can you tell me why? If so I'll write it down.'

She thought for a moment and frowned. 'I think it's because Mummy couldn't look after me properly.'

'I'll write that down then.'

'Is that right? It's what the social worker said.'

'Yes.'

The next question asked: *What do you like about living with your foster family?*

Melody paused thoughtfully and then said, 'I like the food, the house is warm, I like my bed and having my own bedroom. I like Lucy, Paula and Adrian. Oh yes, and I'm starting to like the cat.'

I smiled as I wrote. 'Good.' I hoped she liked me too, but I didn't prompt her on this point. This was her form to express her views. Children who can read and write competently fill in their review forms themselves.

'*What don't you like about where you are living now?*' the next question asked.

'Not seeing Mummy,' she said straight away. I wrote it down.

'Anything else?' She shook her head.

'*What has gone well for you since your last review?* I'll write N/A, which stands for "not applicable", as this is your first review.'

'*What has gone badly since your last review?*' I read out and again wrote N/A.

'*How do you feel most of the time?*' the next question asked, and there were rows of Emoji faces showing a range of emotions – sad, happy, angry, surprised, confused and so forth. I gave Melody the pen; she had to tick which face best represented how she felt. She ticked the sad face. 'I'm sad because I'm not seeing Mummy,' she said. Which comment I then wrote in the space beneath.

The next question was: '*Would you like to know more about your past?*' She shrugged. 'I'll put "don't know" then.'

'*Do you know who your social worker is?*'

'Yes. Neave,' Melody said.

I wrote it down and then read out the next question. *'Would you like to see more of them?'*

'No.' She shook her head vehemently. 'Mummy didn't like her.' Which I supposed was understandable.

I read the next question: *'Who are your friends?'*

'Lizzie,' Melody said.

The next question asked: *'Would you like to see more of them?'*

She shrugged. 'Don't know.'

'I'll write "don't know" then,' I said.

'If you have any problems who do you talk to?' was the next question.

Again Melody looked thoughtful and then said, 'Lucy, Paula and Mummy, but she's not here.' I wrote this but said, 'You know you can always talk to me if there is something worrying you?'

'Yes, I do tell you.'

'Good.' I read out the next question: *'Do you have any questions about what is going to happen in the future?'*

She nodded. 'When can I see my mummy?'

I wrote it down.

'The final question was: *'Is there anything you would like to add?'*

'When will Mummy come out of hospital?' she asked, and again I wrote it down verbatim.

On the back of the booklet was a line where the child had to sign their name, and beneath that another line where the name of any person who had helped the child complete the form had to be entered. Melody wrote her name in the appropriate place and then I wrote mine.

'Well done,' I said, sliding the booklet into the envelope provided. 'I'll take this with me on Monday.'

'So do all those questions mean I'll be seeing Mummy soon?' Melody asked. I smiled.

'I really hope so,' I said, which was all I could say.

Jill telephoned the following day to say she'd spoken to Neave, and Amanda's medical assessment hadn't been completed yet, as a specialist had been asked to look at a brain scan she'd had.

'So there are no plans for Melody to see her mother yet?' I asked.

'No, but we should find out more on Monday at the review.'

'OK, Jill, thanks for letting me know.' She wished us a happy weekend and we said goodbye.

More delay, I thought. Not good news. It was now nearly two weeks since Melody had last seen her mother. Then, just as I was about to leave the house to collect Melody from school, the phone rang and it was Nina French, the Guardian ad Litem.

'Sorry it's such short notice, but can I see Melody later this afternoon? Her first review has been set for Monday and I really need to see her before then.'

'Yes, but we won't be home until around four o'clock.'

'Perfect. I'll be there then. I won't stay for long.'

'All right, see you later.'

When asked what qualities are needed to foster I obviously include a love of working with children, sensitivity, patience, a non-judgemental attitude, but also flexibility – not only in the carer, but in the carer's family. The relaxing end to a busy week had just vanished. I quickly scribbled a note for Paula, Lucy and Adrian saying that the Guardian ad Litem was coming at 4 p.m. and to let her in if she arrived before me.

CHAPTER TEN

SNOW ANGEL

'Will the garden or whatever she's called let me see my mummy?' Melody asked. I'd been explaining the Guardian's role as I drove, and that she was visiting us this afternoon.

'Guardian,' I corrected. 'We can ask her when we see her. She may know.'

'What does she look like?'

'I don't know, I haven't met her yet.'

'Has my mummy met her?' Melody asked.

'I'm not sure, but she will do at some point.'

When we arrived home there was a car parked right outside my house. 'If that's her she's early,' I said, parking behind it.

I let us in the front door and heard voices coming from the living room. Leaving our coats and shoes in the hall, we went through and found Lucy in one armchair and a woman I took to be the Guardian in another, drinking tea from our best china.

'Hello,' I said, 'I'm Cathy. I'm pleased you're being well looked after.' I meant it. Sometimes social workers and other professionals were left to wait outside by my children – especially Lucy – if they arrived early.

'Nina French,' she said, standing to shake my hand. 'Your daughter has made me very welcome. She's been telling me what's wrong with the care system in this country and how to put it right.'

'Has she?' I asked dubiously, glancing at Lucy. I knew how articulate she could be when she got going on one of her pet subjects. What she considered to be the failings of the care system was one of them, having had first-hand experience before coming to me.

'Don't worry, I've been excruciatingly polite and didn't bad-mouth social workers once,' Lucy said.

I smiled weakly.

'I can vouch for that,' Nina said. 'I always appreciate hearing young people's experiences of being in care.'

Melody suddenly found her voice. 'That's good, because I want to see my mummy!'

'I'm sure you do. You must be Melody,' Nina said. Smiling, she went over and shook her hand. 'Very pleased to meet you.' Melody looked a bit taken aback at having to shake hands, but it was a nice gesture. 'Would you like to talk to me now or would you like to play first while I talk to Cathy?' Nina asked her.

'Now,' Lucy put in. 'You don't want five minutes at the end. This is all about you.'

'Thank you, Lucy,' I said pointedly.

'Time for me to go,' Lucy said, standing. 'Oh, and by the way, Mum, Adrian phoned and said he won't be back until after five-thirty. He has to stay behind for an athletics meeting at school.'

'Thanks, love, and is Paula home?'

'Yes, in her bedroom. Nice meeting you,' Lucy said to Nina, with only the faintest hint of sarcasm.

'And you. Thank you for the cup of tea.'

'You're welcome.' Lucy left the room. She had come a long way since she'd first arrived, angry, upset, and feeling unloved and rejected, but occasionally her old resentments resurfaced.

'Do you want me to stay while you and Melody talk?' I now asked Nina, who'd returned to her armchair. Some Guardians want the foster carer present, others don't.

'Stay if Melody is happy with that,' Nina said. Then to Melody, 'Is it OK if Cathy stays?'

'Yes. She can tell you too.'

Melody and I sat on the sofa. Nina — tall, mid-fifties and wearing black trousers and a light blue jersey — set her empty cup and saucer on the floor beside her, then took a notepad and pen from her bag. 'What would you like to tell me?' she asked Melody.

'I want to see my mummy.'

'Yes, I'm sure you do. Anything else?'

'When can Mummy come out of hospital? And why can't I see her now?'

Nina finished writing and looked up. 'I've been talking to your social worker about this, so I think I can answer some of your questions. The reason you haven't been seeing your mother is because the doctor wanted to make sure she was well enough first, so she can talk to you and play games.'

'Can't Mummy talk?' Melody asked, surprised.

'Yes, but I think you've probably had experience of her being difficult to understand sometimes — when she gets confused and says strange things. Do you know why she is in hospital?'

'Yes, Cathy told me. Because she's feeling unwell inside.'

'Yes, in her thoughts.'

'But I still want to see her.'

'I've written that down. I'll talk to your social worker about when it's likely to happen. The doctor will be telling her soon. Is that all right?'

Melody nodded.

'So what do you like about living here with Cathy and her family?' the Guardian now asked.

Melody told her pretty much what she'd told me for her review form – that she liked the food, her bedroom, a bed of her own and that the house was warm. Nina made some notes, then asked her about school. There was then some discussion about what Melody liked at school and the Guardian asked her what she did in the evenings and weekends.

'I used to see my mummy in the evenings,' Melody said, with an attitude that reminded me of Lucy. 'But I don't any more.'

'I know, I've written that down.'

This visit was for Nina to meet and get to know Melody. She would visit again, and during her final visit before the court hearing she would start to prepare Melody for the most likely outcome, as her social worker and I would be doing too. As they continued to talk, with Melody telling the Guardian what she did in the evenings and weekends, I glanced at the clock on the mantelpiece. If I'd had more notice of the Guardian's visit I would have prepared dinner so it could just be popped in the oven later.

'Is there anything else you would like to tell me?' Nina finally asked Melody as five o'clock approached, and Melody had grown fidgety.

'Can I go and play now?'

'Yes, of course.' Nina smiled. 'Thank you for talking to me.'

'You're welcome,' Melody said, in exactly the same tone as Lucy had. She disappeared off to find Lucy and Paula while I made a mental note to remind Lucy that children were impressionable, so it was important to set a good example, which Lucy did most of the time.

'Melody seems happy enough here, considering,' Nina said.

'Yes, she's doing well. She was very anxious when she first arrived, feeling that her mother wouldn't cope without her, and it seems she was right.'

'We think Melody was doing far more for her mother than anyone appreciated. The support worker who visited daily noted that Amanda relied heavily on Melody even for basic tasks, but that was her only comment. Neave is waiting for Amanda's full medical report, but initial tests show that she is likely to be suffering from a form of dementia.'

'Really?' I said, shocked. 'Oh dear. I didn't realize.'

'No one did. Melody was good at covering up her mother's confusion and shortfalls, but her condition has become more obvious since Melody came into care. The police returned Amanda home a number of times after she'd been found wandering, lost. The last time they alerted the social services, as there was evidence that a child had been living in the flat – Melody. It was freezing cold, there was no food in the kitchen and the place was filthy. It seems it was far worse than when Melody lived there.'

'The poor woman. How very sad. She's young to have dementia. Does it have anything to do with her drink and drug addiction?' I knew from my foster carer training there could be a connection.

'Possibly. We're waiting for a fuller diagnosis – when the results of the brain scan are available.'

'Even so, Melody does need to see her mother,' I said.

'Yes, I agree, and I'll be discussing it with Neave first thing on Monday. There is something I need to ask you. If the care plan remains that Melody will stay in long-term foster care, how do you feel about her staying here with you?'

'Yes, although I'd have to discuss it with Adrian, Paula and Lucy first.'

'Thank you.' She made a note. While it was highly likely Melody would remain in long-term foster care, nothing is definite until the judge makes their decision at the final court hearing.

It was 5.30 as the Guardian wound up and I saw her out. Five minutes later Adrian arrived home. With no dinner prepared and four hungry children I suggested we had fish and chips, so I took Melody with me in the car to the shop, while Adrian, Lucy and Paula laid the table.

Foster carers are expected to provide healthy, nutritious meals for the children they look after, and while deep-fried battered fish and chips – like the chicken nuggets and chips we'd had previously – couldn't be described as particularly healthy, they were fine for an occasional meal. We all thoroughly enjoyed them and there was a little titbit for Toscha, who rubbed herself around our legs under the table and meowed loudly as we ate. Melody was more used to Toscha now and had accepted that she didn't have fleas. After we'd finished Adrian took a phone call, Paula offered to hear Melody read her school book and Lucy helped me clear the table, which gave me the opportunity I needed to talk to her.

'Thanks, love, you know I really appreciate all you do, and thanks for looking after the Guardian.'

'I gave her one of our best cups, the ones we usually keep for when Nana and Grandpa come.'

'Yes, I saw. I hope she was suitably impressed.' She returned my smile. Thankfully all my children have a good sense of humour. 'But just a reminder, love, that Melody idolizes you, as do many of the children we foster, so please be careful what you say in front of her.'

'I am careful, aren't I?' she said a little indignantly.

'Yes, usually, but the tone Melody used to the Guardian sounded just like you.'

She looked at me and burst into laughter. I laughed too. 'I'm sorry,' she said. 'I should have realized.'

'It's OK. She did sound quaint and I expect the Guardian has heard worse. But be aware, she copies you.'

'I will.'

Matter dealt with.

That evening it began to snow. All the curtains were closed against the cold winter night, so we didn't know straight away. It wasn't until Toscha went out for her evening run and then shot back in through the cat flap with fresh snowflakes on her fur that I realized. I opened the back door and was met with a flurry of large white snowflakes.

'It's snowing!' I called to the rest of the house.

They opened the curtains of whichever room they were in and I heard cries of delight come from all over the house. Even Adrian, aged sixteen, was delighted, for when it comes to snow I think we are all children at heart. Whether there would be enough to play in the following day remained to be seen, but the weather forecast was hopeful. My mother phoned and said it was snowing where they lived too. We had a chat and then she and Dad spoke to my children.

'I hope it keeps on snowing all night,' Melody declared excitedly. 'Do you think it's snowing where my mummy is?'

'Yes, I would think so.' The hospital was only about a fifteen-minute drive away, so I thought it was likely.

'I hope Mummy sees the snow,' she said, pressing her face against the glass patio doors in the living room. 'It will make her happy. She told me that when she was little she used to make snow angels in the snow. She was going to show me how to make them if it snowed.' A snow angel is a pattern made in the snow that resembles the outline of an angel. It's usually done by a child lying on their back and moving their arms and legs up and down at their sides, which creates the outline of an angel with wings. 'Mummy was happy when she was playing in the snow,' Melody added quietly.

Yet again I felt sadness and regret for Amanda. This and other memories of her early childhood she'd shared with her daughter seemed to show it had been a normal, happy one to begin with before abuse blighted it. I didn't know her early history, but clearly the abuse couldn't have been discovered until it was too late to save her. Early intervention can and does make such a difference and saves lives.

As soon as I woke the following morning I knew we'd had a good fall of snow. The early morning light coming through the curtains was brighter than usual and the sound outside was quieter, muted. I got straight out of bed and crossed to the window. A magical winter wonderland greeted me. A thick blanket of snow covered rooftops, trees, cars, front gardens, the pavements and road, a fairytale landscape where the edges of reality had been smoothed silently during the night. All was as yet untouched, except for a single car track down the centre of the road.

'Cathy! It's snowed!' I heard Melody shout from her bedroom. Throwing on my dressing gown, I hurried round the landing. It was only 7.30, and as it was a Saturday Lucy, Paula and Adrian weren't awake yet.

Giving a brief knock on Melody's door, I went in. She was out of bed, at the window, and peering excitedly through the glass. 'Snow! Can I go outside and play in it?' she asked.

'Yes, of course. But you'd better get dressed first, and not too much noise – everyone else is still asleep.'

She was beside herself with excitement. I took some warm jogging bottoms and a thick jumper from her wardrobe, also the gloves, woollen hat and matching scarf I'd bought, which she hadn't had a chance to wear yet.

'Can I go out as soon as I'm ready?' she asked eagerly.

'Yes, have a drink and then we'll have breakfast later.'

I left her to dress and I quickly showered and dressed and then downstairs I poured her a juice, which she drank straight down. She was wrapped up warm in layers and wearing the bright pink Wellington boots she'd chosen when we'd gone shopping. I unlocked the back door. 'Are you coming out?' she asked.

'Just as soon as I've had a coffee.'

'Will you show me how to make a snow angel?'

'Yes. Give me five minutes.'

I fed Toscha and then watched Melody through the kitchen window as I made and then sipped my coffee. Playing happily in the snow, she could have been any child if you didn't know her past. How much the neglect and chaotic lifestyle she'd experienced would affect her future was impossible to gauge at present. Some children who come into care manage, with help and nurturing, to do well – go to university and form positive relationships – while others really struggle. It is a sad fact that 40 per cent of our prison population has been in the care system at some point and a similar figure is reflected in those living on the streets. Melody was a long way behind in her education and Miss May and I were doing all we could to help her catch up. I assumed that (as with most children who come into care) at some point she would be referred to the Child and Adolescent Mental Health Service (CAMHS) for counselling. Together with the care she was now receiving, I hoped this would give Melody a good chance of enjoying a happy and fulfilling life.

Melody waved for me to come out, so I quickly drained the last of my coffee, fetched my old jacket from the cupboard under the stairs, pulled on my Wellington boots and went out. Toscha sensibly stayed indoors.

The air was crisp and cold and the virgin snow crackled underfoot as I crossed the patio. Birds' footprints were visible in the snow along the top of the fence. 'Make me a snow angel!' Melody cried into the otherwise still air.

'Yes, but quietly.' I glanced up at our neighbour's windows. 'People are still in bed.'

Melody lay on her back and I showed her how to move her limbs up and down to create the pattern. I helped her up so she wouldn't disturb the image, and there was the outline of an angel, complete with a halo from the hat she was wearing. 'It's an angel, just like my mummy said!' she cried, pleased.

'It is. Perfect.'

We stood side by side, gazing at the snow angel, and as we did the sun rose, causing the snow to sparkle.

'Isn't she pretty?' Melody said.

'Yes. Very.'

'I think Mummy is here watching us.'

I smiled. 'Yes, indeed.' For if ever a child needed to feel their mother's presence, Melody did.

CHAPTER ELEVEN

REVIEW

We made the most of the snow while it lasted: after breakfast on Saturday we all went tobogganing in a nearby park, then in the afternoon we made a snowman in the garden and had a snowball fight. But as often happens in England after a snowfall, the thaw quickly set in. On Sunday the garden began to reappear, revealing a few brave crocus flowers that had survived the impact of the snow. By Monday there was just a slushy mess, although Melody's snow angel was the last to melt. This wasn't wholly surprising, as the snow had been compacted by Melody lying on it, and it was in a shaded part of the garden. But for Melody it was a sign her mother was close by and thinking of her; I agreed she was.

I took Melody to school as normal on Monday morning, but my day was very short, as I had to return to the school for 2.30 for her first review. Dressed smartly in what my children refer to as my office outfit – navy skirt, blouse and jacket – I arrived for the review in plenty of time and signed the Visitors' Book. One of the secretaries showed me to the Headmistress's room where I'd gone when I'd first brought Melody into school, and it was now being used for the meeting. Jill and a man I hadn't met before were already seated in the two armchairs. Extra chairs had been brought in and placed either side of the sofa and armchairs to form a circle. Jill smiled, said hello and introduced the man as the Independent Reviewing Officer (IRO), who would chair and minute the meeting. IROs are qualified social workers with extra training, but they are not connected with the social services. Having said hello, I gave him the review forms Melody and I had completed and sat next to Jill.

Almost immediately the door opened and Miss May and Mrs Farnham, the Deputy Head, came in. They said a general hello and sat down, Miss May in the chair to my left. 'Melody is with her class now,' she said to me. 'I'll bring her up later.'

'Is that all right with you?' Mrs Farnham asked the IRO, checking procedure.

'Yes. I think at her age she can come into her review towards the end when we've finished talking.'

The door opened again and Nina, the Guardian, came in. She said, 'Good afternoon,' then crossed to the two-seater sofa that had remained empty. 'Am I all right to sit here? You're not saving it for anyone?'

'No, not at all,' the IRO said.

Neave now entered with a young man I guessed to be in his mid-twenties. She said hello and he smiled a little self-consciously – I wondered if he was a trainee. She sat next to Nina, while he took a free chair on the other side of the circle. Everyone had a folder or notepad with them, including me. It was now 2.30 p.m. and the IRO asked if we were expecting anyone else.

'I don't think so,' Neave said. 'Amanda, Melody's mother, won't be coming. She's still in hospital.'

'Let's begin then,' the IRO said, and he opened the meeting by thanking us for coming. 'This is Melody's first review,' he said. 'Can we start by introducing ourselves?' He gave his name and role, and we then went round the circle giving our names and roles. I learned that the young man who'd come in with Neave, Gareth, was a student social worker on his final work placement. There were eight of us, so it was a medium-sized review. The number attending a review varies depending on factors including the complexity of the case. As is usual at reviews, the foster carer – with up-to-date information on the child – was asked to speak first. I drew myself more upright in my chair and glanced at the sheet of paper I held on my lap. I began by saying that Melody had settled in and was eating and sleeping well, and had reasonably good self-care skills, although she needed reminding to wash and brush her teeth sometimes. I said she'd arrived quite dirty and with head lice, but I'd treated those straight away, and that I'd seen none of the aggression mentioned in the referral.

'So you wouldn't describe Melody's behaviour as challenging?' the IRO asked.

'No. She was obviously upset at being parted from her mother, but generally she's settled in well.' He nodded and made a note. I then spoke a little about Melody's routine and what she liked to do in her spare time.

'Does she attend any clubs outside school?' the IRO asked, looking up from the notes he was taking.

'Not yet, but I'm hoping she will do soon. I'm trying to find out what she's interested in.' Children in care are expected to have the same opportunities as the average child; sometimes they have many more.

'I'll put that as a target then,' he said. Reviews like targets.

'On that subject,' I said, 'Melody has swimming lessons at school and I would like to take her swimming sometimes at the weekends and during the school holidays. I understand from Melody that her mother is very anxious about her drowning and wouldn't be happy if I took her, so I haven't yet. Can I have permission to do so?'

The IRO looked at Neave as he spoke. 'I think that's reasonable, don't you? We can give permission. Melody is on a care order and her mother has been sectioned.'

'Yes,' Neave said. 'I agree.'

'You'll obviously supervise her,' the IRO said to me.

'Yes, and she'll be wearing armbands as she does at school.'

'Good.' He made a note.

'I took her for the medical,' I continued. 'All was well. A copy of the paediatrician's report has gone to the social services. I also took her to the dentist and optician.' I gave the results.

'Has she had the fillings now?' the IRO asked.

'Not yet,' I said and hesitated. This was awkward. 'I'm waiting for the permission slip to be returned.' I looked at Neave.

'Sorry, it's on my desk,' she said. 'I'll let you have it back ASAP.' It's usually parents who sign their children's permission slips, but children in care proceedings generally need them to be signed by their social worker.

The IRO nodded, made a note and looked to me to continue. I glanced at my notes. 'Melody had missed a lot of school before coming into care and is a long way behind. I'm working closely with Miss May, her TA, to try to help her catch up. We do a bit of extra work each evening.'

'And Melody is happy to do schoolwork in the evening, rather than playing or watching television?' the IRO asked.

'Yes, a little,' I said. 'Her mother told her she needs to do well at school and pass her exams to get a good job. She's remembered it.'

'Good,' the IRO said. 'That's positive. And what about contact with her mother? I understand it's been suspended. How does Melody feel about that?'

'She misses her mother a lot. They were very close. Melody helped her mother and now worries about her. My feeling is she needs to see her mother soon. I understand we are waiting for a report from the hospital.'

'Yes, I'll be covering that,' Neave said.

I glanced at my notes again. 'I think that's everything,' I said.

'And you're aware of the care plan?' the IRO asked me.

'Yes.'

He now turned to Neave. She opened the file on her lap and began by giving the background to the case and the reasons for bringing Melody into care – neglect, non-attendance at school and being left home alone. As I already knew, this had been building for years, and despite support being put in the situation at home had deteriorated. Neave gave the date Melody had been brought into care and also when Amanda had been sectioned. She confirmed that Melody was in care under an Interim Care Order and that the social services were applying for a Full Care Order with a final court hearing date in November.

'And the mother's medical condition?' the IRO asked.

Neave nodded. 'She has been diagnosed with clinical depression, acute anxiety and dementia. The former is largely a result of the dementia. Alzheimer's has been mentioned and I'm waiting to speak to the consultant. When she was first admitted it was thought that her confusion and aggression could be a result of still using drugs, but that's been ruled out now. She hasn't had access to drugs or alcohol since she's been in hospital and her condition hasn't improved. The most likely diagnosis is dementia brought on by years of substance misuse. Apparently, those using for prolonged periods are three times more likely to suffer brain damage than those who don't use drugs.' She paused to let the message sink in.

'So is there likely to be any improvement in her condition?' the IRO asked, looking up from writing.

Neave shook her head. 'I'll have a better idea of the prognosis once I've met with the consultant, but Amanda is likely to need long-term care. They are already looking for a care home that can manage her dementia. She will have to leave the hospital where she is, now the assessment is complete.'

There was another moment's silence as the full impact of what Neave had said hit us.

'So there is no chance of Amanda ever going home?' Nina, the Guardian, asked.

'No. The assessment has shown she needs help with even the basics, like washing and dressing herself. Her mood swings and aggression have to be managed too. She could only be discharged home if there was a relative willing and able to look after her, and there isn't.'

'I hadn't realized she was that bad,' I said, shocked.

'I suppose Melody has been helping her a lot,' Jill added.

'Has Melody given you any indication of how much she has been helping her mother?' Neave now asked me. 'The support worker we put in noted that Amanda relied on Melody. The contact supervisor said the same and that Amanda appeared confused sometimes, but those were the only indications we had.'

'Melody was worried about her mother getting lost and she's told me she helped her with the shopping and cooking, but she's never mentioned she needed to wash and dress her.'

'She probably didn't realize that it wasn't normal,' Jill offered. 'I mean, what comparison did she have?'

'True,' Nina said, and the IRO nodded thoughtfully.

'Have you referred Melody to CAMHS?' he now asked Neave.

'Yes, she's on the waiting list, as it's considered non-urgent.' While Melody should have the therapeutic help she needed, NHS resources were scarce. More and more children were being referred for counselling, so a young person who was suicidal or self-harming, for example, would take priority over someone like Melody.

Neave finished by saying that contact would restart once she'd met with the clinician, and that she'd also be visiting Melody later this week, which was news to me.

'So contact will be restarted this week?' the IRO asked.

'Or early next week.'

He finished writing and then asked Nina to speak. Nina didn't have a lot to say as she was still 'familiarizing' herself with the case and had yet to meet Amanda, which she would do shortly. She said that when she'd visited Melody at my house Melody had asked to see her mother, and Nina agreed that contact should be re-established as soon as possible, and added that she wasn't sure why it had stopped. 'Children visit parents in hospital, even in prison,' she said.

'Contact stopped because Amanda was sectioned. She wasn't well enough,' Neave said a little curtly, apparently taking Nina's remarks as criticism.

'But she is stable enough now?' the IRO said. 'The child must have seen her mother like it when she was living at home.'

'I will know more when I've met with the psychiatrist responsible for her care,' Neave said.

The IRO finished writing, thanked Neave, and then looked to Mrs Farnham and Miss May. 'Would you like to tell us how Melody is doing at school?'

Mrs Farnham spoke first and began by pointing out that Melody had only joined the school last September, and prior to that had received very little schooling so was a long way behind. She read out some test results, explained what the school was doing to help her catch up, then she passed to Miss May to speak. She flushed up a little as she spoke, gave some examples of the type of work she set for Melody and said she was an enthusiastic learner and had no behavioural problems, unlike one of the boys on her table. She said Melody did talk about her mother a lot, and that she updated me in the playground at the end of school on most days.

'Has Melody ever talked to you about her life at home before coming into care?' the IRO asked.

'Not really. She tells me she misses her mother and often talks about what she is doing now with Cathy, but not much before then.'

The IRO asked her if she had anything else to say and then, thanking her, turned to Jill. 'Would you like to add anything? Then we'll ask Melody to join us.' Gareth wouldn't be asked to speak; as a student social worker he was there to observe and learn how reviews were conducted.

'My role as Cathy's supervising social worker is to monitor and support her in all aspects of her fostering,' Jill began. 'We are in regular contact and I visit her every month when we discuss the child she is fostering. Cathy is an experienced and dedicated foster carer and I know she will ask for help and advice if necessary. Melody has settled in well and I am satisfied that Cathy is providing a high level of care. I have no concerns and shall be seeing her and Melody again later this week.' Which, like Neave's proposed visit, was news to me.

The IRO thanked Jill and then asked if Melody could be brought into the meeting. Miss May left to fetch her. The bell rang, signalling the end of school, and Mrs Farnham asked if she could go as the Head wasn't in school and she really needed to be in the playground as the children left.

'Yes, you go,' the IRO said. 'Thank you for attending.'

She said goodbye and left. While we waited, the IRO looked through the booklets that Melody and I had filled in and Jill took out her diary and asked if she could visit on Thursday after school.

'We'll be back around four,' I said. I made a note of the visit as Jill entered it in her diary.

'I'll come at the same time then on Friday,' Neave said. I wrote this down too.

'You're popular,' Nina quipped with a smile.

The door opened and Miss May came in with Melody, who looked shyly at me. 'Hello, love, come and have a seat,' I said. It must have taken a lot for her to come into the Head's office and be faced with all those adults. She sat next to Miss May on the chair Mrs Farnham had vacated.

'Thank you for joining us, Melody,' the IRO said. 'How are you?'

'OK,' she replied quietly.

'What do you like doing at school?' he asked.

'Work that Miss May sets,' she said in the same small voice.

'What sort of work is that?' he asked. Melody didn't know. 'Maths? Reading? Art?' he prompted.

'Yes,' she said.

'This meeting is about you,' he continued, 'to make sure you are receiving all the help you need at home and school. Can you think of anything you need here or at Cathy's?'

Melody thought for a moment and shook her head.

'So you're happy at school and being well looked after at home with Cathy,' he said as he wrote. 'That's good. I see from the review form you completed that you like having your own bedroom and playing with Cathy's children.'

'Yes,' she said quietly.

'Good. I've also read that you are sad because you are not seeing your mother at present. Your social worker, Neave, will arrange for you to see her in hospital shortly.'

'When?' Melody asked, suddenly losing her shyness and speaking out.

'I should be able to tell you when I visit you on Friday,' Neave said.

'Is that OK?' the IRO asked.

Melody nodded.

'You also ask on your review form when your mother will come out of hospital. We're not sure yet but Neave will talk to you about that too when she sees you. Is there anything else you'd like to ask the review?'

I thought Melody was going to shake her head shyly or say a small no as she had been doing, but, looking directly at the IRO, she said firmly, 'I really do want to see my mummy. I know she's being looked after in hospital, but I still want to see her very soon.'

The IRO smiled kindly. 'Yes, I understand, and your social worker is going to arrange that. All right?'

She nodded.

The IRO then wound up the meeting by setting the date for the next review – in three months' time – and thanked us all for coming. Having said goodbye, I left with Melody and Miss May to go down to the classroom to collect Melody's school bag and coat.

'So is my social worker going to tell me when I can see my mummy?' Melody asked as we went.

'Yes,' I said, 'when she visits us on Friday after school.'

'That's good then, isn't it?' Miss May said brightly. 'No need for you to worry about that any more.'

Once we'd collected Melody's belongings from the now-empty classroom, I took the opportunity to thank Miss May for all she was doing for Melody, then we said goodbye and Melody and I left the school. As I drove us home I casually asked Melody if she'd ever had to help her mother wash and dress when she was living with her.

'I can't remember,' she said, unable to meet my gaze in the rear-view mirror. I let the matter go. Possibly Melody really couldn't remember with all the other responsibilities she had at home, or maybe she remembered all too well, and wanted to forget. Or maybe she felt that admitting the extent to which she had helped her mother would be disloyal. It was feelings like this that she would be helped to address in therapy. So many children in care are burdened with guilt, shame and remorse.

CHAPTER TWELVE

FOUR SLEEPS

Social workers and supervising social workers usually visit the child in the foster carer's home approximately every four to six weeks. Jill arrived as arranged after school on Thursday and spent time talking to Melody with me in the room before she went off to play. As well as updating Jill, her visit was to check that I was fostering to the required standard, to give support and advice as necessary, to discuss my training needs and finally to sign off my log notes. We spent some time talking about how I would prepare Melody for when she saw her mother in hospital – the details of which I should learn the following day when Neave visited us. 'I just hope it goes ahead,' I said. 'Melody does need to see her mother.'

'I know she does,' Jill agreed.

On Friday Neave was late arriving and Melody's anxiety grew. 'If she doesn't come I won't know about seeing my mummy!' she worried.

'I'm sure Neave will be here soon,' I said. 'If not, I'll phone her and find out what's going on.'

'That man at my review promised I'd see my mummy!' Melody said.

'I know, love.'

Neave finally arrived half an hour later and apologized – a previous meeting had overrun and then she'd got stuck in traffic. Social workers' schedules are always stretched to the limit. I offered her a drink and she gratefully accepted a coffee.

'I'll talk to Melody while you're making it,' she said, hanging up her coat on the hall stand. It's usual for the child's social worker to spend some time alone with the child in case there is anything the child wants to raise that they don't feel comfortable talking about in front of the carer. 'Oh yes, and here's the permission slip for the dental work Melody needs,' she said, taking it from her bag.

'Thank you. I'll book the appointment for after school.'

She went into the living room with Melody while I made the coffee and set some biscuits on a plate. From the kitchen I could hear their voices but not what they were saying. However, when I went into the living room with Neave's coffee, Melody said excitedly, 'I'm seeing my mummy on Monday!'

'That's fantastic,' I said. 'In hospital?'

'Yes, I think so.'

I looked at Neave. 'Do you want some more time alone?'

'No, stay, then I won't have to say everything twice.'

I settled in one of the easy chairs. Neave and Melody were sitting on the sofa, and my children had made themselves scarce and were in their bedrooms. Neave drank some of her coffee and then set the cup and saucer on the occasional table. 'I've explained to Melody that I've spoken to the doctor who's looking after her mother and he has told me that her mummy is well enough to have visitors, but she will need to stay in hospital for the foreseeable future. Melody can visit on

Monday – I'll give you the details. I suggest you go there straight from school so it's not too late for her.'

'Yes, that's fine,' I said, then to Melody, 'That is good news.'

She nodded but then asked, 'What's foreseeable?'

I left Neave to answer, as she'd used the term. 'It means as far as we can see, possibly for good. Some people live in a type of hospital called a care home permanently if they can't look after themselves.'

Melody thought about this. 'So won't Mummy ever be going home?'

'The doctor doesn't think she is well enough,' Neave said.

'When will she be well enough?' Obviously, long-term care was a difficult concept for a child of eight to grasp.

'It's likely your mummy may never be well enough to go home,' Neave said, letting her down as gently as she could. 'So the care home staff will look after her and that will become her home.'

Again, Melody thought about this and then made a connection. 'But if Mummy doesn't go home then I can't.'

'No, but you are being well looked after by Cathy. You said on your review form you liked living here and were happy.'

I watched Melody's face as she took it all in. 'I'd rather be with my mummy at our home,' she said. 'Even if it was cold and there was nothing to eat.'

'I know it's difficult,' Neave said. 'But I think it will become easier for you when you start seeing your mummy regularly.'

I thought she was probably right. Once children in care settle into a routine of seeing their parent(s) at contact, it allows them to concentrate on other aspects of their life.

'How often will I see my mummy?' Melody asked.

'We think once a week to begin with.'

'Then will it be more? I could see her three times a week before.'

'The situation is a bit different now,' Neave said. 'We'll review it as time goes by. Cathy will be with you to answer any questions you may have.'

'Will that lady be there too – the contact supervisor?'

'No, just Cathy.'

'Will Cathy stay with me and Mummy the whole time?'

'Yes.'

'Why? She didn't at the Family Centre.'

'No, but it's different now with your mother being in hospital.'

'How long will I see her for? It used to be four to five-thirty. I know because Cathy and Miss May have been teaching me the time and Cathy showed me on the clock.' I smiled.

'I'm going to leave the exact length of time to Cathy,' Neave said. 'But I think an hour is about right.' Neave glanced at me and I nodded.

'Why not longer?' Melody asked.

'Because we don't want your mummy getting overtired and agitated.' All this must have seemed odd to Melody, who'd been used to living with her mother whether she was tired and agitated or not, but of course Neave was now looking at contact in terms of Amanda being a patient, not just a mother seeing her daughter. 'Let's see how it goes,' Neave said, and drank the rest of her coffee.

'Shall we take Mummy dinner like we used to?' Melody now asked me.

'She'll have plenty to eat in hospital, but we could take her a snack,' I suggested. 'Perhaps some fruit and biscuits, and you could make her a card. That's what people usually do when they visit family in hospital.'

'Yes, I'll make her a card,' Melody said.

'That'll be nice,' Neave agreed. Melody didn't have any more questions, so we spent a little while talking about Melody's routine, then Neave gave me the details of the hospital ward where Amanda was. Satisfied that Melody was being well looked after, Neave then asked to see Melody's bedroom before she went. It's usual for the social worker to check the child's room during their visit. I stayed in the living room while Melody took Neave upstairs. Her room was far more attractive now, more personalized, with the belongings she'd acquired since coming to me. Nothing had come from home and now Amanda was in hospital I doubted any would. They were up there for about five minutes and when they came down Neave said, 'She clearly loves her bedroom.'

'Good.'

Picking up her bag, Neave prepared to leave. 'Have a good weekend then. I'll phone next week to see how contact has gone.'

Melody went off to play while I saw Neave out. It was now nearly six o'clock and I was glad I'd prepared dinner earlier and it was ready in the oven. We all ate and then after dinner Melody made a lovely card for her mother using colouring pens, and sticking on felt shapes and glitter. By the time she'd finished there was glitter everywhere, including on the cat, whose fur sparkled in the light, until, worried she might lick it off, I gave her a good brush.

Despite having been told it was highly unlikely she or her mother would ever return home, Melody was happy because she was seeing her mother on Monday. It overrode everything else. Plus we had a busy weekend. I took Melody swimming on Saturday morning, and Lucy came too. Then in the afternoon I took her to the cinema and Paula joined us. On Sunday we visited my parents and Melody told both of them – jointly and separately – that she was seeing her mother on Monday. 'She's in hospital,' she explained. 'I'm going to see her after school. Cathy will be there too and we are going to take her a snack.'

'That's lovely,' my mother said. 'Your mummy will be so very pleased to see you.'

My family appreciated, as I did, just how important it was for Melody to see her mother. Mum had made cupcakes for our visit and she put some in a stay-fresh box for Melody to give to her. 'Thank you, my mummy will love these,' Melody said gratefully. 'Like she did Cathy's rice pudding. Do you think Mummy will have rice pudding in hospital?'

'I am sure she will,' Mum said.

All Melody's hopes therefore were pinned on seeing her mother on Monday and she planned what they were going to do. I didn't disillusion her by saying that her mother might not be up to playing games, because in all honestly I didn't know. Amanda had played with Melody a few weeks ago when she'd seen her at the Family Centre. She couldn't have deteriorated that much, could she?

On Monday morning Melody was up early and, once dressed, she carefully set by the front door (so I wouldn't forget to bring them later) the card she'd made, the box of cakes, and some fruit and chocolate biscuits she'd selected from the cupboard.

'Don't be late,' she told me when I saw her into school. 'Neave said we're going straight from school to the hospital.'

'I know,' I smiled. 'I won't be late.' And with a hop, skip and a little wave she went happily into school.

On the way home I stopped off at the supermarket, and I was unpacking the shopping in the kitchen when the phone rang. I was slightly surprised to hear Neave's voice, as I wasn't expecting to hear from her again until after Melody had seen her mother this evening.

'A care home has been found for Amanda,' she said. 'She is being transferred there later today, so contact won't take place.'

'Oh no. Can't Melody see her mother before or after the move?'

'No, because I've no idea what time she'll be moved, and the hospital don't know yet either. It'll depend on when transport is available.'

'Oh I see, oh dear. Melody is going to be so disappointed.'

'I appreciate that, but it can't be helped. She'll see her mother as soon as she's settled at the care home.'

'Shall I take her tomorrow then?' I asked.

'No, we want her settled first, and a social worker from the adult safeguarding team will visit her.'

'But Melody will be seeing her mother later this week, won't she? If I could give her a definite day, it might help lessen her disappointment.'

My attitude and persistence must have irritated Neave, and doubtless she was very busy on a Monday morning, for she said tersely, 'Mrs Glass, if I could give you confirmed arrangements I would, but I can't yet. So if you could tell Melody her mother is being moved to a care home and she'll see her as soon as possible, I'd be very grateful.' With a rather curt thank you and goodbye she ended the call and hung up.

'Damn and blast,' I cursed as I returned the handset to its cradle. Not because I'd irritated Neave, but because Melody wouldn't be seeing her mother. While I appreciated that arrangements in fostering can and do change, this wasn't right. Everyone at the review had agreed Melody should be seeing her mother, yet now it had been postponed indefinitely. I realized it wasn't practical for Melody to see her mother today, but I didn't understand why Neave couldn't have given me a firm day, which I felt would make telling Melody that bit easier. *Your mummy is moving today to a care home, so we'll see her on Wednesday* – or Thursday or Friday, or whichever day it was – sounded less harsh than, *We can't visit your mummy today, as she is moving to the care home. Neave will tell us when we can see her.* Children in care have to deal with so many disappointments, especially in respect of their parents, and it's often left to the foster carer to mop up the mess.

I stood in the kitchen, staring into space, feeling Melody's disappointment. I considered telephoning Jill, but she wouldn't be able to offer much beyond commiseration. I then thought about the Guardian, Nina, who'd been advocating the resumption of contact. Going into the front room, I took my fostering folder from the drawer and found Nina's office phone number. As I dialled I hoped Neave wouldn't think I was going behind her back or over her head, then I thought, sod it, I don't care. Melody needs to see her mother.

Nina was out of the office but was expected back in an hour or so, so I left a message with her colleague, giving my details and asking her to call me as soon as she could. She returned my call an hour later and I explained that contact had been arranged for today and how excited Melody had been over the weekend, but that Neave had just telephoned to say Amanda was being transferred to a care home and that she didn't know when Melody could see her mother. 'It's nearly a month since she saw her and this is going to affect her badly.'

'I agree,' Nina said. Then it went quiet. 'My role is really to report to the judge at the final court hearing. I don't usually become involved in social worker practice.' Which I knew. 'But let me see what I can do. Clearly it's in Melody's best interests to see her mother.'

'Thank you.'

Later that afternoon, shortly before I was about to leave for school, the phone rang again and it was Nina. 'I've spoken to Neave and she's suggested you take Melody to see her mother at the care home either Friday after school or Saturday afternoon. Visiting is any time between one-thirty and seven-thirty. If it goes all right then once a week, but she'll speak to you next week.'

'Thank you so much,' I said.

'Do you have the address of the care home?'

'No.' I reached for the paper and pen I kept by the phone and wrote the address. It was an hour's drive away. 'So the care home isn't local?'

'No. It was the nearest that had a free bed and could offer the type of care that Amanda needs. That's why Neave has suggested Friday or Saturday – when Melody doesn't have to be up for school in the morning if you're late back.'

'OK, thank you. I'll tell her.'

As I drove to collect Melody from school that afternoon I considered which day would be best to take her to see her mother – Friday, at the end of the week when she might be tired, or Saturday afternoon, which would limit us going out on any day trips. I decided to try Friday and see how it went. If Melody was too tired, I would switch it to Saturday the following week. Neave had said Friday or Saturday and left it for me to decide. I was pleased that I could now give Melody a definite day, although of course she was coming out of school expecting to see her mother that afternoon.

I waited in my usual place in the playground and when Melody's class came out she was near the front, smiling broadly and with Miss May at her side. Miss May also thought we would be going straight to the hospital to see Amanda so didn't come over to talk, but just gave a little wave. Melody ran to my side full of joy and anticipation. I steeled myself for what I had to say.

'Look, love,' I said, taking her hand. 'There has been a slight change of plan.'

'I'm not seeing my mother, am I?' she cried, snatching her hand away.

'Yes, you are, but not this afternoon.'

'That's not fair!' she shouted, and stamped her foot. Others turned to look.

'Come on, I'll explain as we walk to the car.' I didn't want a scene in the playground. With her face set like thunder, Melody reluctantly fell into step beside me.

'What?' she demanded. I saw her old anger return and who could blame her?

'You remember Neave said that they were looking for a nice care home for your mummy?' I began steadily. 'Well, they've found it and she's moving there this afternoon. That's why we can't see her today, but we are going to see her on Friday after school.'

'But Friday is ages!' she moaned.

'It's not ages,' I said. 'It's four sleeps, which isn't long at all.'

She thought about this for a moment. 'But I wanted to see her today.'

'I know, love, but it can't be helped, and Friday isn't so long.'

'What about all the food I got ready to take and your mum's cakes?'

'The biscuits will be fine and you can choose some more fruit. But I think we should eat those cakes and then you and me can make some more.'

Most children like to make cakes and Melody was no exception. 'All right,' she said begrudgingly, but her anger was receding.

'Excellent,' I said and opened her car door. 'I've just had another good idea.'

'What?' she asked suspiciously, pausing before getting in.

'Let's stop off on the way home and you can choose a box of chocolates to take to your mother on Friday.'

'Yes, my mummy likes chocolate, and we'll make the cakes too?'

'Yes, of course.'

'With icing on?'

'Yes, if you like.'

So while Melody was disappointed, it could have been far worse.

CHAPTER THIRTEEN

HEARTBREAKING

Adrian, Lucy and Paula obviously knew that Melody was supposed to be seeing her mother that afternoon, so I'd left a note in the kitchen saying contact had been postponed so they wouldn't accidentally say something insensitive when we walked in earlier than expected. Melody and I stopped off on the way home to buy the chocolates for her mother and she also chose some pink icing for the cupcakes we were going to make. By the time we arrived home her anger had subsided, my family were in, and the afternoon and evening continued as most school evenings did, with Melody playing or watching television before dinner, then me helping her with her homework, and reading her a story before her bath and bed.

While Paula, Lucy and Adrian didn't bring up the subject of contact, Melody told each of them in turn that she hadn't seen her mother because she was being moved to a care home, and she would see her on Friday and take her chocolates, biscuits, fruit and the cakes we were going to make.

'Sounds good to me,' Lucy said.

'That's nice, she'll like those,' Paula said.

'She'll explode eating that lot!' Adrian joked.

'No, silly, she won't eat them all at once,' Melody told him firmly. 'You are daft sometimes.'

Melody loved being around my children, but sometimes I had to subtly intervene and suggest she and I did something together, for clearly at their ages, apart from having home-work, Adrian, Lucy and Paula needed time to themselves to do what they wanted. I was very lucky that they were so patient and understanding with all the children we fostered, but they had their own lives to lead.

The week passed. Melody counted down the sleeps until Friday and became increasingly excited, while I worried that something might happen to postpone contact again – either with Amanda or possibly the weather. If we had another heavy snowfall we wouldn't be able to make the journey until the roads were clear, so I kept an eye on the weather forecast. On Thursday evening, with no snow forecast, Melody and I made the cupcakes for her mother and, once they were cool, Melody covered them in pink icing. We put some aside to take to her mother and we all ate the rest. I knew there was a reason I didn't bake cakes often – they're irresistible!

I'd planned the route to the care home and I also made a lasagne for Lucy, Paula and Adrian to put in the oven and have when they were ready. Melody and I would eat when we returned from seeing her mother. I estimated it would take at least an hour to drive from Melody's school to the care home, then we'd probably spend about an hour there, and an hour to drive back again meant that we wouldn't be home until 7 p.m. Melody had school lunch around 12.30, so I made her a little picnic to eat in the car to tide her over until dinner.

It had been difficult for me to prepare Melody for what to expect at the care home, as I'd never been in one specializing in the care of dementia patients before. From time to time I visited an elderly neighbour who'd gone into a nursing home, so I modelled what I said on that when I explained to Melody what a care home was or answered her questions.

It was a relief when Friday came and the contact arrangements were still in place and the skies were clear. At the end of school I waited in my usual spot in the playground and Miss May, whom Melody had excitedly told a number of times that she was seeing her mother in the care home today, came over. 'I know you need to get going so I won't keep you, but I just wanted to say have a lovely evening and weekend.'

'Thank you, and you,' I said.

'And please tell Amanda how well Melody is doing at school.'

Melody glowed with the praise.

'I will. Thanks again.'

Miss May was a wonderful woman and I thought Melody was very lucky to have her as her TA.

As we crossed the playground Melody skipped for joy. 'I'm going to see my mummy! Did you remember to bring everything?'

'Yes. It's all in a bag in the car.'

But just to be sure, once we were in the car Melody unpacked the bag and checked off all the items: 'The card I made for Mummy, the cakes we made, biscuits, grapes and the box of chocolates we bought.'

I smiled to myself. Melody was so excited to finally be seeing her mother and she talked non-stop as I drove. 'Do you think Mummy has made any friends, like I'm doing at school?'

'Yes, I expect she has.'

'Does she have her own bedroom, like I do with you?'

'Yes.'

'Do they watch television at the care home?'

'I think so. I'm sure there'll be a television in the lounge, but I'm not sure if each bedroom will have one.'

'We could watch my favourite programme.' I nodded.

'Will Mummy's carer buy her new clothes, like you do me?'

'If she doesn't have any of her clothes from home, they'll give her some.'

'From spares? Like you did with me when I first arrived?'

'Yes, I expect so.' I thought that Melody was viewing her mother's care home as similar to her being in foster care, which I suppose in some respects it was.

Then revealingly Melody asked, 'Will they give Mummy shampoo and tell her when to wash her hair?'

'Yes, if necessary,' I said. 'Why? Did you have to do that for your mother?' I glanced at her in the rear-view mirror.

'Sometimes.'

'And remind her to bath or shower?'

'Can't remember,' she said and, closing the subject, she began eating the sandwiches I'd made for her.

No one really knew exactly how much Melody had been supporting her mother at home, and the chances were they never would. But given Amanda's diagnoses and her need for long-term care, Melody must have been doing an awful lot, far more than the social services had realized – partly due to Melody and her mother covering up their need for help.

* * *

The traffic was heavy as we crossed the town, but once on the dual carriageway we made good progress. Melody finished her sandwiches, crisps and packet of juice and then gazed through her side window.

'It's a long way,' she said. 'Are we nearly there?'

'Not too far now. Would you like to listen to a CD?'

'The nursery rhyme one.'

It was already in the player from the last time we'd played it and I switched it on. Although the songs were really for younger children, Melody loved hearing them over and over again. While riding in a car and listening to music is nothing unusual for most children, it hadn't been part of Melody's life with her mother. Impoverished, with a chaotic lifestyle, moving from one cheap rented room to another and with Amanda's memory failing, they'd struggled even with the basics, let alone had CDs or a car. I was pleased that Melody was now able to listen to her favourite rhymes, was being looked after and didn't have to worry about where her next meal was coming from, just as her mother was being looked after too. It wasn't long before I found myself joining in with the sing-along. As I drove our singing got louder and louder until the CD finished, when Melody clapped.

Shortly before five o'clock I pulled into the road where the care home was and slowed the car to a crawl. I knew it was on the far side of a relatively new housing estate and we followed a residential road of semi-detached houses to the end.

'There it is,' I said. 'Oak Lane House Care Home.' It was a two-storey red-brick building and I drew into the car park where about half a dozen other cars were already parked and cut the engine. Because the care home was right at the edge of the estate it had a backdrop of rolling hills stretching into the distance, over which the wintry sun was now descending. The home itself was set in beautiful landscaped gardens; even at this time of year they were well tended and green with shrubs.

'Which is Mum's room?' Melody asked, peering through her car window.

'I don't know yet, we'll have to ask.'

I opened Melody's door. 'Bag,' I reminded her. She'd been about to leave it on the back seat.

I brushed the crumbs of bread and crisps from her school uniform and locked the car. It was quiet and peaceful here, very tranquil. A lone blackbird trilled from somewhere in the shrubbery. A short path led up to the main entrance, either side of which were more neatly tended gardens. Wooden chairs and benches were set out ready for summer, although I noticed these areas were surrounded by a high wire-netting fence discreetly hidden by ivy and other evergreen climbers. A pair of large stone planters filled with brightly coloured pansies stood either side of the main door and the doormat had 'Welcome' printed across it, which gave the place a warm, homely feel.

The outer door wasn't locked, so I pushed it open and let us in. We now stood in a lobby with a set of double doors in front of us. On our right was a small oblong table covered with a lace cloth, on which stood a beautiful vase of cut flowers. Beside the vase lay an open Visitors' Book, and a notice on the wall behind it told visitors to sign in, then press the bell to be admitted. Using the pen provided, I filled in the columns with the date, my name, the time and the reason for my visit. Then passed the pen to Melody. 'Write your name there,' I said, pointing.

'It's like at the Family Centre,' she said, and carefully printed her name below mine.

I pressed the bell and heard it ring somewhere inside.

'Why can't we go straight in?' Melody asked.

'We have to wait for someone to open the doors.' This and the wire-netting fence surrounding the gardens were the only differences so far from the nursing home I'd visited, and suggested the residents here needed a higher level of protection. We were soon to find out why.

As we waited for the doors to be opened a man and a woman, who I guessed to be in their seventies, appeared on the other side. Dressed in casual day clothes, they could have been visitors about to leave the building, except there was something in their manner, the way they held themselves, and the distant look in their eyes that suggested otherwise. Melody was watching them carefully and had gone quiet. The man began banging on the glass of the door, while the woman pointed to the lock.

'I can't open the door from this side,' I said, and shook my head, unsure if they could hear me. Even if I had been able to open it, I clearly wouldn't have done. It was locked for a reason.

I glanced at Melody, who was looking at them, very worried. 'I hope they're not Mummy's friends,' she said quietly.

I smiled reassuringly and held her hand. 'Don't worry, love, your mummy is being well looked after.' Although I was feeling a little apprehensive. It wasn't the best start to her first visit to be greeted by a couple desperately trying to get out. People suffering from dementia can act in strange and sometimes disturbing ways. Thankfully, a care assistant appeared behind the couple and slowly and gently moved them aside, then opened one of the doors to let us in.

'Sorry,' she said with a small sigh. 'It happens every time the bell rings. They think they're being taken out.'

The care assistant took the couple's behaviour in her stride and I guessed she was used to it, but I thought how sad it was, and exhausting for the care assistants, to keep having to go to the door to move the couple every time anyone arrived, instead of just releasing the doors from the office as they did at the Family Centre. I guessed they probably had to be there when anyone left the building too, as clearly the couple were determined to leave. Even though the door was now closed, the man had resumed banging on the glass while the woman was rattling the door handle.

'We've come to see Amanda –' I said, giving her full name to the care assistant.

'I think she's in the lounge.'

'Could you tell me where that is please. This is our first visit. Melody has come to see her mother.'

'Yes, sure, this way,' she said, throwing Melody a smile. Melody held my hand as we followed the care assistant down the corridor. The walls were painted magnolia and had framed prints of country scenes. We passed residents' bedrooms. Some of the doors were open and I glanced in. Carpeted, with brightly coloured curtains at the windows, they were decorated in warm colours and personalized with the resident's belongings. We also passed a meeting room with chairs facing a projection screen and then more bedrooms. A man called out from inside one, 'Nurse! Nurse! Come quickly, I have a plane to catch.'

'It's all right, Mr Wilson,' the care assistant replied kindly. 'There's plenty of time.' We continued by.

'Nurse! Come quickly, I have a plane to catch,' he called again and again.

I felt Melody's hand tighten in mine and I gave it a comforting squeeze. We turned left and into the lounge. It was a spacious carpeted room and light, with patio doors, closed now in winter, leading to a courtyard. The hills could be seen in the distance beyond. Around the edge of the room were about twenty high-backed armchairs, some with residents sitting in them, their feet resting on the rising footstools. In the centre of the room was a table with four dining chairs, where an occupational therapist sat with two residents, helping them weave small baskets using brightly coloured raffia. I couldn't see Amanda; neither apparently could Melody, for she too was looking around. The care assistant saw our hesitation. 'Your mummy is over there, love,' she said kindly to Melody. Even then I didn't immediately recognize Amanda.

We followed the care assistant to a chair in one corner where I now saw Amanda was slumped. Head back and jaw hanging open in sleep, she was snoring quietly. With her missing teeth at the front now more visible and the grey roots of her hair growing through, she could have been an elderly woman in her eighties. I was shocked by the change in her in little over a month.

'Should we wake her?' I asked the care assistant.

'Yes, she'll want to see her daughter.' She gently touched Amanda's shoulder. 'Amanda, your daughter is here to see you.'

Amanda woke with a start, sat bolt upright and stared around. Clearly disorientated, I assumed from having just been woken, she appeared not to know where she was or who we were. Even when she looked directly at Melody she didn't immediately show any signs of recognizing her. It was only when Melody said, 'Hello, Mummy, I've brought you lots of nice things to eat,' that she looked more closely at her daughter.

'Melody,' she said. 'Melody, well, fancy finding you here. How did you do that?'

Melody looked confused. She didn't know what to say and tried to smile.

'I brought her here in the car, Amanda,' I said, which would have been obvious to someone who wasn't suffering from dementia. 'Do you remember that Melody is living with me for now?' I asked her. 'I'm Cathy Glass, Melody's foster carer.'

The care assistant who'd shown us in had gone to attend to a lady who was struggling to get out of her chair.

'Are you taking me home?' Amanda asked me, ignoring her daughter.

'No, love,' I said. 'You're living here now. So you can be looked after.'

'It's very damp,' Amanda said, 'and that bloody social worker keeps poking her nose in.' Of course, she was referring to the past, not the present, but for her it was very real. Melody didn't know what to say.

'Amanda,' I said, leaning in slightly so I could make eye contact, 'you don't have to worry about that any more. Your room isn't damp and the social worker is pleased you are being looked after here. I am looking after Melody.'

'That's good,' she said, but I wasn't sure she'd understood. She appeared to have little grasp of the present, and from her expression and the look in her eyes I doubted she knew where she was. Her condition had dramatically deteriorated.

Melody, who'd been standing beside me watching her mother, not sure what to do for the best, now put down the bag she'd been carrying and threw her arms around her mother. Amanda looked surprised at first, as though she didn't know who was hugging her, and sat upright and unyielding. Then she appeared to realize – perhaps from the smell and feel of Melody – that this was her daughter. Her expression changed. Her face softened and she slipped her arms around Melody and hugged her back. As she did, a tear slipped from her eye.

'I knew you'd find me. You always do when I get lost,' she said.

I swallowed hard. It was heartbreaking.

CHAPTER FOURTEEN

PRECIOUS FREEDOM

Past and present merged again for Amanda, and as quickly as she had recognized her daughter it vanished and the light went out of her eyes. She took her arms from around Melody, sat back in her chair and looked at us as if we'd just arrived.

'Mummy's gone again,' Melody said. Her comment surprised me. I supposed she must have recognized the distant look in her mother's gaze from when they'd lived together and at contact. Thinking back, I too had seen it at contact, but, not knowing that Amanda had dementia, I'd assumed it was a result of substance misuse.

There were empty chairs either side of Amanda, so I suggested to Melody that we sit down and she could show her mother what she'd brought for her. Amanda was still staring across the room with apparently no interest in us at all.

'Look, Mum, I've made cakes for you,' Melody said, and she took the box containing the cupcakes from the bag and set it on her mother's lap. 'I bought you a box of chocolates,' she said, taking that from the bag and placing it on her mother's lap too. 'And biscuits, and grapes. Here's the card I made.' The pile grew, yet Amanda appeared not to notice and didn't give them so much as a glance. Then suddenly she stood up, jettisoning all the items onto the floor. Melody and I scrambled to pick them up. Amanda left her chair and began walking slowly across the room.

'Amanda, where are you going?' the care assistant called. Leaving the lady she was with, she went to Amanda.

Amanda heard her and stopped. It was as if her words had for a moment meant something.

'You've got visitors. Come and sit down and talk to them,' the care assistant encouraged. Amanda turned and began walking back towards us, seemingly recognizing Melody as if for the first time.

'You found me, you always do,' she said again as she sat in her chair. I thought Melody was coping very well.

'Look, Mum, I've made you some cakes,' she tried again. Leaving the other items in the bag this time, she took out the box of cakes and, peeling off the lid, offered them to her mother. 'They've got pink icing on, your favourite colour,' she encouraged.

Amanda took one and so did Melody.

As they ate I took the opportunity to look around the room. The wall-mounted plasma-screen television was turned off, but light classical music was playing softly in the background. It was all women in this room and they were quiet, just the occasional cries of 'Nurse! Come quickly, I have a plane to catch' could be heard in the distance coming from Mr Wilson's room. No one took any notice, so I guessed they were used to it.

There were eight residents in the lounge, plus the female occupational therapist, and the care assistant who'd shown us in. All the residents were dressed smartly in their day clothes, were clean and had their hair brushed and styled. They wore slippers or light indoor shoes. Most of them seemed to be in their seventies, although there was one woman who could have been Amanda's age. The two women sitting at the table with the occupational therapist were still concentrating hard on their basket making, weaving the raffia in and out of the frames. It was a simple activity, one enjoyed by quite young children, but they needed a lot of help. Other residents were slumped asleep in their chairs as Amanda had been, or sat gazing across the room, some making involuntary and repetitive movements. One was continuously tapping her feet, while another kept rubbing her hands together as if she were cold, although the room was stiflingly hot.

Melody and Amanda were quickly finishing off the cakes, although Amanda hadn't said anything – that they were nice or that she was enjoying them. Melody thought to offer me the last one, but of course I refused and she ate it. I was actually thirsty – it was a long time since I'd had a drink and I hadn't thought to bring a bottle of water with me. A man shuffled in, tall and willowy, with his gaze down. He was making a strange 'boo-boo' noise with his lips. Melody looked over while the other residents ignored him. A care assistant appeared behind him, having followed him into the room. She lightly touched his shoulder. 'Come on, Mr Andrews, this is the ladies' lounge. The gentlemen's lounge is this way.' So I learnt that the men and women had separate lounges.

He ignored her and, still making the 'boo-boo' noise, went right up to one of the women and just stood in front of her, shuffling his feet. Goodness knows what was going through his mind; perhaps he liked her and wanted her company. His care assistant gently turned him around and, once he was pointing in the right direction, he walked out again. She followed him, but a few minutes later he was in again, this time going to a different woman.

'We know how much you like the ladies,' the care assistant said with a smile, and steered him out. Again I thought how much patience these care assistants needed to do their job compassionately and competently.

Amanda and Melody had finished the cakes and Melody brushed the crumbs off her mother, as I did sometimes to her. Returning the empty box to the bag, she took out the chocolates. 'Just a couple,' I said, 'and we'll leave the rest for your mother to have later.'

Amanda shook her head, signalling she didn't want a chocolate, so once Melody had eaten two I told her to close the lid and that her mother would enjoy them after we'd gone. She did as I asked and put them in the bag.

'Perhaps your mother would like some grapes?' I suggested. She didn't. Amanda was now gazing absently across the room and I wondered if her medication included a sedative. Whenever I'd seen her before at the contact centre she'd been quite nervy and agitated. But if she was on medication it was nothing to do with me; it was a matter between her doctor and social worker.

'Can we see Mummy's room?' Melody now asked me.

'I would think so. Ask your mum.'

'Mum,' she said, tapping Amanda's arm to get her attention. 'Can we see your room?'

'If you must, it's very damp,' Amanda replied. I guessed she was again remembering the flat where she'd lived before. But she stood, so I picked up the bag of food and my handbag, and Melody and I went with her.

144

As we passed the care assistant I thought I should mention where we were going. 'Amanda is going to show us her room. Is that OK?'

'Yes, of course.'

Amanda seemed to know her way, so we followed her out of the lounge, down the corridor, then turned right and passed Mr Wilson's room. 'Nurse! Come quickly, I have a plane to catch,' he cried.

'No, you haven't, you silly old bugger!' Amanda returned, and continued on.

I stifled a smile. A care assistant who'd heard this exchange walked on without comment – I supposed the staff were used to it – but it struck me as funny and bizarre. Despite her dementia, Amanda had known that Mr Wilson couldn't possibly have a plane to catch and had retorted with a witty, if not polite, remark.

The bedroom doors had the residents' names printed on a small colourful card with their photograph beneath it, which would help them identify their room. Amanda knew where her room was without a problem and led us straight to it. It was large, comfortable and well furnished with a single bed, wardrobe, chest of drawers, a small table and two dining chairs in the recess. An armchair was by the bed and an oblong mirror was mounted on the wall. Floral curtains matched the duvet cover and some scatter cushions, and an en-suite bathroom was through a door on our left. Yet despite the room being light, airy and comfortable, it had none of Amanda's personal belongings in it as the rooms of other residents we'd passed had. The bookshelves and surfaces were empty, without the usual clutter you'd expect to find in a bed/sitting room – ornaments, books, magazines, CDs and so forth. The cork pinboard on the wall had one photograph on it and that was of Amanda – a copy of the one on the door – which I guessed had been taken when she'd first arrived.

Melody was looking around the room, then began opening and closing the drawers and doors, exploring. 'Those aren't Mum's clothes,' she said, looking in the wardrobe.

'Perhaps the home has given them to her,' I said. 'I'll ask Neave where her own clothes are.'

Melody opened the bathroom door and went in. 'This is nice.'

'Yes, it is,' I said. Scrupulously clean, tiled from ceiling to floor, and with a gleaming white porcelain bathroom suite, it wouldn't have looked out of place in a decent hotel.

'Her room is much nicer than the flats we lived in,' Melody said, coming out of the bathroom. Then to her mother, 'It's not damp, Mum.'

'That's because I scrubbed all the mould off before you came,' Amanda replied.

'I think your mum is getting confused with some of the flats you lived in,' I said, for Melody might have believed it was true.

'She often gets confused,' Melody said, then, 'I need to use the bathroom. Can I use this one?'

'Yes, I don't see why not,' I replied.

She went in and closed the door.

Amanda was standing in the centre of the room and I went up to her. 'Amanda, I'll put your grapes in the bowl here, shall I?' There was an empty wooden bowl on the table. I took the grapes from the bag – I'd washed them before we'd come – and set them in the bowl. Melody had also put a banana, apple and tangerine in the bag and I set those in the bowl too.

Amanda was watching me, but her face was expressionless. She could always take them out if she didn't want them there. 'I'll put your box of chocolates and packet of biscuits here,' I said, and placed them on the table beside the fruit bowl. Then I took out the card Melody had so carefully made and, opening it, set it on her bedside cabinet.

'Melody made the card for you,' I told her.

'Who are you?' she asked.

'Cathy, Melody's foster carer.' I smiled. What a frightening place dementia must be, not being able to retain information. 'Melody is staying with me for now,' I added.

Amanda gave no indication she'd understood but was looking at the card. 'You'll be able to see it at night before you go to sleep and first thing in the morning. Melody made it for you,' I repeated. 'Next time we visit I'll bring in some photographs of Melody and we can put those on your pinboard.'

Her gaze went to the pinboard, so I thought she'd understood at least some of what I'd said. Melody came out of the bathroom and I showed her where I'd put the items – the food on the table and her card by the bed.

'Do you like the card I made for you?' she asked her mother.

'Yes,' Amanda said blankly without any emotion, and she headed out of the room.

'Can't we stay here, Mum?' Melody called after her, but she'd gone.

'I think we should go with your mother,' I said. It didn't feel right staying in her room without her.

Amanda was waiting for us in the corridor and we followed her in the direction of the lounge. There were always plenty of care assistants around and I guessed homes like this one must need a very high staff–patient ratio to look after so many vulnerable patients. As we approached Mr Wilson's room it was quiet, but as soon as he heard our footsteps outside he called, 'Nurse! Nurse! Come quickly, I have a plane to catch.' We couldn't see him and he couldn't see us, so I guessed his calling out was triggered by hearing someone pass his room. What had led to this was impossible to know; perhaps he'd missed a plane in the past and it was playing on his mind. I didn't know if he was in bed or sitting in his armchair – his door, like many others, seemed to be left ajar, but it didn't allow you to see that far into the room.

Amanda led us back into the lounge and we returned to the chairs we'd been in before. A male care assistant was now sitting in the chair next to me and he smiled and said, 'Hello, you've come to visit Amanda?'

'Yes. I've brought her daughter.'

'That's nice. Amanda doesn't have many visitors. Are you a relative?'

'No. Foster carer. Her daughter is staying with me.'

He nodded. 'It must be difficult for her.'

'Yes,' I agreed.

He was very pleasant, softly spoken, slightly built, with a kind and caring nature, and seemed genuinely interested in his patients' welfare. Amanda was staring blankly across the room, while Melody was looking longingly at the basket-weaving going on at the table. The occupational therapist saw her looking.

'Would you like to make a basket?' she asked Melody.

Melody was immediately on her feet. 'Yes, please.'

'Bring Amanda with you and you can make one together.'

'Mum, come on, we're going to make a basket,' Melody said, tugging at her mother's arm. Amanda didn't appear very interested but eventually succumbed to her daughter's insistence and went with her to join the other two ladies at the table. The occupational therapist gave them a basket frame and raffia and explained what to do. Amanda held the frame while Melody began weaving the raffia in and out.

'Being a foster carer must be a difficult job,' the male care assistant sitting next to me said, making conversation.

'Not as difficult as yours,' I replied.

He smiled. 'I like my job. Some of my family and friends don't understand why I would want to do it.'

'I think I can.'

As Melody and her mother wove their basket, we continued talking and I learnt that he'd been a nurse in the Philippines before coming to England five years ago. He was married, with a six-month-old baby. 'Some of my patients are like babies,' he said, but in the nicest possible way. I asked him when the residents had dinner, for it was about the time we usually had our dinner. He said they had their main meal at lunchtime, then a light meal around four o'clock, as it was better for their digestion and they went to bed early. While we talked he was continually looking around the room to see if any of the residents needed anything, when he would immediately go to them to give them a drink, raise or lower their footstool, or adjust a cushion so they were more comfortable. I saw that many of the patients had dementia far worse then Amanda and it was affecting their motor skills, as I assumed it would Amanda's eventually. It's a cruel disease that can't be cured at present, so all the carers could do was to make their patients as comfortable as possible while they deteriorated – unlike my role as a foster carer, where I saw the children I looked after grow and flourish.

On one of the male carer's trips to fetch a cup of water for a resident I asked if it would be possible for me to have one too. 'Of course, and Melody,' he said, and brought us both a cup of water. 'Any time you want a drink just ask at the kitchen.'

'Thank you.'

He sat beside me again. It was dark outside now and through the glass patio doors blue and white fairy lights could be seen strung across the courtyard, giving it a magical feel – quite a contrast to the grim reality inside. I took the opportunity to ask him about the residents' belongings. 'When Amanda showed us her room I noticed there was nothing of hers in there. No personal items.'

'Some patients don't have much from home, while others have a lot and their rooms are crammed full,' he said. 'It relies on the next of kin bringing in their belongings.'

'I'll have to ask Amanda's social worker,' I said. 'There are clothes in her wardrobe, but her daughter doesn't think they're her mother's.'

'If patients don't bring clothes from home then we provide what they need from clothing donated by relatives when a person passes.' I nodded. It was a sad but practical solution. 'We also give them toiletries, toothbrushes – in fact, whatever they need,' he added. He then had to leave to take a patient to the bathroom.

A young woman in her twenties came in and sat beside one of the elderly residents. I heard her say, 'Hello, Gran, how are you?' The old lady muttered something unintelligible and dribbled. Her granddaughter wiped the saliva away with a cotton handkerchief kept on the woman's lap, and then began talking to her in an upbeat voice, telling her about her day. I thought how sad it must be for her to see her beloved gran like this. I greatly admired her courage to see through the old lady's dementia to the person she once knew and cherished.

It was now 6.30 p.m.; we'd stayed longer than I'd anticipated. I waited until Melody and her mother had finished their basket-weaving, and then said to Melody we needed to leave now.

'She can take her basket home with her,' the occupational therapist said. 'Amanda can always make another one.'

I thanked her and then told Melody to say goodbye to her mother. I was wondering if she'd resist, wanting to stay longer, but with the basket in one hand, she gave her mother a hug with the other and kissed her cheek. 'Bye, Mummy. See you soon.'

'Bye,' Amanda said spontaneously, then her expression changed and she looked very anxious. 'Before you go you need to help me clear up. That social worker will be here soon and the place is a mess.' Clearly she'd reverted again to another time and place.

'Everything is fine, Amanda,' the occupational therapist reassured her.

'Everything is fine,' Amanda repeated.

Melody kissed her mother's cheek again. I said goodbye and we left the lounge. We walked down the corridor, and passed a man trying to take his trousers off; a care assistant rushed to stop him and Melody giggled. Then we approached Mr Wilson's room. 'Nurse! Nurse! Come quickly, I have a plane to catch.'

Neither of us commented; we were already getting used to it.

At the main door I signed us out in the Visitors' Book, then pressed the bell for a care assistant. There was a swipe-card entry system and a notice above it asked visitors to ring for assistance. Almost as soon as I'd rung the bell, the couple who'd been at the door when we arrived appeared. Pushing in front of us, they began knocking on the door again, wanting to be let out, although there was no one on the other side. Melody looked worried. I took her hand and whispered, 'Don't worry.' A few moments later a care assistant arrived, gently moved the couple away from the door and then swiped her card in the reader. I thanked her and we left quickly before the couple could follow us. As soon as the door closed they were on the other side, knocking on the glass. I glanced back. Clearly they needed secure residential care, but never before had I been so aware of how precious our freedom is. Freedom of mind and thought, freedom of movement – to come and go as we want. Like many, I took my freedom for granted, but I wouldn't again. It was a chilling thought that possibly one day I might be behind that door, in need of full-time care but desperate to get out.

CHAPTER FIFTEEN

STAYING POSITIVE

Outside the night air had chilled and the rural setting that had seemed so pleasant and tranquil on the way in now felt isolated and eerily quiet. The street lamps glimmered in the distance, but the gardens at the front of the care home weren't illuminated as the central courtyard had been. The shrubs, chairs and benches loomed now as menacing shadows and the dark hills beyond blended in with the skyline. As our solitary footsteps echoed down the path Melody held my arm and neither of us spoke until we were in the car.

'Why can't the people who live here get out?' Melody asked as I closed my car door.

I turned in my seat to look at her. 'Because everyone living here needs to be protected. You remember how worried you used to be when your mummy got lost? Well, I think most of the residents here would get lost too.'

'Some of them are very odd and a bit scary.'

'I know, love, but they can't help it. It's part of their illness. It can seem strange, but they won't hurt you.'

'I forgot to tell Mummy what Miss May said about me doing well at school,' Melody said sadly.

'We will tell her next time.'

'And I didn't watch my television programme,' she lamented.

'No, but you made a basket instead.' She was holding it on her lap. 'I'll get us home now and we can have another chat later.' It was getting late and I expected Melody would have plenty of questions about her mother and the care home.

It was a relief to be driving through the housing estate again – a welcome return to normality – then into the bright lights of the town. Every so often I glanced in the rear-view mirror at Melody, who was gazing through her side window deep in thought. It was a lot for a child to process: not only seeing her mother's worsening dementia, but the behaviour of the other residents. While they weren't responsible for their behaviour – as I'd told Melody – it was still quite an experience to see so many people together exhibiting erratic and sometimes bizarre behaviour.

As I drove my thoughts too were with Amanda and the care home. Visiting a home like Oak Lane House wasn't the same as taking a child to see a parent in hospital recovering from an illness or operation, which I'd done before. Those parents had physical conditions from which they would recover. Amanda was going to get steadily worse, and if Melody was going to see her mother then it would need to be at the care home. There wasn't an alternative. Amanda could no longer live independently or attend the Family Centre and Melody needed to see her mother, didn't she? But was there a cut-off point where Neave would take the decision that it wasn't appropriate for a child to see their parent in the final stages of dementia? I didn't know. This was all new to me. But I had concerns.

As we settled on the dual carriageway I glanced again in the rear-view mirror. Melody was still staring through her side window, clutching the basket on her lap.

'Are you pleased you saw your mother?' I asked.

'Yes,' she replied without hesitation.

'She said some strange things, but you understand she couldn't help it? I'm sure she knew who you were and was pleased to see you.'

'I know she still loves me, but she's got worse.' How quickly this poor child had had to grow up, I thought.

'Would you like to see her again?'

'Yes. Can we go Monday, Wednesday and Friday like we did at the Family Centre?'

'The care home is too far away to go on a school night. Neave said once a week, on a Friday evening or at the weekend when you don't have to be up early in the morning.'

'Can we make Mummy some more cakes?'

'Yes.'

'Will I be able to make another basket?'

'I think that will depend on the activity the occupational therapist is doing. The occupational therapist is the lady who organized the basket-weaving and sat with you at the table,' I explained. 'I expect she does lots of different activities.'

'Good.'

So I thought that, overall, seeing her mother had been a positive experience for Melody and one she was eager to repeat. Had it not been, I would have had grave concerns about taking her regularly, although ultimately it would be the social worker's decision.

* * *

It was nearly eight o'clock by the time we arrived home. The rest of the family had had dinner and were doing their own thing. Having taken off our coats and shoes, Melody and I stopped off first at the living room where Lucy and Paula were watching television.

'Hi,' Lucy said, glancing at Melody. 'Did you see your mother?'

'Yes. We made a basket.' She proudly held it up.

'Wonderful,' Lucy said.

'So you had a good time?' Paula said. 'Did your mum like the cakes?'

'Yes, we ate them all.'

'Good.'

They returned their attention to the television and Melody and I went into the kitchen where Adrian was making himself a sandwich. At his age he was constantly hungry.

'Look what Mummy and me made!' Melody said, holding up the basket.

'That's very good, but won't it leak?'

It took Melody a moment to realize Adrian was joking. 'You don't put water in it, silly. It's for fruit and sweets and things in my bedroom.'

'Oh, I see,' he said, feigning amazement. 'Well, that's a relief.'

'Did he really think you put water in it?' Melody asked me after Adrian had left.

'No. Adrian likes a joke. It's a lovely basket.'

I pinged our dinners in the microwave and Melody and I ate together. It was nearly nine o'clock when we'd finished, and Melody was yawning. I was exhausted too, not just from the drive at the end of a busy week, but emotionally – from seeing her mother's dementia and experiencing this type of care home for the first time. It had been draining, although I thought it would probably be a bit easier the next time, now we knew what to expect.

Lucy and Paula had turned off the television and were in their rooms. Melody called goodnight as we passed their bedroom doors. She had a quick wash and I went with her to her room. She positioned the basket on a shelf and then put in some of the small toys and knick-knacks she'd been buying with her pocket money. I admired the result, then, yawning again, she climbed into bed.

'Do you think Mummy will be in bed now?' she asked.

'Yes. I would think so.'

I sat with Melody for a while, wondering if she'd want to talk more about her mother, but she was so tired she fell asleep straight away, her face resting against her teddy bear.

Downstairs I cleared up our dishes and then sat in the living room and wrote up my log notes. As well as wanting to do it while it was still fresh in my mind, I find writing cathartic, and my thoughts were full of Amanda. Now I'd seen her in the care home I could picture her in the lounge and her bedroom. She was one of the youngest residents and it was so sad knowing her life would end like this – her condition steadily worsening until she lost all grasp of reality and couldn't do even the most basic tasks.

Paula, Lucy and Adrian came into the living room for a quick chat before going to bed, which brightened my mood. I felt I hadn't seen much of them today, but we had a reasonably leisurely weekend ahead when we would all be together.

At eleven o'clock I went up to bed and surprisingly slept well, although my first thoughts on waking were of Amanda, as were Melody's.

'Do you think Mummy is getting dressed?' she asked me as I went into her room.

'Yes, or she might already be up,' I said. I put her clothes out ready.

'What will she do today?'

'Get dressed, I suppose, have her breakfast, then perhaps do an activity or watch television.' Or just sit in a chair and stare into space, I thought but didn't say.

'Can we go swimming?' Melody asked.

'Yes, it'll be tomorrow this week, as we need to go shopping today.'

I left Melody to get dressed and when she came down to breakfast Lucy and Paula were already at the table eating theirs. Adrian had left earlier to go to football practice. Melody joined the girls at the table and as I made her breakfast in the kitchen I could hear her telling Paula and Lucy about her visit to the care home – not so much about her mother but the other residents there.

'One man tried to pull his trousers down,' she giggled, 'and another kept going "boo-boo" and walked like this.' She stood and demonstrated, shuffling her feet and drooping her bottom lip as the man had done. I heard Lucy and Paula laugh too.

I didn't feel comfortable hearing those poor residents being mocked, so, leaving what I was doing, I went over.

'Those people can't help it,' I said. 'All the residents at the care home have dementia. I don't think we should laugh at them.'

They took my point. Melody sat down; she was too young to appreciate why ridiculing them was unkind, and Lucy and Paula hadn't really thought about it.

'So you were pleased to see your mum?' Lucy said, understanding – and changing – the subject. 'And you're going again?'

'Yes. Next Friday or Saturday.'

'And she liked the cakes?' Paula said.

'We're going to make some more for next time.'

I returned to the kitchen. They were good kids, but all children need correcting sometimes, and for Melody, laughing at the men was probably also a coping mechanism.

Paula came shopping too, as she needed some more shoes, while Lucy stayed at home. I went shopping most weekends and I was gradually building up Melody's wardrobe. Melody liked to spend her pocket money, but whereas before she'd been spending it on herself, now she wanted to buy things for her mother.

'I want Mummy to have ornaments on her shelves in her room like I do,' she said.

She spotted a charity shop and knew from when she'd lived with her mother that the donated items stocked by these shops were much cheaper than in the stores. Inside it was a treasure trove with plenty of choice. Apart from the rails of clothes, shoes, belts, handbags and so on, there were shelves of books, CDs, vinyl records, china and glass ornaments and general bric-a-brac. Melody was delighted and Paula helped her to take the items she was interested in from the shelves for a closer look while I browsed. I bought a pair of new oven gloves and a tea towel – it was for a good cause – and half an hour later we emerged from the shop with Melody having spent all her pocket money on her mother and carefully holding a carrier bag containing the tissue-wrapped ornaments. I hoped Amanda would appreciate how much care and love had gone into choosing those gifts, but I doubted it. Much of the joy of giving for a child is to see their parent's face light up as they present them with the gift, but Amanda's face was largely expressionless now. I feared she might not even understand the gifts were from her daughter.

Again and again my thoughts kept returning to Amanda even as we shopped, for it occurred to me that here was another experience she'd probably never have again, unless a care assistant took her to the shops. But would there be any point? How much would any experience mean to her now? It was impossible to know. Then I started to wonder if my own parents would ever need to go into a care home. I'd assumed that eventually, if they couldn't look after themselves, they'd live with me or my brother. But that was in relation to them growing old and needing extra help, not dementia. If one or both of them suffered from dementia, would I still be able to have them live with me? It's a dilemma faced by many families. Seeing Amanda at Oak Lane House had forced me to confront difficult issues that previously I hadn't given much thought to.

On a positive note, Paula found some shoes she liked and I bought Melody some more casual clothes. I also bought some photograph frames and an album to mount photographs of Melody in for her mother. Having pictures of her daughter should help keep her memory alive. Melody had plenty of photographs of herself in her Life Story Book, which I'd begun when she arrived. I'd have copies made for Amanda and take them with us on our next visit. Before we left the town I stocked up on groceries from the supermarket, and that evening we had a Chinese takeaway.

'Do you think Mummy has Chinese food?' Melody asked as we ate, which was a coincidence, for I'd been thinking something similar.

'I expect the cook at the care home makes a variety of food,' I replied.

'I used to have takeaways with Mum – Indian and Chinese,' Melody said.

I nodded, although I was surprised they could afford takeaways given how poor they'd been.

'The man who lived in the house next door had lots of takeaways,' Melody continued. 'Mum said he got them on the way home from work because he couldn't be bothered to cook. He could never eat them all, so we used to have them.'

'He shared them with you?' I asked.

'No. Mum and me used to sneak round when he'd finished after he'd put them out.'

'Put them out where?' I asked, pausing from eating.

'In the dustbin,' Melody replied.

'Oh no! Gross!' Lucy exclaimed. While Adrian and Paula stared at Melody, horrified.

'The food was still in the boxes, and he put the lids back on,' Melody said, as if that made it OK.

'You won't have to do that again,' I said, 'and neither will your mother.'

'Good. It was always cold,' she said. 'I don't like cold food.'

'How do you know he hadn't spat in the food?' Lucy asked, grimacing.

Melody looked very worried.

'I'm sure he hadn't,' I said, and moved on to another topic.

I'd fostered children before who'd had to scavenge for food or ask neighbours to feed them. If the parent(s) had an expensive drug habit then that always had first claim on any money, with food, clothes, rent and so on coming a poor second. But despite this revelation, we all enjoyed the takeaway and I told Melody we'd do it again another time.

On Sunday morning after breakfast we all went swimming at the local leisure centre. Adrian, Lucy and Paula were growing up quickly and increasingly wanted to do their own thing, so the number of times we went out together as a family was sadly decreasing, but swimming was an activity that appealed to everyone. Melody was still quite timid in the water despite wearing armbands, and I stayed with her in the learners' pool while the rest of my family swam in the main pool. There weren't many there, which helped, as Melody didn't like to be splashed. Now I was taking her swimming regularly, and with the lessons at school, hopefully her confidence in the water would grow. After we'd dried off and got dressed, we had a hot drink and a snack in the café and then had to make a dash for the car, as it was pouring with rain. We all got soaked – 'A car load of drips,' as Adrian put it.

Once home, I cooked a roast dinner while the family amused themselves, and then we had a leisurely afternoon and evening, during which time I telephoned my parents. They spoke to everyone in turn, including Melody, and I arranged to see them the following weekend.

That night as I saw Melody into bed she asked when we'd make the cakes to take to her mother, and I said probably Thursday evening.

'I can't wait,' she said. 'Mummy loved the cakes.' So I was pleased she was remembering the good parts of her visit. How long that would be possible, I didn't know.

CHAPTER SIXTEEN

AMANDA – A MOTHER

On Monday morning, having taken Melody to school, I returned home and telephoned Jill to update her on our visit to Oak Lane House and the weekend in general. Jill felt as I did that overall Melody's visit had been a positive experience and, as long as it continued to be so, she should see her mother every week. She reminded me to include the visit in my log notes, which I had done. I intended to telephone Neave straight after Jill, but a friend phoned first. She and her partner were hoping to foster and she had some questions about the 'Skills to Foster' assessment, which was part of the application process. It was therefore around midday before I spoke to Neave and I began by updating her, much as I had done to Jill. I then asked, 'Will Amanda live at Oak Lane House permanently or will she have to move again?' Melody wanted to know and I was concerned that if she was moved then the next care home might be even further away.

'As far as I know Amanda will stay there until she needs a nursing home,' Neave said.

'When is that likely to be?'

'It's impossible to predict, as it will depend on the progression of her illness, but it's likely she'll be there for at least a few years. When she can no longer feed herself she'll be reassessed and then will very likely be transferred to a nursing home.'

'I see.' It was sad. 'Thank you. Amanda's room is very bare,' I said, moving to my next question. 'I was wondering what happened to all her belongings. Melody hasn't had anything from home either.'

'Everything went into a skip, so it's gone,' Neave said. 'Amanda owed the landlord a lot of rent so once they'd left he changed the locks and cleared out the flat. He said there was nothing of value, and I know from when I visited there wasn't much. But Melody should have everything she needs now she is in foster care.'

'Yes, she has,' I said.

'And the care home will provide for Amanda.'

Even so, it seemed dreadful that all their possessions had been thrown away. I then asked Neave if the choice of visiting time – Friday evening or the weekend – could be left to me, as I was thinking of alternating it. She said that was fine but she then had to go, as she was due in a meeting. I'd covered what I'd needed to say.

That afternoon I sorted through the photographs I'd taken of Melody and noted which I wanted copies of, ready to have them printed when I went into the high street the following day. While it was only Monday I knew how quickly the week could disappear. I had a full day's training on Wednesday (all foster carers in the UK have ongoing training), Thursday was set aside for the clerical work I did part-time and Thursday evening we would be baking cupcakes, so I needed to check we had all the ingredients, and also at some point give the house a good tidy and hoover.

That afternoon, when I collected Melody from school, Miss May – smiling as usual – came over to me. 'Melody has done some really nice work,' she said, as she did most days. 'I'm very pleased with her. She has literacy and numeracy home-work in her school bag. She's been telling me about the visit to her mother. I'm so pleased it all went well. It seems she's in the same care home my father was in.'

'Really? Oak Lane?'

'Yes, he was there for three years until he passed last October.'

'Oh, I am sorry.'

'Thank you, although to be honest it was a release in the end; he was very poorly. But it's a lovely home and he was well looked after. A bit of a drive, though.'

'Yes, it is.'

I was pleased that Melody had heard Miss May speak highly of the care home, and that she'd spoken positively about her visit there to Miss May, but later in the car on the way home she asked, 'Why isn't Miss May's father still in Mummy's care home? She said he passed, but what does that mean?'

There was no easy way to explain the euphemism. 'It means he died, love.'

'Why?'

'Because he was very ill and maybe old. Miss May said he was poorly.'

'Is my mummy poorly?'

'Yes, but not as poorly as Miss May's father was.'

'Will my mummy die there too?'

I met her gaze in the rear-view mirror. 'I don't know, love, but it's possible, eventually.'

'How long before my mummy dies?'

'I don't know. No one knows when they are going to die. But Miss May said her father was very well looked after. So that's good.'

'She said it was a release. What did she mean?'

'That he's at peace now.'

Melody nodded. 'I told her about Mr Boo-Boo and she said he was there when she went. But she didn't see anyone pull down their trousers.'

'Good.' Any conversation about dementia and dying was going to be difficult, but Miss May, having had the experience of her father being in the care home, was well qualified to answer Melody's questions and reassure her. I knew she'd have handled Melody's comments sensitively and appropriately.

'Lizzie doesn't know anyone in a care home,' Melody declared as though she was missing out. 'So I told her what it was like, but I didn't laugh about Mr Boo-Boo.'

'Good girl.'

'Lizzie did, though.'

'She doesn't understand,' I said. 'It sounds as though you are good friends with Lizzie so shall we invite her to tea next week?'

'Yeah.'

'Great. I'll speak to her mother in the playground tomorrow and arrange it.'

The week progressed more or less as I'd anticipated, although with four children in the house there was always a minor drama or catastrophe to sort out – often as a result of an item becoming lost due to it not being put away in the first place.

On Thursday evening Melody and I made the cupcakes and we all ate two each while they were still warm and the rest I put on a cooling rack for icing later. Melody wrote a large sign (I helped her with the spelling) – KEEP AWAY. MUM'S CAKES – and propped it by the rack.

As we were seeing my parents at the weekend I was planning to take Melody to visit her mother on Friday after school as we had done the previous week – I'd take sandwiches, crisps and a drink to see Melody through to dinner. It was March now; tulips had joined the daffodils in the garden and the days were gradually lengthening. I was looking forward to being able to drive back from the care home in the daylight, although that wouldn't be for another couple of weeks yet.

On Friday I made dinner before I left, with a note to Adrian, Lucy and Paula telling them the time it needed to be put in the oven and the heat setting. I then checked I had everything we were taking. There were two carrier bags ready in the hall, one of which contained, among other things, a potted plant I thought Amanda might like. I collected Melody from school and drove to the care home. We arrived just before five o'clock, let ourselves in the outer doors, signed the Visitors' Book and then Melody pressed the bell to be admitted. Within seconds the couple we'd seen the week before appeared on the other side of the door, the man knocking on the glass and the woman, now with her handbag over her arm, pointing to the lock. It was sad but whereas the first time we'd met them Melody had found their behaviour unsettling (as indeed I had), now they were more familiar they didn't hold the same threat. Melody said simply, 'They're here again,' and then gave them a little wave.

'I can't unlock the door,' I said, and shook my head. It didn't stop them trying, though, and they continued their fruitless attempts to leave until a care assistant appeared. She moved them aside and quickly let us in.

'Thank you,' I said. 'We've come to see Amanda. Is she in the lounge?'

'I think so, most residents are. Do you know where it is?'

'Yes, thanks.'

We left her talking to the couple, trying to persuade them to do something else. 'Mr and Mrs Bennett, we're not going out today, it's too cold.' So they were married, which seemed bittersweet: lovely that they were together, I thought, but sad that they had both succumbed to dementia and had to live here rather than in their own home.

Melody slipped her hand into mine as we set off along the corridor. 'I wonder if Mr Aeroplane Man is in his room,' she whispered, giving him a name as she had Mr Boo-Boo.

Mr Wilson was in his room, and as we approached his slightly open door he called out, 'Nurse! Come quickly, I have a plane to catch.'

Again, Melody didn't seem quite so perturbed by this as she had last week. I think giving the patients names helped; it made them seem more like characters in a film and therefore less intimidating.

'Can we take Mummy straight to her room so we can put her things on her shelves?' Melody asked.

'Yes, if she wants to.'

The lounge was fuller than on our last visit and most of the chairs were occupied. Not only were there more residents in there, but there were three visitors, including the granddaughter we'd seen the week before, and two care assistants. The table in the centre where the occupational therapist had been was empty. I saw Amanda on the far side of the room, curled into a chair. With her legs drawn up under her she seemed even smaller in the high-backed chair, child-like and vulnerable. 'Over there,' I said to Melody. Amanda was gazing at the television on the wall that was switched on but with the sound off. As we approached her gaze shifted to us.

'Hello, Mummy,' Melody said, and kissed her cheek.

Amanda looked at her daughter, but her expression remained blank as if she could have been anyone.

'Hello, Amanda,' I said. 'How are you?'

She looked at me, but again without any sign of recognition.

Melody and I stood as the seats either side were occupied, then I squatted a little so I was at eye level. 'Melody's had a good week at school,' I said. 'Her TA wanted you to know.'

'Good,' Amanda said.

'I've made you some more cakes,' Melody said. 'And I've bought ornaments for your room. Can we go to your room now?'

Amanda must have understood, for, unfolding her legs, she stood and made her way across the lounge. We followed, and as we left the lounge Mr Andrews shuffled in on his regular route to visit the ladies, and making his 'boo-boo' noise. I saw a smile cross Melody's face, but to her credit she didn't laugh, although his behaviour was bizarre. A care assistant had followed him in and now said, 'Come on, Mr Andrews, you've seen the ladies, let's go to the men's lounge now.'

Amanda didn't give him a second glance, apparently seeing nothing unusual in his behaviour, but as we passed Mr

Wilson's room and he called out that he had a plane to catch she responded with, 'Be quiet, you daft bugger!' She'd said similar the week before and these flashes of apparent lucidity struck me as odd. What was in her mind that allowed her these glimpses, when she didn't immediately recognize her daughter? A lot of research has been done into the workings of the brain with dementia, but it has raised more questions than it's answered. I suppose eventually we'll understand more and find a cure, although sadly that is still a long way off.

Amanda led us straight to her room without any hesitation and opened the door. I saw that the card Melody had made the week before was still on her bedside cabinet. Melody saw it too.

'You've kept my card!' she exclaimed, delighted. 'I've got lots more things for you.' She began unpacking the carrier bag.

I watched Amanda's face as she stood looking at her daughter, who took the ornaments from the bag one at a time and, carefully removing the tissue paper, placed them on the shelves.

'Very nice,' I said encouragingly as Amanda continued to watch, her face blank.

With the ornaments neatly arranged on the shelves, Melody took out some drawings she'd done especially for her mother and I helped her pin them on the cork board. 'Those look good,' I said.

Amanda's face remained expressionless, although when Melody took out the box of cakes she exclaimed, 'My cakes!' and snatched the box from Melody like a child who'd yet to learn good manners.

Melody looked taken aback, but I could hardly tell Amanda not to snatch at her age. Ripping off the box lid, she began eating the cakes without offering one to Melody.

'They were for us to share,' Melody said, hurt. 'Like we did last time.'

Amanda didn't reply.

'We'll make some more,' I reassured Melody. But when Amanda had gobbled down three and had taken another one, I thought she'd had enough for now and gently eased the box from her hand. I gave one cake to Melody, put the lid on the box and left it on her bedside cabinet for later. Amanda didn't protest. 'Do you like this plant?' I asked, taking the potted orchid I'd bought her from the carrier bag. 'Where shall I put it?'

'Up your bum,' she said.

'Mum!' Melody exclaimed. 'You can't say that, it's rude.' I had to smile. Melody said to me, 'Mum said that to the bus driver and people who wouldn't give us things for free. She thinks you want money for it.'

'Amanda, I'm giving you the plant,' I said. 'I saw it in a shop and I thought it would look nice in your room. I bought it for you. I don't want paying. It's a gift.'

She took the plant from my hands and stood it on the floor, which wasn't the best place for it. 'Mum's never had a plant before,' Melody said.

I picked it up, removed its cellophane cover and placed it on the table in the bay window. 'It looks nice there and will thrive in the light,' I told Amanda. She hadn't had the experience of receiving a plant before dementia, so there was no chance of her relating to it now, I supposed. Often in fostering I have to remind myself that the child I look after

172

and their family haven't had the same life experiences as I have.

Although Amanda didn't take any notice of the plant, she left it where it was and watched us carefully as Melody and I continued to unpack the bags. I put the fruit we'd brought in the bowl and Melody put the biscuits in the drawer in her bedside cabinet. I then took out the photograph album I'd made for her. 'Why don't you sit on the bed with your mum and show her the album?' I suggested to Melody. I'd previously shown her the album and she'd been delighted. As far as she knew her mother had never owned a photograph album, or if she had it had been lost a long time ago in all the moves. When you think of all the photographs parents usually collect, yet Amanda had five children but not a single photograph of any of them. It was as though their history had been wiped out, even more so now Amanda had dementia, so it was important I took plenty of photographs and kept Melody's Life Story Book going.

'Come and sit next to me, Mum,' Melody said, patting the bed beside her. 'This is for you.' She held up the album. 'It's got lots of photos of me.'

Amanda hesitated, then went over and sat beside her daughter but with no sense of expectation or delight. Melody positioned the album between them so they could both see it and opened the first page. 'There's me outside Cathy's house,' she said, and allowed her mother time to look at the photo before moving to the next. 'That's my bedroom … that's the garden … that's me on a swing in the park.' And so on. There were some posed photographs of Melody and I'd put three of those (including a head-and-shoulders shot) into the frames I'd bought. But the pictures in the album mostly showed

Melody involved in some activity or on an outing, which would hopefully give Amanda a sense of Melody's life with me and reassure her she was happy and doing well.

As Melody continued talking her mother through the album I took the framed photos from my bag and set them on the shelves. Amanda took no notice but kept her attention on the album. She hadn't said anything about the photos, but halfway through it was as though the door into her memory suddenly opened again and she realized she was looking at photos of her daughter, who was sitting beside her. 'Melody!' she cried, looking at her. She slipped her arm around her daughter's waist and rested her head on her shoulder. 'My Melody, my darling daughter.' Amanda's face crumpled and her voice shook. 'I'm so sorry, love, for being a shit mother, really I am.'

My eyes filled.

'It's all right, Mum,' Melody said. 'I don't blame you.'

'You should,' Amanda said, and she began to cry.

I went over and, taking a tissue from the box, passed it to her to wipe her eyes. 'Amanda, it's Cathy, Melody's foster carer. You mustn't worry. Melody is fine, she's living with me and I'm taking good care of her.'

'Are you?' she asked, meeting my gaze.

'Yes, honestly. She has everything she needs and her social worker visits us regularly. I promise you, Melody is happy.'

'That's good.' Her eyes went blank again, but I knew that for those brief moments I had made contact with the real Amanda, the mother, before drugs and dementia had taken it all away. It was all so very sad.

CHAPTER SEVENTEEN

NOT THURSDAY

The following week on Thursday Melody's friend Lizzie came to tea. Melody had chosen Thursday so they could make the cupcakes for her mother together. Lizzie was a lovely child, gentle and polite, who had two younger brothers. After dinner – sausage and mash, which was what Melody and Lizzie had wanted – I helped them make and ice the fairy cakes, with extra so that Lizzie could take some home for her family. The girls played together nicely – before and after dinner – and when I took Lizzie home at seven o'clock her mother thanked me and asked if Melody would like to go there for tea.

'Yes!' Melody screeched at the top of her voice, then added solemnly, 'But not on Thursday. I make Mum's cakes then.' It had become something of a ritual.

'I know.' Lizzie's mother smiled. 'Lizzie told me. What about Wednesday then?'

'Yes!' Melody cried again.

'Thank you,' I said, 'that would be great.' I'd see her in the playground nearer the time to confirm the arrangements.

I was pleased Melody now had at least one good friend at school and I knew from what she was telling me that she was playing with other children too. One of the targets from her review had been that she should attend an after-school club, but whenever I raised the matter with Melody, suggesting various activities, she said she didn't want to do any of them, but liked to come straight home. I suggested an evening activity such as ballet or the Girls' Brigade, but she didn't want to do those either. I wasn't going to force her. She'd had a lot of adjustments to make; it wasn't that long ago she'd been described as feral and uncontrollable and hadn't been attending school at all. I was pleased with the progress she was making, not only at school, but also generally, and I hoped that in time she might want to join an activity club. If she didn't then so be it.

We visited Amanda on Saturday afternoon that week as we had a free weekend, which was better as it was less of a rush and the traffic was lighter. As usual, the couple we now knew to be Mr and Mrs Bennett arrived on the other side of the door as soon as Melody pressed the bell. I guessed they must wait just out of sight of the door to appear so quickly. We went through the routine of Mr Bennett knocking on the glass with his wife pointing to the lock, while I shook my head and said, 'No, I can't unlock it.' Melody, far more relaxed about them now, threw them a smile. A care assistant let us in and I said hello to her and Mr and Mrs Bennett. They obviously didn't know who I was, but it seemed as if we knew them now. Likewise, when Mr Andrews shuffled along the corridor towards us, having been shooed out of the ladies' lounge, both Melody and I said hello to him and his care assistant as they passed. Oak Lane House was starting to feel like a home from home for us; we were seeing familiar faces and we knew our way around.

Amanda was sitting in the lounge, staring into space. The occupational therapist was at the table with one resident threading beads to make a bracelet. She asked Melody if she'd like to bring her mother over to join in the activity. She said she hadn't been able to persuade Amanda or any of the others to join in, although to be honest I thought that many of the residents were past the stage of being able to thread beads to make bracelets.

Melody went over to fetch her mother. 'We didn't see you last Friday,' I said to the occupational therapist.

'No, I'm shared between two care homes on a two-week timetable. I come here on alternate Fridays,' she explained.

Melody arrived at the table with her mother. I said hello to Amanda and asked her how she was.

'Fine,' Amanda said tersely, although I'm pretty sure she didn't know who I was.

'How's school?' the occupational therapist asked Melody as she and her mother settled at the table.

'Fine,' Melody said, just as her mother had. 'My friend Lizzie came to tea and I'm going to hers next week.'

'That's nice. My children like to do that too.'

The occupational therapist cut them both a length of cord and, taking a few beads from the box on the table that held hundreds of different colours, showed them what to do. Melody began threading the beads while the occupational therapist had to help Amanda. Like the basket-weaving, this was an activity a young child could easily master, but it took Amanda numerous attempts to thread one bead onto the cord. It seemed her hand–eye coordination (needed for controlled movement) had deteriorated, which I thought could be part of the disease's progression.

The care assistant I'd been talking to on our first visit was on duty and while Amanda and Melody threaded their beads I went over and sat in the chair beside him and asked him how he was. He said he'd just finished a week of nights and was pleased to be on the day shift again. I asked after his baby and he said he was teething. I sympathized, as I knew how fractious infants could be when cutting teeth. As we talked he kept a watchful eye on his patients. I mentioned Mr and Mrs Bennett and asked how long they'd been living here. He said nearly a year and that they'd celebrated their golden wedding anniversary last month. 'We gave them a little party, and decorated their room,' he said, smiling. 'We celebrate as much as possible – birthdays, Christmas, a birth in the family. Any excuse.'

'That's lovely.'

Inevitably it wasn't long before Mr Andrews shuffled in making his 'boo-boo' noise, followed by a care assistant. I thought she must walk miles in a day keeping an eye on him. The care assistant I was talking to said Mr Andrews had been a qualified accountant before becoming ill, and still liked numbers, often reading them from the doors and the calendar in his room. It was a sobering thought that very likely everyone in the home would at some point have had a career and led an independent life before dementia set in.

Once Melody and Amanda had made a bracelet each, Melody was eager to go to her mother's room. I thanked the occupational therapist and, with Amanda and Melody wearing the bracelets they'd made, we left the lounge. As before, Amanda took us straight to her room without any hesitation, which again struck me as odd given how much she forgot.

Her room was as we'd left it the week before, with the plant on the table, the card Melody had made on the bedside cabinet, the ornaments and photos on her shelves and Melody's drawings on the pinboard. Melody added another drawing to the pinboard first, and then as Amanda watched she set a new ornament on her shelf. She then took out the box of cakes, but this time stayed in charge of it. She gave her mother one, had one for herself and put the box in the bedside cabinet for her mother for later. I retrieved the old stay-fresh box from the cabinet. The photograph album was in there too and Melody now took it out. Encouraging her mother to sit beside her on the bed, she began going through the photographs as she had the week before, telling her mother a bit about each picture. Every so often I saw a flash of recognition cross Amanda's eyes, as if she might remember seeing the photograph before. Had she remembered it from last week or had she been looking at them since? I didn't know. Then, as if to prove she remembered, she suddenly said, 'Melody looking very smart in her school uniform,' before Melody had said it.

'Yes, well done,' I said.

Melody was ecstatic. 'You remembered!' she exclaimed, kissing her cheek. 'You remembered what I told you.' Then to me, 'Mummy's getting better!'

My heart sank. 'It's good she could remember the photograph,' I said carefully. I'd have to explain again later that people didn't recover from dementia. It was very difficult. I knew from what I'd read that dementia didn't always progress evenly but in fits and starts, which allowed snatches of memory and lucidity from time to time until the final stage when it all disappeared for good.

We spent the rest of the afternoon in Amanda's room and then, when it was time to go, she came with us to the main door. There was no sign of Mr and Mrs Bennett, but as soon as I rang the bell for a care assistant to let us out they appeared from just around the corner. I looked round the corner and saw an open door leading to another, much smaller sitting room. So that was where they waited for the bell to ring. While it seemed a bit depressing that their lives centred on the doorbell ringing, they weren't distressed and appeared reasonably content. So I told myself it was just part of their ritualistic behaviour, similar to Mr Andrews visiting the ladies' lounge and Mr Wilson calling out he had a plane to catch. The alternative – that they were really desperate to get out – was too painful to contemplate.

The care assistant arrived and Melody kissed her mother goodbye. Mrs Bennett then offered her cheek for kissing, which moved me. 'She has a granddaughter about your age,' the care assistant said to Melody. 'She always kisses her goodbye.' I was so pleased to hear they had family who visited them, and Melody was happy to kiss her cheek. The care assistant then moved them aside to let us out. As we went down the path we turned to wave goodbye. Amanda was standing between Mr and Mrs Bennett and the three of them waved back.

'I don't mind Mummy being friends with them now,' Melody said. 'I think they're nice.' Now she'd got to know them their behaviour was no longer intimidating and frightening, as it had been on our first visit.

* * *

From then on we visited Amanda either Friday after school or Saturday afternoon, depending on what I'd planned for the weekend. We always baked cakes on Thursday evening and also took in the ornaments Melody had bought with her pocket money, fruit, a packet of biscuits and any other food Melody thought her mother might like. I'm sure Amanda was very well fed at the care home, and I'd reassured Melody this was so, but like many children who come from homes where food has been scarce, she was still anxious about it. It can take months, sometimes years, before they stop worrying about where their next meal will come from. At each visit we spent some time in Amanda's room and Melody took pride in making it look nice, tidying it, rearranging the shelves, adding to and adjusting the pictures on the pinboard and so on. The room looked far more homely now and while it pleased Melody and me, I doubted Amanda knew or cared, or perhaps she did. With so little language she rarely expressed her thoughts and feelings.

Towards the end of March, Neave and Jill visited us for their statutory visits. We discussed Melody's progress and Jill checked and signed off my log notes. Neave also spent a short time alone with Melody and checked her bedroom before she left. Neave hadn't seen Amanda since she'd been admitted to Oak Lane House, as once Amanda had been diagnosed and assessed a social worker from a different team was responsible for her. From what Neave said she wasn't in regular contact with Amanda's new social worker, so it was left to me (and Melody) to tell Neave how Amanda was. Melody's version was slightly different to mine. She told Neave about the cakes, the ornaments, the drawings she'd done for her mother, and of course Mr Boo-Boo, Mr Aeroplane Man, and Mr and Mrs

Bennett 'trying to escape' as she put it, while I told Neave (out of earshot of Melody) that Amanda's dementia seemed to be advancing very quickly.

'Does she still recognize Melody?' Neave asked.

'Sometimes. But those times are getting fewer.' She made a note.

Melody also told Miss May about her visits to her mother, so that when I collected her from school on Monday Miss May always had something positive to say about the visit; for example, 'Melody tells me she and her mother made some lovely bracelets.' Or, 'I hear Amanda's room is looking pretty.' Although Miss May would know the grim reality from watching her father's decline.

At the start of April the schools broke up for the two-week Easter holiday. Adrian planned to spend most of it studying, as his exams began in May, so I took the girls on plenty of daytrips, which allowed some quiet in the house. Melody and I also visited Amanda on both Friday afternoons, while Lucy and Paula stayed at home 'chilling'. I suppose they could have come with us, but neither of them nor Melody had suggested it, and I knew they would find the experience very upsetting. And part of me felt this was Melody's special one-to-one with her mother and that she needed to make the most of whatever time there was left.

I received a letter in the post from CAMHS (Child and Adolescent Mental Health Service) with details of Melody's long-awaited appointment to see a therapist. It was in ten days' time. While there didn't seem such a pressing need now for Melody to have therapy, as she was doing so well, she must still have many dark thoughts and unresolved issues that she needed to talk about, and a trained therapist would help her. I noted the appointment in my diary and let Neave know the next time we spoke.

Fostering is often marked with flurries of activity when the phone seems to be constantly ringing and there is a steady procession of professionals coming into the house, then it eases off, and you all fall into a routine and the household runs relatively smoothly. It's always very hectic when a child first arrives and then it tends to settle down (unless anything untoward happens) until the final court hearing approaches, when there is renewed activity. The final court hearing wasn't until November and at present everything seemed to be ticking along. School returned for the summer term and the air was warmer and the sun shone (well, sometimes – it was the UK, after all!). The days were longer now and I was driving back from Oak Lane House in daylight.

I took Melody for her CAMHS appointment. The unit was sited in a separate wing at our local hospital and I knew its location from having taken other children I'd fostered there. I gave our names to the receptionist and then we sat in the waiting room. It was very child-friendly, with bright collages of birds, butterflies and animals on the walls and plenty of toys and books for all ages of children. We were the only ones there and Melody didn't want to play with anything, so I read to her from one of the books. After about five minutes a woman came in and introduced herself as Dr Marina Short, 'But call me Marina,' she said pleasantly. She was indeed short and I hoped Melody didn't comment. I guessed Marina to be in her mid-fifties; she had grey hair knotted tightly in a tall bun on top of her head, which I thought perhaps was intended to give her some height. She told Melody it was very nice to meet her and then showed us into a consulting room. I remembered being in it before with another child but not with this therapist. It was carpeted and contained a desk, filing cabinets, shelves of books, toy boxes and a circle of chairs around a low coffee table in the centre, on which was a box of tissues.

Melody and I sat down as Marina collected a notepad and pen from her desk and then joined us, facing Melody and me. I knew from experience that the first appointment is largely an assessment. Marina would have received the background information from Neave, and this session was to find out how Melody was and what CAMHS could do to help her. Marina began by asking Melody how she felt she'd settled in with me.

'OK,' Melody said with a nervous shrug. I threw her a reassuring smile.

'How do you think Melody has settled in?' Marina asked me. 'I believe you have older children in the family?'

'Yes, two daughters and a son. Melody has settled in very well.' I outlined the progress she'd made at home and school as Marina made some notes.

'Excellent,' she said, smiling at Melody. Then she asked her what she liked about school.

'Miss May,' Melody said. 'She's nice and helps me with my work.' Marina asked her about friends and Melody said, 'Lizzie is my best friend,' and told her about going to each other's houses for tea.

'Do you have any problems making friends?' Marina asked.

'No,' Melody said. 'Sometimes.'

Marina looked at me. 'Because Melody hadn't been in school mixing with her peer group, she struggled a little to make friends to begin with,' I said. 'Her TA, Miss May, and her teacher tell me she is doing well now.'

'Good. That is progress,' Marina said and made another note.

'What about your family?' she asked Melody. 'You're seeing your mother three times a week at contact. How is that going?'

Melody looked confused, as well she might.

'Amanda is in a care home,' I said. 'Didn't you know?'

'No. The referral was made in January from her social worker. It says Melody has supervised contact at the Family Centre on Monday, Wednesday and Friday. I assume I haven't been updated.'

'Apparently not.' I then went over as concisely as I could what had happened in the interim, including Amanda being sectioned, her stay in hospital, diagnosis, move to Oak Lane House and the present contact arrangements. It was a pity Melody had to hear all this, but there was no alternative.

'I see,' Marina said as I finished, frowning as she wrote. 'Things have changed.' I thought she really should have known all this, although whose responsibility it was to update her I didn't know – Neave's? Or perhaps it was up to Marina to check she had the latest information.

'So you see your mother once a week at the care home?' she now said to Melody. Melody nodded. 'How is that going?'

'OK,' Melody said. Marina waited for more to follow and I wondered if Melody would start talking about Mr Boo-Boo and so on, but she didn't.

'How do you feel when you see your mother?' Marina now asked.

'I want to see Mummy,' Melody said a little defensively, as though she thought Marina might stop her.

'Good, and after you've seen her at the care home do you think about her a lot?'

Melody shrugged. 'Sometimes.'

'We always have a talk about our visit in the car on the way home,' I said. 'And if Melody has any questions or if there is anything worrying her, I hope she feels she can tell me.'

Marina nodded as she wrote, then, glancing up at me, she said, 'I'm sure Melody must have many emotions, some of them conflicting.'

'I'm sure she does, and I try to help her deal with them as best I can.'

'When you see your mother, do you feel sad?' she asked Melody.

'Sometimes, but I know the care assistants look after Mummy. She has a nice room and it's warm, and there's plenty of food. On Thursday we bake cakes for her, and Cathy always takes in fruit.'

'Good. What was life like with your mother before you came into care? Can you remember?'

'Some of it,' Melody said guardedly.

'Would you like to tell me about it?'

Melody thought for a moment and then shook her head.

'OK, maybe another time. What do you like about living at Cathy's?'

Melody looked embarrassed and self-conscious. 'Lots of things.'

'What do you like doing?' Marina asked, rephrasing.

'Baking cakes and playing with Lucy and Paula. I like Adrian too, but he's always in his room, studying.'

I smiled. 'He has exams starting next week.'

'Do you go to any clubs or activities?' she asked.

Melody shook her head. I thought that before long the poor child would sign up to an activity just to keep the professionals in her life happy.

'We go swimming most weekends,' I said. 'Melody knows if she wants to join an after-school activity then she only has to say, but at present she prefers to come home and relax.'

'Sounds good to me,' Marina said with a smile. Then to Melody, 'Is there anything you would like to tell me? Our hour is nearly up.'

Melody shook her head.

'All right,' she said, addressing us both. 'I think that's enough for now. Here at CAMHS we offer a number of different therapies, and for a child of Melody's age play therapy is usually considered more appropriate than a talking therapy. We have two therapy rooms here that are equipped with a variety of toys and art materials. The children usually come for an hour a week and work in small groups, but at their own pace. It allows them the space and time to explore issues that are affecting them, past and present.' Then, looking at Melody, she asked, 'Would you like to come here once a week and do some painting and play with other children? I can arrange it for after school so you don't miss any more school.'

'OK, but not Thursday,' Melody said. 'I bake cakes for Mummy on Thursday.'

'I'll make sure it's not Thursday then,' Marina said.

'Thank you,' I said.

'You're welcome. I'll have the appointment letter sent to you with a copy to her social worker. You shouldn't have to wait too long.'

I thanked her again and, saying goodbye, we left. Once outside I told Melody she had done well.

'It was boring,' she said. 'Why did she ask me all those questions?'

'Marina was trying to find out more about you and if there was anything worrying you, so she can help.'

'I'm not going if she keeps asking me questions. That's what the social workers did before they took me away.' So I wondered if some of Melody's reluctance to talk to Marina had been due to that.

'Next time will be different. You'll be playing and doing art work with the other children.'

She didn't look convinced.

'We'll see how it goes,' I said, and left it at that.

Therapy doesn't suit everyone and I'd fostered children before who had stopped going. Therapy has to come at the right time in a child or young person's life and they have to be able to relate to the therapist just as an adult in therapy does. We all have different coping mechanisms and some find therapy helpful, others not so much. But at least Melody was being given the chance, and CAMHS has helped thousands of children and young people. It is available to them whether they are in foster care or living with their family and is funded by our National Health Service, so is free for the user.

CHAPTER EIGHTEEN

DEVELOPMENTS

Melody's second LAC review was approaching and we received the review forms in the post for us to complete. My form had changed a little since the first review and now included a section entitled 'Staying Safe', with details of any accidents or notifiable incidents. I wrote 'None'. Melody's form was unchanged and I sat with her after dinner one evening to help her complete it. She could write well enough now to form her own letters and some words but still needed help with spelling and reading the questions. When we got to the question, *What has gone well for you since your last review?* she said without hesitation, 'Seeing Mummy.' I was relieved. *What has gone badly since your last review?* I helped her read.

'Having to keep answering questions!' she said vehemently.

I laughed out loud. 'Very good.'

'Can I put that then?'

'Yes, if you want to, it's your review form.' Why shouldn't she put that if it was what she felt? Her social worker always asked her questions, so too did Jill when she saw her, the Guardian ad Litem, Marina and now another review form. Compared with the average child living with their family,

Melody must have felt that her life was full of questions, although of course they were all being asked in her best interests.

In response to the question, *If you have any problems, who do you talk to?* Melody said, 'You, Lucy, Paula and Lizzie. I used to talk to Mummy, but she doesn't understand any more.'

'But it's still important we talk to her,' I said. 'I know she doesn't say much, but we don't know what she understands.'

'What's the next question?' Melody asked, not wanting to dwell on this, and she moved on.

The following week, as I set off for the review, I wasn't expecting any big surprises, which was naïve. Fostering should have taught me never to become complacent. As far as I knew this second review was routine – to make sure everything was being done to help Melody and that the care plan was up to date. Again it was being held at Melody's school and she would come in towards the end. I dressed smartly and arrived in plenty of time, signed in, and then one of the school secretaries took me to the Head's room for the meeting. The IRO and Miss May were already there and we said hello.

'Cathy Glass, Melody's foster carer,' the IRO said, remembering me, and ticked off my name from his list of those who'd been invited.

Jill arrived, quickly followed by Neave but without her student social worker, whom I guessed had finished his placement. The IRO checked off their names, then the Deputy Head Mrs Farnham came in with a bright, 'Good afternoon all.'

'I think that's everyone,' the IRO said, glancing around the room. 'I've had apologies of absence from the Guardian and also Dr Marina Short, who has sent in a short letter. I'm assuming no one from Melody's family will be attending?'

'No,' Neave confirmed.

The IRO opened the meeting by thanking us for attending and then asked us to introduce ourselves – standard practice at reviews even though we had all met before. The introductions over, he began by saying, 'I understand there have been some developments since Melody's first review.' At that point I assumed he was referring to contact being established, so I would mention that early on when I spoke. 'Cathy,' he said, looking at me, 'thank you for sending in the review forms. I've read them. Would you like to start by telling us how Melody is doing now?'

'Yes, of course.' I straightened in my seat, glanced at my notes and then met the gaze of the others in the room. I said that Melody continued to do well at home and school, and I took her to see her mother once a week at the care home. I covered what Melody liked to do in her spare time and that, while she hadn't joined an after-school club, I was taking her swimming most weekends. I included that she was healthy, up to date with her dental and optician's check-ups, and since the first review she had seen Dr Marina Short at CAMHS for an initial appointment and was going to be offered play therapy. I concluded by saying she was generally more confident, was making friends and had one special friend, Lizzie, whom she saw out of school.

The IRO thanked me and then asked, 'When you take Melody to the care home to see her mother do you stay with her the whole time?'

'Yes. Always.'

'Does her mother talk to you or her daughter?' he asked.

'Not really. She says things sometimes, but it's not really talking as in having a conversation. She has very little language now.'

'Because of her dementia?' he asked.

'Yes.'

'And the prognosis?' he now asked Neave, glancing at her.

'Not good. I'll cover that and say more about contact in my report.'

The IRO nodded and made a note. I had an uncomfortable feeling. Neave hadn't observed contact; indeed, as far as I knew she hadn't been to the care home, so what could she possible have to say about contact?

'Does Melody find her visits to the care home and seeing her mother distressing?' the IRO now asked me.

'Not distressing, but obviously it's a lot for a child of eight to cope with. We talk about it after and Melody knows if she has any questions she can ask me. Play therapy should help too.'

He nodded. 'Thank you for all you are doing. And Melody can stay with you for as long as necessary?' This was a stand- ard question asked by most IROs.

'Yes.'

He made a note and then asked Neave for her report. I looked at her carefully.

'I visit Melody every four to six weeks at the foster carer's home,' she began – a standard opening. 'Melody attends school regularly and punctually and is making steady progress. I haven't seen Melody's mother, Amanda, since she was diagnosed and her case was transferred to the adult social-care team. Amanda will remain at the care home for the foreseeable future, until she needs nursing care.' Which I knew, but then Neave said, 'The care plan has been revised and the family-finding team has begun to look for an adoptive family for Melody. In line with this, contact is going to be reduced from weekly to fortnightly.' So these were the developments the IRO had referred to! I struggled to concentrate on what Neave was now saying.

'When Melody first came into care,' Neave continued, 'she wasn't considered adoptable because of her very challenging behaviour, and she had a strong bond with her mother. Her behaviour has improved dramatically, which has allowed a chance for her to be adopted. Obviously it's going to be difficult to place an eight-year-old – most adoptive families want babies or young children – but the department believes it's worth exploring.'

'But Melody still has a strong bond with her mother,' I said, speaking out of turn.

'That bond will lessen with time as her mother's dementia progresses,' Neave said. 'Her prognosis is poor and it is likely that Amanda will die before Melody reaches adulthood, effectively making her an orphan.' Blunt but true. 'She has no relatives to look after her, so the alternative to adoption is for her to remain in long-term foster care. We expect to be granted a Full Care Order in November, so the permanency team has started family finding. Contact will be reduced now and then again if a suitable adoptive family is found. These are the changes; everything else in Melody's life remains the same.' Neave stopped and while I could see the logic in reducing contact and trying to find an adoptive family, it had still come as a huge shock.

'When will the reduction in contact start?' the IRO asked as he wrote.

'From this week,' Neave said, and turned to me. 'Can you tell Melody tonight and then I'll explain in more detail the reason behind the reduction when I see her next week?'

'So Melody isn't going to see her mother this week?' I asked, seeking clarification.

'No. Next week, so fortnightly from now on.'

'She won't be pleased,' I said.

'No. But we all have to deliver unpalatable news some-times. As you're an experienced foster carer, I'm sure you'll know how to handle it.' That told me, I thought.

'Can you send a copy of the new care plan to the agency and to Cathy?' Jill said.

'Yes,' Neave confirmed.

'If Melody is adopted, will she be able to remain at the same school?' Mrs Farnham, the Deputy Head, asked. 'She's only just settled in here and with so many changes going on in her personal life, it would give her some stability.' I knew the answer.

'It will depend on where the adoptive family live,' Neave said. 'We keep children at the same school when possible. But family finding is nationwide and we haven't identified a family yet. Please don't tell Melody there's a chance she might have to move. It could make her unsettled.'

'No, of course I won't tell her,' Mrs Farnham said, affronted at being told what she considered obvious. 'But the school does need to be kept informed. The staff here work very closely with the children and we pride ourselves on our pasto-ral care.'

Neave nodded. The IRO finished writing and looked up at

me. 'It shows what a good job you've done that Melody can now be considered for adoption,' he said.

I smiled weakly.

That was all Neave had to say and the IRO asked Mrs Farnham to give her report. As she talked about Melody's IEP (Individual Education Plan), I thought over what I'd just heard. While it had come as a shock, I thought it was highly unlikely that Melody would be leaving us any time soon. She was eight, and as Neave had pointed out it wasn't going to be easy finding an adoptive family. I knew plenty of foster carers with a child or sibling group where they'd been told the department was family finding for an adoptive home and years later the children were still with the carer. Eventually, the family-finding team gave up and the child or children stayed with the carer long term and became permanent members of their family. I was more worried that Melody would only be seeing her mother every two weeks and the effect that would have on her.

Mrs Farnham finished her report and passed to Miss May, who, a little nervously, told us about the work she was doing with Melody. The IRO then read out the letter from Dr Marina Short, which just confirmed that she'd seen Melody in the clinic with her foster carer and play therapy was being offered. He then ticked off the swimming target as having been reached and carried over 'out-of-school activity' as an ongoing target. Jill was asked to speak and as usual explained her role, said we were in regular contact and that I was providing a good standard of care.

The IRO thanked her and then asked Miss May if she would bring Melody to her review. Melody came in far more confidently than at her first review. Sitting beside Miss May, she threw me a lovely smile, and I felt guilty, as though I was part of a conspiracy to stop her from seeing her mother. As she answered the IRO's questions, bright and bubbly and blissfully unaware, I knew I'd have to tell her as soon as we got home, and I steeled myself for the anger and upset that I knew would follow.

CHAPTER NINETEEN

CAUGHT HIS PLANE

'They can't do that!' Melody screamed at the top of her voice. 'It's not fair!'

'I know it's upsetting, love,' I said. 'But two weeks isn't so long.'

'Yes, it is! I hate you, I hate you all!'

'Some children in care only see their parents two or three times a year,' I offered.

'I don't care about them!' she stormed. 'I want to see my mummy every week! I want to live with Mummy again like I used to!'

Then her anger gave way to tears and, throwing herself face down on her bed, she sobbed as if her heart would break. I sat beside her, my hand lightly resting on her back, waiting for her upset to subside. Sometimes it helps to have a good cry and let out all that bottled-up emotion.

This scene was playing out exactly as I'd imagined it would since I'd been told at the review that Melody's contact with her mother was being reduced to fortnightly. Needing to get it over with, I'd told Melody as soon as we were home, with just the two of us in the living room. I'd approached it as sensitively as I could. There'd been no easy way of telling

197

her and unsurprisingly she had reacted angrily and fled to her bedroom, slamming the door behind her. I'd followed her up, and reassured Paula and Lucy who, having heard Melody screaming, were concerned. I'd been talking to Melody ever since, offering her platitudes that sounded feeble even to me.

After a few minutes, her sobbing reached a climax and then began to ease. I lightly rubbed her back, trying to soothe away the pain, then she sat up and looked at me through tear-filled eyes. 'It's not fair,' she said, defeated, her bottom lip trembling. 'I want to visit my mummy every week.'

'I know, love. Come on, let's dry those eyes.' I took a tissue from the box and gently wiped her face. 'I know it's difficult, but two weeks will pass very quickly. You saw Mummy last Friday and you'll see her again next Friday, so not many sleeps. Some of the children I've looked after have found that writing a letter to someone they miss can help.'

'I like writing,' she said, brightening a little. 'Can we post it like a proper letter?'

'Yes, or we can take it with us next week and you can read it to your mother.'

'I want to post it,' she said.

'OK.'

Strictly speaking, sending a letter was considered a form of contact by the social services, but Amanda wasn't going to be able to read it and probably wouldn't even know who it was from. The letter was to help Melody, so I'd have no qualms about posting it. Some older children I've fostered have found that writing their thoughts and feelings in a diary helps – journal therapy is sometimes used by therapists.

'Can we still bake cakes on Thursday?' Melody asked as I wiped away the last of her tears.

'Yes, but we'll have to eat them ourselves, as they won't keep, and then make fresh ones to take the following week.'

'I don't mind eating them,' she said.

'All of them!' I exclaimed. 'You'll go off pop!' Finally she smiled.

'Good girl, come on, let's go downstairs.' I helped her off the bed.

'Can I go to Paula's room and play with her doll's house?' she asked.

'Yes, if it's OK with her.'

Paula had a beautiful doll's house with collectable furniture, which she'd added to over the years. Even now, aged twelve, she valued it, and although she didn't play with it as such herself, she allowed other young children to when she was present.

She was sitting on her bed listening to music and was happy for Melody to stay and play. I thanked her, came out and then looked in on Lucy, who was also listening to music, then Adrian, who was studying hard as his first exam was the following day. 'See you at dinner,' I said, and left him to it.

Melody stayed with Paula until dinner was ready, then once we'd eaten and Melody had done her homework I sat with her at the table and helped her with the spelling as she wrote the letter to her mother.

Dear Mummy
I am sorry I can't see you this week. I can only see you
every two weeks now, but I am thinking about you. I hope
you can think about me. I know it's hard because you forget
things. Don't forget me. Look at the photos. Don't worry
about me. Cathy and her kids look after me. I am doing
well. Bye for now.
Lots of love
  Melody
xxxxxxxxxxxx

Her words touched me and I thought it was a very mature and insightful letter for an eight-year-old. Although it was written in a young child's writing, it seemed to show that Melody understood and accepted her mother's condition – that she did forget things and might eventually forget her.

I fetched an envelope and stamp and helped Melody write the address on the front of the envelope.

'Can we post it now?' she asked as she sealed it.

'Yes, but then it's straight to bed after. It's getting late.'

We could have posted it on the way to school the following morning as it would have caught the same post, but I knew that sending it on its way now would help Melody settle.

I told the rest of the family where we were going and then we changed into our outdoor shoes, left the house and walked up the road to the post box in the high street. It was a pleasantly mild evening in May and Melody held my hand as we went and chatted about school, Lizzie and how pleased her mummy would be to receive the letter. At the post box I pointed out the collection times on the front. 'The postman will collect your letter from here at 9 a.m. tomorrow morning and your mother should have it the following day.'

'Good. Night, Mummy,' she said as she dropped the letter into the post box. 'See you next week.' Writing to her mother had made her feel that little bit closer. She slipped her hand into mine and we turned and retraced our steps home.

The following morning, Miss May was waiting in the play-ground for us. Melody ran off to play with her friends and Miss May told me she'd had a restless night after the review, worrying about how Melody had taken the news of not seeing her mother.

'That's kind of you,' I said. Miss May was a treasure. I told her that Melody had been angry and upset to begin with, but had written to her mother and had become less anxious, and was now looking forward to seeing her the following week. Miss May said she'd keep an eye on her, and I thanked her. I think that having had her father at the care home and suffer-ing from dementia, she was even more sympathetic to what Melody was going through.

On Thursday evening, Melody and I baked and iced cupcakes – the same number we usually made. I said I'd put the extra (those we would normally have taken to Amanda) in a container for us to eat the following day, to stop everyone devouring the lot in one go. However, on Friday morning I woke with a different thought. Although Melody couldn't visit her mother, there was nothing to stop me going – I could take her a few of the cakes she enjoyed. As far as I knew, Amanda didn't have any visitors apart from us, and the social worker responsible for her wouldn't be seeing her more than once a month maximum. Why shouldn't I go? If I went that morning and spent an hour with Amanda I'd be back in plenty of time to collect Melody from school in the afternoon. No one need ever know. So often in fostering bonds are formed with the child's family as well as with the child.

The thought grew as I woke the rest of the house and made breakfast. I wouldn't tell Melody I was going, as she'd find it confusing and possibly upsetting that I could visit her mother but she couldn't. Neither would I tell Paula, Lucy or Adrian, because if I did it would come with the rider that they weren't to tell Melody. Secrets are generally not good between siblings in foster families. Surprises are fine, but secrets often have negative connotations.

On returning home from taking Melody to school, I set aside cakes for the children and put the rest in a box for Amanda, together with some grapes. I'd been replenishing the fruit bowl in her room every week, so I assumed she was eating the fruit. As I locked up and left the house I felt like a child on a secret mission. Adrian would be home first as he was now only in school for his exams, so I'd left a note saying that I'd gone to see a friend and would be back in the afternoon. That was all he needed to know.

The roads were clear and I made good time, although it was strange driving to the care home without Melody in the back, either chatting or listening to her favourite CD. It was 11.30 a.m. when I arrived. The care home's visiting times weren't like a general hospital's, which were strictly controlled. Visitors to the care home could go in between 10 a.m. and 8 p.m., and even these times were relaxed.

Retrieving the carrier bag and my handbag from the passenger seat, I made my way to the main entrance. The air smelt fresher here and the skyline stretched as far as I could see to the distant hills beyond. As I let myself in the outer door there was no sign of Mr and Mrs Bennett, but I now knew they'd be waiting for the bell to ring in the small lounge just around the corner. I signed the Visitors' Book and pressed the bell. Sure enough, a few seconds later they appeared on the other side of the door and we went through the usual routine of them gesturing for me to open it while I shook my head and said I couldn't. As with most of the residents, there was nothing in their manner to say they recognized me or that I looked familiar, although they'd seen me many times before.

'Good morning, you're early today,' the care assistant who let me in said. Many of the staff knew us now, as we did them. 'No daughter?'

'No, not today. She'll be coming every two weeks in future.'

'Amanda is in the lounge,' she said, relocking the door.

'Thank you.'

Having said hello to Mr and Mrs Bennett, I headed off along the corridor in the direction of the lounge, but as I passed Mr Wilson's room he didn't call out, so I assumed his routine was different in the morning and that perhaps he was in the men's lounge.

The women's lounge was fuller than I'd seen it before and Amanda was sitting on the far side with a care assistant beside her. I went over and said hello to them both.

'Hi, how are you?' the care assistant asked with a smile.

'Very well, thank you, and you?' I replied while Amanda stared at me.

'Good. No daughter with you today?'

'No, not today. She will be coming fortnightly from now on.'

The care assistant nodded. From what I'd seen, not many residents had regular visitors. Some we'd seen – like the young woman who came to visit her grandmother and an elderly lady who visited her husband each day – but most residents had only the occasional visitor, some none at all.

Amanda was still staring at me and I said hello again and smiled. It was impossible to guess what she was thinking. I drew up one of the chairs from the table.

'Melody is at school,' I said. 'She sends her love and will see you next week.'

There was no response, but she continued to look at me quite intently, as if trying to work out something.

'Melody has made you some cakes,' I said, and took the box from the carrier bag.

She suddenly snatched it from my hand, quite aggressively, making me start.

'It's rude to snatch,' the care assistant said evenly.

Amanda took no notice but began struggling to get the lid off the box.

'Shall I help you?' I offered.

She thrust the box back at me and I took off the lid. I gave her a couple of cakes and resealed the box and returned it to the carrier bag. Having eaten them, she grabbed the bag.

'Don't snatch,' the care worker said again. Amanda's aggressiveness was a new development, although perhaps she was confused because Melody wasn't with me. She rummaged in the bag.

'We can put the box of cakes and fruit in your room later if you like,' I said.

She threw the bag in my direction, stood and set off across the lounge.

'She wants to go to her room now,' the care assistant said, which I'd rather guessed.

I followed her out and as we left the lounge Mr Andrews entered, making his usual 'boo-boo' noise. A young care assistant I hadn't seen before followed him.

'This must keep you fit,' I said as I passed her.

'Absolutely!' she returned, laughing. 'I've cancelled my gym membership!' Not for the first time since I'd been visiting the care home, I thought how much good humour and patience were required to do their job. They really were saints.

Amanda stopped outside Mr Wilson's room and cocked her ear, listening out for him. 'I don't think he can be in his room,' I said. 'Perhaps he's in the men's lounge.'

She looked at me oddly, waited for a while longer and then continued along the corridor to her room.

As we went in I immediately saw the letter from Melody open on the bed with the envelope beside it. It must have arrived that morning. Had someone read the letter to her and explained who it was from?

'You got the letter from Melody then,' I said, pointing.

Amanda looked at me blankly.

'The letter on your bed,' I said, and pointed again.

'Letter,' she repeated. I went over and picked it up.

She made a rush and snatched it back. Perhaps she thought I was going to take it.

'I know it's yours,' I said. 'It's from Melody. I helped her write it. Shall I read it to you?'

She didn't reply but stuffed the letter under her pillow for safe keeping, so I assumed she must at least feel it was precious and possibly know it was from her daughter. I took the box of cakes from the carrier bag and put it in her bedside cabinet where we had been leaving them. At the same time I retrieved the box from last time, telling her what I was doing as I did it. I put the grapes into the fruit bowl, which was empty again. Amanda was watching me carefully, possibly a little confused, for in whatever memory she had of my previous visits Melody would have been there too.

'Melody is at school,' I said again. 'She will be coming next week.' At the mention of her daughter's name Amanda's gaze went to the framed photographs of her on the bookshelves, which I took as proof she still knew who Melody was.

'Would you like to look at the photograph album?' I asked her. It was on the bottom shelf. 'I could show you the photos as Melody does.'

The poor woman just stared at me but then suddenly seemed to make the connection and understand. She went to the bookshelf, picked up the album, sat on the bed and then patted the place beside her for me to sit as Melody did. I smiled and sat next to her. As she turned the pages I told her about each photograph: Melody on the swings, Melody having her dinner, Melody's bedroom and so forth. When she came to the end she returned the album to the shelf, walked around the room a few times, then looked directly at me.

'Photos,' she said and went back to the shelf. Taking the album, she returned to sit beside me and we began to go through the album again exactly as we had the first time. Sadly there was nothing from her to say she remembered any of them from looking at them before. Part-way through a knock sounded on the door and a member of staff put her head round. 'Amanda, it's lunchtime,' she said. 'Come to the dining room, please.'

She said hello to me and closed the door, so I assumed Amanda understood and knew where the dining room was. Clearly she did, for snapping shut the album she threw it on the bed and headed for the door. I followed her out. It was 12.20 now. I'd been there nearly an hour so I thought that once I'd seen her into the dining room I'd say goodbye and leave. We passed Mr Wilson's room and it remained quiet, but Amanda didn't stop or give it a second glance now. She was more intent on going to dinner. We turned right down a corridor I hadn't been through before, passed a kitchen and then went into the dining room, where residents were arriving. The room was about the same size as the lounge and six small dining tables were set with cutlery, condiments, glasses and a jug of water. Some residents were making their own way in, others were being guided in by care assistants, some were being pushed to the tables in wheelchairs, and three large pressure-relieving air chairs had been parked to one side, their occupants the most disabled. Men and women were in here and I thought it was nice that everyone came together at mealtimes, like a family. Apart from the elderly lady who seemed to spend most of each day with her husband, I was the only visitor present.

An assistant standing by a catering trolley began taking plated food to the residents and setting it on the table in front of them. Not everyone had identical food so I assumed some were on special diets. Mr and Mrs Bennett had temporarily left their post by the main door and now sat together, while Mr Andrews had joined a table of ladies but interestingly had stopped making his 'boo-boo' noise while he ate. The smell of food was making me hungry. I poured water for Amanda and the other lady at the table and then, when their food arrived, I said, 'Amanda, I'm going now. I'll see you next week.'

She didn't respond – I hadn't expected her to – but she had picked up her cutlery and was concentrating on the food on her plate. 'See you next week,' I said again, and kissed her cheek as Melody always did.

I left the dining room, returned down the corridor and passed Mr Wilson's room. It remained quiet. Perhaps he'd been in the dining room; I wouldn't have recognized him, as I'd never seen him, only heard him. I assumed the plane he had to catch must wait until he'd eaten, for until now his calling out had been constant. When a member of staff arrived at the main door to let me out I remarked, 'I haven't heard Mr Wilson today.'

'Didn't you know?' she asked, concerned.

'Know what?' A chill ran down my spine.

'He passed away in his sleep two nights ago.'

'Oh, I am sorry,' I said. 'It's so quiet without him.'

'Yes, we do miss him, but I guess he's finally caught his plane – to heaven.'

I nodded and hurried out, for ridiculously I'd teared up. I'd never met Mr Wilson, yet I felt I knew him. He was one of the characters in the care home and now he'd made his final journey – to heaven – as the care assistant had said. Goodbye, you finally caught your plane, Sir.

CHAPTER TWENTY

A TIMELY REMINDER

Bad news never seems to come alone. I had time to go home first before I needed to collect Melody from school, but as I let myself in Adrian immediately appeared in the hall looking very worried. My first thought was that the exam he'd sat that morning hadn't gone well, but then he said, 'Mum, there's something wrong with Toscha. She's in her bed and won't get up. I've tried to tempt her with food, but she's just lying there and her nose is running.'

I quickly followed him into the kitchen-diner where Toscha had her basket in one corner. She was never in her bed during the day. We knelt beside her and I stroked her. She looked so poorly and hadn't the energy to raise her head, and her eyes were watering. 'I'll phone the vet,' I said, straightening.

'Here's the number,' Adrian said, handing me a piece of paper. 'I was going to phone them, then you came in.'

'Thanks, love. Can you get the pet carrier from the cupboard under the stairs? It's right at the back.' The carrier was only normally used once a year to take Toscha to the vet for her annual check-up and vaccination – I couldn't remember her ever being ill before.

I used the handset in the kitchen to phone the vet. They ran an appointments system, but when I described Toscha's symptoms the receptionist said to bring her in straight away, as there was a nasty flu-type virus appearing in local cats, which could be fatal in older animals. I felt my heart twist and said I'd be there in ten minutes. Adrian and I gently lifted Toscha into the carrier. Normally she had to be tempted in with treats, but now she was too ill to protest. A lump rose in my throat. Toscha had been part of our family for as long as anyone could remember.

'I'll come with you,' Adrian said, picking up the carrier.

'Thanks but what about studying for your exam tomorrow?'

'I won't be able to concentrate until I know she's OK.'

He carried her to the car and then sat on the back seat with her on his lap, talking to her in a soothing voice. It was only ten minutes to the vet and I was able to park right outside. Adrian carried her in. I went to the reception desk to check in as Adrian sat on a chair with Toscha in the carrier on his lap. There was one other lady in the waiting room, elderly, with a small dog on her lap. Usually Toscha would have hissed at a dog, but now she remained unnaturally quiet.

'The vet won't be long,' the receptionist said. 'She's with another emergency, but you'll go in next.'

'Thank you so much,' I said, and sat next to Adrian.

'Are you the ones with the very sick cat?' the woman asked.

'Yes.' I guessed the receptionist had told her and that we would see the vet ahead of her.

'I hope your cat is OK. Albert is just here for his check-up.'

I raised a smile and nodded and assumed Albert was her dog. I think she would have liked to chat, but I was too worried about Toscha to make conversation. I also had one eye on the clock. If I was going to be late collecting Melody from school I'd have to phone and let them know. Five minutes ticked by with Toscha remaining unnaturally quiet and still, and then a veterinary assistant came out and showed us through to a consultation room.

The vet was waiting there and we carefully lifted Toscha out of the carrier and put her on the examination table. Adrian and I were silent as the vet looked in Toscha's eyes, ears and throat, then listened to her chest and took her temperature.

'When did she fall ill?' the vet asked.

'This morning,' I said. 'It was very sudden. She seemed fine first thing, although I noticed she didn't eat all her breakfast. Then when my son came home at midday he found her in her basket like this.'

'I'm sure it's the new strain of feline influenza that's appeared. It comes on very quickly, even in cats that have been vaccinated. I'll give her a shot of antibiotics now and a course of oral antibiotics for you to continue at home. I want to see her again on Monday, but if she worsens over the weekend then phone our emergency out-of-hours number.' I nodded. 'Keep her calm and try to get her to drink. Don't worry too much about food. She won't feel much like eating while she's feeling poorly. She's an old cat, so let's hope for the best.' I heard her warning, as did Adrian.

'She will be all right, won't she?' he asked.

'The next forty-eight hours are crucial,' she said. 'Do you have any other cats?'

'No.'

'Keep her in and away from other cats, as the virus is very contagious. I'll get the medicine.'

She left and Adrian and I stroked Toscha, who was on her front, legs tucked under her and head down. I could see how worried Adrian was. He doesn't easily show his feelings, but he was close to tears.

'She's strong,' I said, touching his arm. 'I'm sure she'll pull through.'

'I hope so,' he said. 'I know she's old, but I'm not ready to say goodbye to her yet.' His voice broke.

The vet returned and prepared the antibiotic injection. I steeled myself for the needle going in, but Toscha was so poorly she didn't murmur. Adrian and I stroked her as the vet talked us through how and when to give the oral antibiotics, then we gently lifted Toscha back into the carrier. I thanked the vet and we returned to reception to pay and make the follow-up appointment for Monday. Another couple with a pet carrier had joined the woman with her lapdog, Albert. As we left she said goodbye and hoped our cat was better soon. I thanked her.

Toscha was quiet on the drive home. Usually by now – on her annual trip to the vet – she would have had enough of being in the carrier and would meow constantly, calling us all sorts of names. Her silence deepened our concern, and Adrian and I were quiet too.

Once home, we settled Toscha in her basket again and I left Adrian trying to tempt her to drink some water, as I had to collect Melody from school. I arrived in the playground a few minutes late and Miss May was waiting with Melody. I walked swiftly over.

'I'm so sorry I'm late. I had to take our cat to the vet,' I explained. 'She's got cat flu.'

'Oh dear, I hope she's all right,' Miss May said, concerned. 'Melody's told me all about her. Toscha, isn't it?'

'Yes, that's right. She's on antibiotics.'

'She'll be better soon then,' she said positively.

I didn't go into more detail and sound the warnings the vet had done – that the disease could be fatal in older cats. I thanked Miss May for looking after Melody, wished her a nice weekend and said goodbye.

'What's the matter with Toscha?' Melody asked, worried, as we walked away. Despite her early animosity towards Toscha, she was now very good with her and often stroked and talked to her just as we did.

'She's got cat flu,' I said. 'We have to look after her and keep her quiet so she can rest.'

'My mum knew a man who died from flu,' Melody said.

'Yes, it can happen.'

'I hope Toscha doesn't die.'

'So do I, love.' I put off telling her about Mr Wilson.

At home I found Lucy and Paula sitting beside Toscha's bed, stroking her, clearly very concerned. Adrian had told them how ill she was, and was now in his room trying to study. I explained to them what the vet had said – that the next forty-eight hours were crucial and she needed water but not to worry if she didn't want to eat. Melody joined them for a while and then I suggested they left Toscha to rest.

That evening we had fish for dinner and normally Toscha would have been purring around our legs, hoping for a titbit, but now she stayed in her bed with her eyes closed and with no interest in food.

'I expect the antibiotics have made her tired,' I suggested, but it was clear to all of us that she was very ill.

I cancelled the visit to my parents that weekend. They under-stood I needed to be at home to take Toscha to the vet if her condition worsened. I was the first one downstairs on Satur-day morning and I opened the door to the kitchen-diner with some trepidation, scared of what I might find. But as I approached Toscha's bed her head moved and she opened her eyes a little, although she made no attempt to stand. Normally she would have already been out of bed by now, meowing for her breakfast. I saw that the food and water in her bowl were untouched. I stroked her, made myself a coffee, and then gave her the first dose of the liquid antibiotic using the pipette provided. She couldn't be bothered to resist and swallowed the medication I squirted into her mouth. I then had the idea of using the pipette to give her some water. I filled a tumbler, drew water into the pipette and slowly released it into her mouth. She swallowed and I refilled the pipette twice more, then her eyes closed and she went back to sleep. The next forty-eight hours were crucial, the vet had said.

As the rest of the family came down their first question was, 'How is Toscha?' They went to her bed and stroked her, and then I suggested they left her to sleep. Toscha stayed in her bed all day Saturday and had nothing to eat, although when I gave her the other two doses of medicine – midday and evening – I managed to give her some water using the pipette. That evening everyone made a point of stroking and saying goodnight to her before they went to bed. I knew what they were doing – saying goodbye, just in case.

I was the last to go to bed and before I went I found the old cat litter tray in the cupboard under the stairs and set it beside her bed in case she needed the toilet in the night. Normally Toscha was very clean and went to the toilet in the garden, but she hadn't been out since early Friday morning.

I didn't sleep well and was wide-awake at 2 a.m. so I went downstairs to check on her. She was just as I'd left her the night before – no better, but no worse. However, when I went down on Sunday morning I found that the litter tray was wet, which I took as a very good sign. Toscha was in her bed, but her eyes were open. I stroked her and offered her some food, but she didn't want any. I gave her the antibiotics in the pipette, followed by some water.

She was still in her bed when the children came down, but everyone agreed she was looking a bit better. Our hopes were up, although I sounded a note of caution that she was still very poorly. Melody hadn't been out at all on Saturday, so I said I'd take her swimming and left Adrian, Paula and Lucy at home, keeping an eye on Toscha. Melody was slowly gaining confidence in the water and we were gradually building on this each week, although she still relied on armbands even in the shallow water. We didn't stay for a drink in the café as we usually did but went straight home. As we entered the house the smell of fish greeted us. In the kitchen we found Lucy and Paula beside Toscha's bed with an open tin of smoked salmon.

'Look, Mum! She's eating again!' Paula cried excitedly.

'She's had a lot,' Lucy added.

I wasn't sure about 'a lot', but Toscha was licking little

flakes of salmon from their fingers. 'Wonderful,' I said. 'That's a really good sign.' The atmosphere in the house lightened.

Lucy, Paula and Melody fed Toscha flakes of salmon in her basket from time to time throughout the day, and I gave her the antibiotics and water in the pipette. That evening as we sat down to dinner Toscha finally left her basket and walked unsteadily to the back door. 'She wants to do her toilet in the garden,' I said, immediately standing to let her out. 'She must be feeling better.'

She was very slow in her movements and unsteady on her feet, just as humans are when they first get up after flu. She'd also lost weight, but she'd put that back on once she started eating properly again; that she was well enough to go outside and dig a hole to do her business in was huge progress. I waited outside for her and she made a brave attempt to cover over her toilet but was clearly exhausted and staggered back indoors. She sat in the kitchen just looking around, probably pleased to be feeling a bit better. Her eyes had stopped watering and her nose running, but she didn't want anything else to eat or drink. Reassured by her progress, we all went to bed that night feeling much easier.

When I came down on Monday morning I was delighted to find Toscha out of bed and meowing for something to eat. Her food and water bowls were empty, so she must have eaten and drunk in the night. I gave her the rest of the salmon and replenished her water, and told her she was going to be fine. Her movements were still a little uncertain, but I knew she was out of danger now. When the family came down they were relieved and delighted. So often we take our pets for granted. Toscha had always been part of our family and we'd assumed she always would be. This was a timely reminder that we are all mortal. I know some parents don't have pets, as they believe it's too upsetting when they pass, but I think that the joy they bring outweighs the loss when they do pass. Thankfully we didn't have to face that yet.

I took Toscha to the vet that morning for her follow-up appointment and the vet was delighted she was looking so much better. She examined her and took her temperature, which was now normal. She said her throat was still a little sore and I should continue giving her the antibiotics until the end of the week, but that I needn't bring her in again unless I had any concerns. I thanked the vet for all she'd done and as I lifted Toscha into the carer she meowed in protest. Never had her meow sounded so sweet!

Crisis over, normality returned. Neave visited on Wednesday after school, mainly to explain to Melody why contact with her mother had been reduced and the plans they had for her. Neave said I could stay in the living room with them. She sat opposite us and leaned slightly forward towards Melody as she spoke.

'You've done really well while you've been living at Cathy's, and have surprised us all. Because you've made such good progress we think you would be very happy in an adoptive home. Do you know what that means?'

Melody shook her head.

'It's a forever family where you stay for good and become a permanent member of that family. All families are different. Some have one parent, some two, and some families have a lot of children, while others only have one, so they have all the attention. We are looking for a special family for you where there will just be you and the mummy, like you used to have before you came here.'

I see, I thought, so she certainly wouldn't be staying with me then. I looked at Melody sitting beside me as Neave continued her spiel, selling Melody the idea of a single-parent adoptive family where she would be the only child. The family-finding team usually come up with a profile of the family they are looking for, which includes factors like ethnicity, whether the child should be the only child and, if not, should they be the youngest in the family (or didn't that matter). This was to ensure the child felt comfortable and to give them the best chance of bonding with their new family, and the family with the child. However, in profiling the ideal family, the social services were of course limiting their options. I thought the chances of finding a single woman with no other children who wanted to adopt an eight-year-old with a history of challenging behaviour were pretty slim. When Neave got to the end she asked Melody if she had any questions.

'Why can't I see my mummy every week?'

'Mummy is very ill,' Neave said. 'It must be difficult for you, seeing her so poorly.'

'No, it's not, I have fun. I make jewellery and things.'

'Good. But your mummy doesn't know you are there.'

'Yes, she does.'

'Maybe she still does sometimes, but there will come a time when she doesn't know who you are, which will be very upsetting for you.' While this was harsh, it was also true and something I'd considered. I did have concerns about Melody witnessing her mother's decline and for this reason I hadn't opposed the reduction in contact.

'You will still see your birth mummy,' Neave said, introducing the term, 'but not as often. And when we find an adoptive mother you will be seeing her lots before you go to live with her.'

Melody just stared at Neave. It was a lot for her to take in all in one go: the idea of loosening the bond with her birth mother so she could transfer her affection to someone she had yet to meet. But it was standard practice to introduce the idea of a forever family early on – if that was in the care plan – so the child had time to adjust and get used to the idea.

'I know it's difficult for you,' Neave said with a reassuring smile. 'You did a great job looking after your mother and now it's time to let others look after her so you can get on with your life.'

True, I thought, but easier said than done.

CHAPTER TWENTY-ONE

MATCH

The following day, the letter I'd been waiting for from CAMHS arrived. Melody was to start play therapy the following Tuesday, for an hour a week, 4–5 p.m. When I told Melody she shrugged dismissively and said she could do painting and artwork here with me.

'It's a bit more than that,' I said. 'Marina will help you to sort out your feelings about what has happened.'

'How?' she asked.

I hesitated and realized I didn't know. I'd taken plenty of children I'd fostered to CAMHS, but the carer or parent always stays in the waiting room while the child is with the therapist and there is virtually no feedback. I knew play therapy involved artwork and appeared to help some children, though not all, but I didn't know any more than that. It occurred to me that perhaps foster carers should experience a play therapy session as part of their training so we had some understanding of how it worked. I made a mental note to suggest it to Jill when she next visited.

'I'm not sure exactly how the play therapy does work,' I admitted to Melody. 'You could tell me if you like once you've started going.' Which seemed to appeal to Melody.

'OK. I'll go, and give it a try,' she said.
'Good girl.'

I purposely hadn't told Melody that Mr Wilson had died, for
it would have raised the question – how did I know? Also, I
rather hoped I wouldn't need to tell her, as I felt she had
enough sadness in her life to deal with without adding to it. I
hoped she wouldn't notice that he was no longer calling out
from his room. How wrong I was.

On Friday, armed with our usual batch of iced cakes, fruit,
biscuits and another card made by Melody for her mother, we
went to the care home straight after school. I'd also put my
camera in my bag, as I wanted to try to take at least one good
photo of Melody with her mother and give them both a copy.
We were greeted at the door by Mr and Mrs Bennett, gesticu-
lating to be let out. The care assistant who opened it said that
Amanda was in the lounge and we headed down the corridor.
As we passed Mr Wilson's room I glanced at Melody. A call
buzzer could be heard bleeping from another room close by,
but Mr Wilson's door was closed and the room silent.

'No Mr Aeroplane Man,' Melody remarked.

'No,' I agreed. It was a statement, not a question, so I didn't
add anything and thought I'd got away with it.

Amanda was sitting as usual in one of the high-backed
chairs at the edge of the room, looking clean and well dressed
in the clothes donated to the care home. They kept all the
residents looking very presentable. The patio doors leading to
the courtyard were open and two residents were pacing up
and down outside. Many of the residents paced from time to
time and I supposed it was part of their illness, although I
hadn't seen Amanda do it yet. The occupational therapist sat

at the table, helping two ladies play a game of cards. She said a welcoming hello and asked Melody if she'd liked to bring her mother to join in. I went with Melody to Amanda and said hello as Melody kissed her cheek. She asked her if she wanted to play cards and, without replying, Amanda stood and went to the table.

Once they were settled, I sat in the chair Amanda had vacated with a resident on either side. The two care assistants in the room were busy with other patients. From where I sat I could see the game of cards and it was very slow. It seemed to be a form of snap where the players were meant to shout 'Snap!' when two cards that were the same appeared from the pack, but it had lost its usual fervour as Amanda and the other two residents had to be told when to call 'Snap'. I think it was more to help them recognize the cards than win a game, although of course at her age Melody couldn't appreciate that. After two very slow, laborious games, when there was no competition and Melody won easily, she lost interest and asked her mother if she wanted to go to her room. Amanda ignored her and the occupational therapist began to collect up the cards, ready to deal again for another game. I saw Melody place her hand on her mother's arm and tug slightly, as children do when they want to attract a parent's attention. Amanda reacted by slapping her daughter sharply on her bare arm.

'Ouch!' Melody said, rubbing her arm. 'That hurt, Mum!'

'You mustn't slap,' the occupational therapist told Amanda firmly.

I went over. 'Are you OK?'

'Mum slapped me,' Melody said, clearly shocked.

'She didn't mean to,' I said. I'd heard care assistants before tell residents not to slap, pinch, thump or grab, but Amanda hadn't behaved like this towards Melody before. I assumed it was another indication that her illness was progressing. Amanda remained unconcerned by what she'd done.

'Amanda,' I said, leaning in towards her. 'Melody would like to go to your room with you now. Is that OK?'

Amanda looked at me and then at Melody, as if seeing her for the first time. 'Go to my room,' she repeated, and she stood and left the table.

I thanked the occupational therapist, and Melody and I followed Amanda out of the lounge and along the corridor. Although Mr Wilson's room remained silent, Mr Andrews appeared from the opposite direction on his way to the ladies' lounge making his 'boo-boo' sound.

'Boo-boo,' Amanda imitated as he passed.

Mr Andrews immediately stopped, turned and squared up to her. 'Booooooo!' he shouted loudly, jutting out his chin aggressively.

'Booooooo!' Amanda yelled back, mimicking his posture.

Melody giggled, but I was concerned.

'Come on, Mr Andrews,' his care assistant said and, taking him by the arm, led him away.

Amanda looked as though she might go after him, so I linked my arm in hers and, drawing her away, said, 'Melody wants to go to your room now.' Which seemed to work and we continued along the corridor, Mr Andrews' 'boo-boo' sound steadily receding. While the scene had had some comical elements, they had squared up to each other quite aggressively and if left unchecked it could have turned nasty. The care assistants often had to deal with small acts of aggression between the patients.

Once in Amanda's room, Melody shared some of the cakes with her mother and then put the rest in the bedside cabinet and gave me the box from the previous week. At some point during our visits to her mother's room Melody usually checked the cupboards and drawers to make sure her mother had everything she needed. Today in the top drawer she found the letter she'd written and was delighted. 'Look, my letter! Did you read it, Mum?'

Amanda took the few steps across the room and snatched the letter, as she had with me the week before, and stuffed it into her pocket. Melody looked taken aback.

'She probably thought you were going to take it from her,' I suggested. 'It's very precious to her.'

'I'm not going to take it, Mum,' Melody told her. 'I wrote it for you.'

Yet despite incidents like this Amanda still had flashes of lucidity and recognition. With the letter in her pocket for safekeeping, she took the photograph album from her bedside cabinet and, sitting on the bed, began looking through it, associating this act with Melody. Melody joined her, and as Amanda turned the pages Melody talked about each photograph as they had many times before. I thought it would make a nice picture – the two of them together – and I took my camera from my bag.

Melody, always happy to have her picture taken, smiled at the camera, but Amanda just looked blank.

'Smile,' I encouraged as I looked through the viewfinder. 'Smile, Amanda.' But no smile came. I hadn't seen her smile in a long time and I knew that smiling was lost in patients with advanced dementia. I tried again without success and then took a picture. Although it wasn't full face, it was nice and showed the two of them sitting close and looking at the album.

We stayed for an hour; it was long enough. When I said it was time to go Melody didn't protest. 'See you next week, Mum,' she said. Then realized her mistake. 'No. See you in two weeks.' Neither of which meant anything to Amanda, for she'd long lost any sense of time.

She came out of the room with us and as we passed Mr Wilson's room it remained quiet. Intrigued, Melody stopped and retraced her footsteps, stamping a little to see if she'd get a response. I knew then I'd have to tell her, but Amanda beat me to it. Having hardly said a word all visit, she suddenly said very clearly, 'He's dead.' Then continued along the corridor to the main door.

Melody caught up with her. 'What did you say, Mum?' she asked.

Amanda looked at her nonplussed and didn't repeat it.

'I'll explain once we're outside,' I told Melody.

Mr and Mrs Bennett appeared by the door and I saw Amanda looking at them with hostility for reasons I didn't understand. Then, before the care assistant arrived to let us out, Amanda left and walked down the corridor in the direction of her room.

'Bye, Mum!' Melody called after her, but there was no reply.

As soon as we were outside Melody asked, 'What did Mummy mean about Mr Aeroplane Man?'

I took her hand. 'I'm afraid he's died, love,' I said gently as we walked. 'He was very ill.'

'Oh. My mummy is very ill. Will she die soon?' Melody had asked me similar before and I always tried to be honest. 'I don't think your mummy will die yet,' I said, 'but you're right, she is very ill.' Melody accepted this, but again I wondered how much of her mother's decline she should witness. It was impossible to predict how quickly the disease would progress, but from what I knew I thought it was likely that Amanda had many years before it proved fatal, by which time Melody would be older and hopefully able to understand and cope with what was happening. She'd also be in a better position to decide how often she wanted to see her.

On Saturday the weather was very warm for the end of May and while Adrian continued studying in his room, the girls and I went for a long walk in the woods – a local beauty spot not far away. On Sunday we went to see my parents, again leaving Adrian behind to study. He only had a couple more exams to do the following week and then he was finished, so it was worth making this last all-out effort. My parents were sorry he couldn't make it but appreciated why he hadn't come with us.

On Monday, once I'd taken Melody to school, I went into town and had two copies of the photograph I'd taken of Melody with her mother printed. I also bought two frames. Melody was delighted when I gave her one of the framed prints and she positioned it on the bookshelf in her bedroom so she could see it from her bed. She was looking forward to being able to do similar in her mother's room when she saw her the following week. On Tuesday after school Melody began play therapy and she wasn't impressed. She was fine going in with the other three children, but when she came out at the end of the session she was scowling. Dr Marina Short had brought the children into the waiting room to return them to their parents and carers and said to me, 'I've had to explain to Melody that the artwork she's done has to stay in the room and can't be taken home.'

I knew this from other children I'd fostered who'd attended play therapy, but not the reason behind it. 'Why is that?' I now asked.

'I wondered the same thing,' another parent said.

Marina looked slightly taken aback. Perhaps no one had ever asked before. She took a breath and addressed us all.

'Play therapy is designed to encourage the child to explore their personal world through art and craft. We provide a safe environment that allows them to get in touch with their innermost thoughts and feelings through the process of creation. These are sensory-based experiences – visual, tactile, kinaesthetic – which encourage the child to express and record their experiences, perceptions, feelings and imagination, which they may not be able to verbalize. What they produce is very personal to them and they may want to return to explore it at a later date, so we keep it here safe.'

There was a moment's silence. 'Thank you,' I said. 'I think I understand.'

'I don't,' the other woman said under her breath.

On Thursday evening we baked and iced cupcakes, ate two each and put the rest in the cake tin. This was the week Melody didn't visit her mother, but I would still go. The following day I took some out for Amanda and wondered if any of my family would notice that the cakes were disappearing faster than would have been expected had it just been us eating them. My visit to Amanda that afternoon was very similar to my previous one. We spent some time in the lounge and then went to her room, where we looked through the photograph album. I'd no idea if Amanda knew who I was, although I told her a few times. Once she said Melody's name as we looked at her photo. I said, 'Yes, well done. That's your daughter, Melody. She's at school now. She'll see you next week.' But that was it. As usual I left her the box of cakes and replenished the fruit bowl. I also asked a care assistant if Amanda needed anything, but was reassured she didn't.

Friday was also the last day of Adrian's exams and when I returned home he was already in and relaxing. He would still have to go into school until the end of term, but the lessons were vocational for those who'd taken exams to help them decide on a career and choose the subjects they wanted to study at a higher level.

Jill paid one of her statutory visits the following week and, having updated her, I made my suggestion for including play therapy in foster-carer training to give us a better understanding of what happened in a session. She thought it was a good idea and said she'd pass on my suggestion. I also told her I was seeing Amanda every other Friday when Melody didn't. She couldn't see a problem with that but pointed out that if Melody found out I'd have to explain my reasons for not telling her. She also said it was nice of me to go. I shrugged off her comment. I wasn't visiting Amanda to 'be nice'. I was going because I had got to know her, was looking after her daughter, and because she was very much alone in the world. It reassured me as much as anything that she was being well looked after. I told Jill that I doubted Amanda knew who I was or remembered my visit after I'd gone.

'Or maybe she does,' Jill said, 'in which case your visits are even more important.'

* * *

Our weekday routine continued and towards the end of June Lucy and Paula had end-of-year exams, and Neave visited. She didn't have any more to tell me but said family finding was ongoing for Melody. I updated her on how Melody was doing, including swimming and her visits to her mother. I said I felt that Amanda's disease had plateaued for the time being, as I hadn't noticed much change in her in the last month, and Neave agreed that was the nature of the illness. I told her that Melody was a little ambivalent towards the play therapy but didn't mind going. At some point Marina would write a report for Neave.

School broke up the third week in July for the long summer holidays, and as Melody was now at home I had to suspend my visits to Amanda on alternate Fridays, but obviously still took Melody as normal. Although the weather was lovely and some residents were outside in the courtyard, Amanda never wanted to go out – unlike Mr and Mrs Bennett. We always followed the same routine: spent time in the lounge (doing occupational therapy if the therapist was there), then went to Amanda's room. One day when we arrived there was a police car parked outside.

'I wonder what's happened?' Melody asked excitedly.

As we let ourselves in through the outer door we could see two police officers through the inner glass door talking to three members of staff, one of whom I recognized as the manager. Mr and Mrs Bennett were also there. Once we'd signed in and were admitted, I heard the manager thanking the police officers for returning them. I guessed she was referring to Mr and Mrs Bennett. In the lounge, I soon learnt that they had slipped out when the door had been left open during a delivery of catering supplies. Thankfully their absence had been noticed as soon as the lorry had left and the police had been called. They were found just ten minutes away, but the care home's security was being reviewed, as clearly they and the other residents were highly vulnerable and could easily come to harm out alone. Having said that, you have to admire their persistence.

I hadn't booked for us to go away during the school summer holidays, but we had plenty of days out, including trips to the coast, theme parks, the zoo and other places of interest that suited everyone. My children were growing up quickly and I knew it wouldn't be long before they didn't all want to come on every family outing, so I was making the most of it while they did. Adrian and Paula also saw their father. Lucy saw her birth mother very occasionally. She phoned if she was in the area, but we hadn't heard from her for a while. Lucy had grown used to this and, although she loved her, she accepted her mother's shortcomings.

Neave telephoned in respect of Melody's next review, which was due in August. The previous two reviews had been held at Melody's school but the school was closed for the summer holidays, so Neave asked if it could be held at my house – reviews are sometimes held in the foster carer's home. I said that was fine and Melody could play in another part of the house until it was her turn to speak. Then, almost as an afterthought, Neave added, 'The family-finding team think they may have found a good match. I'm going with them to meet the woman at the start of September. She's away on holiday at present.'

'Oh, really?'

'Nothing is definite yet, so please don't say anything to Melody.'

MATCH

'No, of course not. Who is she?'

'A single woman in her forties with a responsible job. She has no other children, but her work is demanding. I have some concerns that I'll discuss with her when I meet her. That's about it for now, really. Can you tell Melody I'll see her at her review?'

'Yes,' and we said goodbye.

Sharing information with foster carers has improved dramatically since I first started fostering – see my book *Cut* – but it still has some way to go. I now felt marginalized; I'd been told virtually nothing about this prospective adopter who could become Melody's new mother, not even her name. Where did she live? What was the nature of her work? What were the concerns Neave had? She'd said she was in her forties with a demanding job and no experience of children, so was she really right for Melody? I doubted it.

CHAPTER TWENTY-TWO

COPING?

The forms arrived for Melody's next review and as I helped her with the spellings it struck me how much her literacy skills had improved since she'd been with me. I praised her. She wanted to learn and do well, for as her mother had told her, if she studied and passed her exams, she'd get a good job. I thought it was a great pity that Amanda didn't know how well her daughter was doing, and I suggested to Melody that she took in some of her schoolwork to show her mother on our next visit. I assumed she'd think it was a good idea, but Melody said dejectedly, 'What's the point? Mum won't know what it is or that I've done it. She doesn't even know me anymore.'

I looked at her carefully. 'Melody, we can't be sure of that. No one knows how much your mother understands – or any of the patients there. She still likes looking at the photographs of you and has kept the letter you wrote. I think she'd like to see your schoolwork.'

'All right,' she agreed with a shrug. 'I'll take some in.'

'Excellent. Good girl.'

So on our next visit Melody took in a large folder containing selected items of her schoolwork, but unfortunately

Amanda wasn't interested. We both tried showing her the work – in the lounge and in her room – but she just kept pushing it away and then standing and walking around. Indeed, she spent most of the time walking and didn't sit still for long, not even in her room to look at the photograph album. Understandably, Melody was hurt and lost patience. 'I don't know why I come to see you,' she snapped.

I tried again to engage Amanda in the schoolwork and photographs but without success. Eventually I decided to cut short our visit, as clearly it wasn't a positive experience for Melody. I suggested to Melody that she could leave her schoolwork in her mother's room so she could look at it later. She left it on the bed and we said goodbye. Amanda didn't so much as look at her daughter and simply walked out of the room and along the corridor in the direction of the lounge.

Melody and I signed out of the Visitors' Book and left. 'I expect your mum will look at your work later when she is more settled,' I said.

'Who cares!' Melody replied moodily.

I paused by the car before we got in and looked at her. A warm breeze blew from the hills. 'Melody, I know it's difficult for you, seeing your mother like this. If ever you feel you want to visit less often or not at all, you must tell me. You know you don't have to come. You could write letters and send her cards instead.'

She shrugged. 'I want to keep coming, but why has she started walking up and down like Mr Boo-Boo and the others? She didn't used to.'

'No. I think it's part of her illness. A stage she might be going through.'

The next time we visited, Amanda was the same, so I assumed her dementia had advanced some more.

There were only four of us at Melody's review. No one from her school was able to come as they were all on their summer holidays, as was the Guardian. So Neave, Jill, the IRO and me settled in my living room. The patio door was slightly open and through the gap came the distant cries of happy children playing in a garden further up the road.

'Reviews in August are often sparse,' the IRO said, but we still went through the formality of introducing ourselves. Paula and Lucy were keeping Melody amused in the front room.

The IRO noted apologies for absence and as usual I was asked to speak first. I said that Melody was healthy, up to date with her dental and optician's check-ups and continued to do well at home and at school. I said she had begun attending CAMHS but was questioning the point of it, as she wasn't allowed to bring home the artwork she made there each week. I then explained what Dr Marina Short had said and the IRO made a note. I read out Melody's teacher's comments on her end-of-year report – a copy of which had been sent to Neave. I talked candidly about our visits to see Amanda and that sometimes they could be very difficult, but that Melody still wanted to go. I confirmed I was keeping Melody's Life Story Book up to date. This is a record of the child's time with me and includes photographs and memorabilia and is theirs to keep. I said that her swimming was going well, although she hadn't joined any out-of-school activities yet – something I'd raise with her again at the start of the new term. I mentioned the outings we were going on during the summer holidays and I finished by adding that I understood from Neave that a possible adoptive match had been found, although Melody wasn't to be told yet.

The IRO wrote, thanked me, and asked Neave to speak. She confirmed what I'd said – that Melody was happy and continued to make steady progress. She said that the application the family-finding team had received in respect of Melody was from a single woman who had already been approved to adopt. She said she was going to visit her on the 3rd of September and that this was one of two matches for Melody. I wondered why the other one had been discounted, but we weren't told.

'If it goes ahead, when would you take this to panel?' the IRO asked Neave. Although the prospective adopter had been approved to adopt, the match would still need to be passed by the adoption panel – this was usually before the child and adopter met.

'October,' Neave said, 'so we'll have it for the final court hearing in November.'

I met Jill's gaze. 'So you'd be looking to move Melody in late November or early December?' Jill asked Neave.

'Yes, if it is a good match and it goes ahead. I have some reservations, which need addressing first. Then I'll draw up the Adoption Placement Plan in October with a view to moving Melody after the final court hearing.'

'What about contact?' Jill asked. 'It's fortnightly now.'

'We'll reduce it again in preparation for the move.'

The IRO nodded and wrote, while I considered what I'd heard. I'd learnt no more about the prospective adopter or what Neave's reservations were, and it wasn't appropriate for

WHERE HAS MUMMY GONE?

me to ask now. If the adoption did go ahead, I'd learn more and be part of the process for introducing Melody to her adoptive mother and then the move, which sounded as if it would be taking place not long before Christmas. While I still had doubts it was going to happen at all, foster carers have to be prepared to accept that at some point the child they are looking after, and have grown close to and loved, might be moved. It's for this reason that some people who would like to foster don't, and I fully understand why. I liken a child leaving a carer to a type of bereavement – the loss, sorrow and adjustment. Sometimes they keep in touch, but that relies on the child's parent or guardian doing so, and many do not.

Jill was then asked to speak and as usual stated her role, said she monitored all aspects of my fostering and that I continued to provide a high level of care. She concluded by saying, 'I have no doubt that if Melody is moved to an adoptive home, Cathy will ensure that the transition goes smoothly.'

'Thank you,' the IRO said. He made a note and then looked up. 'Does anyone want to add anything to this review? If not I'll ask Melody to join us.'

'I'm finished,' Neave said, and Jill and I both nodded.

I went into the front room where the girls were engrossed in a game of Monopoly. 'Melody, can you come in now, love?'

'In a minute,' she said, concentrating and without looking up. 'It's my go next.'

'It needs to be now,' I said. 'We can't keep them waiting. You can play the game again later.'

Lucy and Paula were still intent on the board, but then realized Melody was needed now.

'I know it's a bummer, but you have to go to your review,' Lucy said.

'Language,' I lightly admonished.

'We'll play when you've finished,' Paula told Melody.

Reluctantly she stood. 'I won't be long,' she said and, leaving the game, came with me. In the living room, faced with three official-looking adults, notepad and pens on their laps and briefcases beside them, Melody lost her bravado. She stopped dead and looked at them.

'Hello, Melody,' the IRO said, smiling encouragingly. 'You remember me from your last review?' Melody nodded. 'Have a seat, next to Cathy if you like.' Jill moved along to make room.

'So tell us how you have been doing since your last review,' the IRO said.

'OK,' Melody said quietly.

'I hear you are doing well at school.'

'Yes,' she said in the same small voice.

'You like school then?'

She nodded.

'And you're still seeing your mother at the care home. How is that going?'

'OK, but she doesn't always know who I am.'

'That must be difficult for you,' the IRO said.

'Sometimes it is.'

'Thank you for completing your review form.' It was on his lap and he now opened it. 'I'll read some of it out, if that's all right?' Melody nodded. 'You've put that you feel happy most of the time, which is very positive.'

'Yes, I wrote all those sentences myself.'

'I know Cathy told me. That's excellent.'

'Well done,' Jill added.

'I see that Lizzie is still your friend,' the IRO continued, going through the booklet, 'but you have other friends too. And if you have any problems you tell Miss May, Cathy, Lucy and Paula, which I believe is what you put last time.'

'Well, it's true,' Melody said a little indignantly. I saw Jill smile.

'Do you have any problems now?' the IRO asked.

Melody shook her head.

As he neared the end of the booklet I saw Melody shift to the edge of the sofa ready to leave. The IRO paused and cleared his throat before reading out the next question and Melody's response, and I knew why. Her reply had choked me up when she'd written it.

'The next question asks if you have any questions about what is going to happen in the future?' the IRO said. 'And you've written, *When will my mummy die?*'

The room fell silent. Even the cries of the children playing outside seemed to stop in sympathy. No one spoke for a few moments or made eye-contact. I heard Jill give a heartfelt sigh.

'I reassured Melody as best I could,' I said, touching her hand. 'It's a question that has come up before, usually after we've visited her mother. I try to explain to Melody that her mother is very ill, but it's impossible to know when she will die. I've told her I don't think it will be soon, but a man at the care home died in May and it seems to have stayed with Melody and played on her mind.'

'Understandably,' the IRO said. 'Is it something that could be addressed by CAMHS?'

'I don't know if she's spoken about it to the therapist,' I said.

'I'll speak to Dr Short,' Neave said, making a note.

'I used to call him Mr Aeroplane Man,' Melody said, 'because every time anyone walked past his room he called out, "Quick, nurse! I have a plane to catch." I never saw him, but I heard him. I was sad when he died and stopped calling out. Not many people there can talk and the corridor outside his room is too quiet now.'

I gave her hand an encouraging squeeze as I looked at the expressions on the faces of those around me. Mr Wilson's death had affected Melody. They were heartfelt words, and I could tell what Neave was going to say before she spoke. 'It's a lot for a child to cope with.' It was indeed, and would add to the argument for reducing contact sooner rather than later – and maybe that was best for Melody.

'Do you still want to visit Mummy in the care home?' Jill asked, turning to Melody.

'Yes,' she said without hesitation.

'Children don't always know what's best for them,' Neave said, which of course was true.

'Can I go now and finish my game?' Melody asked.

'Yes, unless there is anything else you want to tell your review?' the IRO asked.

Melody thought for a moment and then said, 'Tell the doctors to try to make my mummy better.' Standing, she quickly left the room.

I went after her to check she was all right. She was on her way upstairs. 'I'm going to find Lucy and Paula,' she said, 'so we can finish the game.'

'OK, love. You did very well in there.'

She seemed all right, so I returned to the living room and said that Melody was going to play with Paula and Lucy. The

IRO thanked me and said he'd minute that Neave would ask Dr Short to do some work with Melody around bereavement and her mother's illness. Then, with no other business, he set the date for the next review in three months' time and, thanking us all for coming, closed the meeting.

I was pleased that bereavement and Amanda's illness were hopefully going to be addressed in Melody's therapy. I felt I'd said all I could to try to reassure her, and the input of a skilled therapist should help, for as Neave said, Melody had a lot to cope with. I thought she was coping very well. I'm sure I wouldn't have done so well if I'd been subjected to all the years of neglect, uncertainty and hardship Melody had, and then on top of that to see her mother's dementia take away the person she knew. Melody's half-brothers and sisters, all adopted as children many years ago, had been spared all of this. It was a great pity, I thought, that Melody hadn't been taken into care much sooner. Whether she would ever fully recover from her experiences only time would tell. On the surface she seemed to be doing well, but it was impossible to know how she would be affected in the future. Some survivors of abuse (neglect is a form of abuse) manage to move on and lead successful lives, while others don't, and have their adulthood blighted by their early years' experiences.

CHAPTER TWENTY-THREE

ROBBED OF DIGNITY

Adrian received his exam results on the 24th of August and thankfully achieved what he needed to continue studying in the sixth form. We celebrated with a meal out. A week later, the school holidays drew to a close and the new school term began. Melody was pleased to be seeing her friends again; Lizzie and her family had been away for most of the summer, staying with family in France. Miss May was in the playground on the first day to greet the children and Melody ran to her and gave her a big hug. Miss May looked very pleased. I asked her if she'd had a nice summer and she said she had, although it had been very quiet and she was pleased to be back.

That afternoon, Melody came out of school smiling proudly with Miss May at her side.

'I've put my name down to join the after-school sports club!' Melody declared.

'Fantastic! Well done!' I said.

I could see Miss May was pleased too. She knew it had been a target set by the review, and it was a sign of Melody's ongoing improvement that she had finally found the confidence to achieve it. Miss May then gave me the details of the club with a permission slip to sign. It was held on Wednesdays, was open to all year groups and offered a variety of sports activities, including table tennis, indoor football, badminton, yoga, keep fit and dance.

Play therapy continued on Tuesdays. I didn't know if Neave had spoken to Marina about helping Melody come to terms with her mother's illness and bereavement issues – Marina didn't say. She came into the waiting room to collect the children at the start of the session and then returned them at the end, but gave no feedback. With school having resumed, I began visiting Amanda on alternate Fridays again. Her pacing had grown worse so that she wasn't still for a minute. Not sure what to do for the best, but wanting to spend time with her, I followed her up and down the corridors and in and out of the rooms, some of which she wasn't supposed to be in, like the men's washrooms. She didn't appear to be looking for anything but paced in an agitated manner – something I'd seen others there do. We weren't in her room for long enough to sit and look at the photographs, but I did manage to replenish the fruit bowl and leave the box of cakes in her bedside cabinet before we continued our endless journey. If she stopped for a few seconds I tried to engage her attention, but it was hopeless. Because this and other such behaviours weren't unusual in the care home, the care assistants accepted it and just smiled as we walked by yet again.

Amanda was the same when I took Melody the following week and Melody and I both walked up and down with her, but the week after, when I visited alone, Amanda was much calmer. I wondered if she'd been given a sedative, although a care assistant told me that pacing was a phase dementia patients went through from time to time and it often settled of its own accord. Amanda was calm the next time, when I took Melody, and they sat at the table with the occupational therapist and filled lavender bags, and also spent time in Amanda's room looking at photographs. However, I'm pretty sure that Amanda didn't recognize Melody at all; the flashes of recognition seemed to have gone and her face was blank with a slightly downward turn, like most of the other residents there.

At the end of September, Jill telephoned to say she needed to see me before our next scheduled meeting. I knew she had something important to say, otherwise she would have told me over the phone. Aware that Neave by now had visited the woman who wanted to adopt Melody, I guessed it was to do with her.

'So has Neave decided this lady is a good match?' I asked Jill over the phone.

'Yes, but I'll tell you more when I see you.'

Two days later, Jill and I settled in my living room with a cup of coffee each and she began telling me what, as Melody's foster carer, I needed to know about the woman who was hoping to adopt Melody. 'She's called Dana, she's forty-one and is a social worker in child protection.'

'Oh, really?' I said. 'In this area? Perhaps I know her.'

'No. She doesn't work here and I'll come to that later. Neave is obviously aware of how demanding her job as a social worker is and the hours involved, and she had concerns that Dana wouldn't be able to meet Melody's needs, especially if Melody became unsettled after the move. However, when Neave visited Dana at her home with a member of the family-finding team, she was able to reassure her. She is proposing to take three months' adoption leave to settle Melody in – more if necessary. She has a married sister who lives in the next street who will be her support carer so that if, for example, Dana is delayed at work her sister will meet Melody from school and give her dinner and look after her until Dana is free. So there are no issues there.'

I nodded. All foster carers and prospective adopters are expected to have a good support network.

'Neave had another concern,' Jill continued, taking a sip of her coffee. 'In respect of Dana's child.'

'I thought Neave said Dana didn't have any children.'

'She doesn't now,' Jill said. 'Sadly, twelve years ago she lost her only child, Katie, at the age of three from a rare genetic condition.'

'Oh dear, I am sorry. How dreadful.'

'Yes. Dana made the decision not to have any more children in case the same thing happened again. There is no screening yet for the condition she had and it can be passed on from parent to child. Her marriage folded as a result of their loss and Dana has been living alone for over eight years. Although time has passed, Neave was concerned that Dana might be trying to replace her daughter with an adopted child, which was never going to work. That concern was also raised during Dana's adoption assessment. Neave discussed this with Dana and has been reassured. Dana appreciates that Melody will arrive with her own personality, and that the needs of a child Melody's age with her early years' experiences will be very different to those of Katie. One of the reasons she put herself forward to adopt Melody was because she is very different to the child she lost, not only in age and disposition, but physically they look very dissimilar. She has some photos of her daughter on display in the house and she had dark hair and brown eyes and was quite sturdy before her illness. Melody is fair haired with blue eyes and slightly built.'

'So why does she want to adopt?' I asked.

'Dana always intended to have a family and would have applied to adopt with her husband had he not left her. She believes she has a lot to offer and with her experience as a social worker in child protection she won't be under any illusions. Neave is satisfied her expectations are realistic and she appreciates Melody's past cannot be undone and they will have to work with it.'

'Good.' I knew how important this was, for sometimes adoptions of older children fail because the parents have unrealistic expectations of the child – see *Nobody's Son*.

'Neave and the family-finding team believe it is a good match and that Dana is in an ideal position to meet Melody's needs. And of course with Melody being an only child, Dana can devote all her spare time to her.'

I nodded, but I felt sad. It was bittersweet, for while I clearly wanted what was best for Melody, it would mean that she was going to leave us after all. 'So it's definitely going ahead?'

'Neave is planning to take it to the October panel, but obviously don't say anything to Melody yet. Introductions won't start until after it's been to court, but Neave wants to reduce contact in preparation for a move in December. She would like you to start going to the care home every three weeks instead of two.' Jill looked at me as if waiting for my objection, but I didn't object.

'It will be difficult for Melody, but I think that reducing contact is probably for the best. Not only to prepare her for meeting and bonding with her adoptive mother, but I am concerned the effect that seeing her mother's deterioration is having on Melody.'

Jill nodded and made a note. 'I'll pass this on to Neave.'

'But, Jill, what will happen after the move? I think Melody should have some contact with her mother.'

'Dana is aware of the situation and she has suggested she takes Melody to see Amanda once a month for as long as it is beneficial to Melody. She also wants to keep in touch with you.'

'That's good,' I said, and I meant it, although time would tell if this happened. I knew that adopters often promised to keep in touch with the carer prior to the adoption, but once it had all gone through they didn't maintain contact and there was no legal requirement to do so.

'Dana is planning on combining the visits to Amanda with seeing you, as she lives over a hundred miles away.'

'Does she? So Melody will have to change schools.'

'Yes, but there are plenty of good schools in the area where she lives. Dana's sister's children go to a very good school a ten-minute walk away. Dana has already seen the headmistress and secured a place for Melody.'

Clearly Dana had done all the right things. She would, I thought uncharitably, being a social worker; of course she'd know what was expected. But putting aside my selfish thoughts, I acknowledged that if Dana was right for Melody then that was all that mattered, and from the sound of it she was a good match. Jill's next comment helped too.

'Dana would like to meet you to learn more about Melody so the move runs smoothly. If you're happy, Neave will pass on your contact details so you can arrange something.'

'Yes, that's fine with me,' I said.

That evening, once we'd had dinner, and there was just Melody and me, I gently broke the news to her that Neave had said we were to visit her mother every three weeks from now on.

'Why? What's it got to do with her?' she demanded.

'She's your social worker and she can make these decisions if it's best for you. Neave feels it's upsetting for you to see your mother like she is now and I think she is right.'

Melody looked taken aback. 'But I don't cry when I see Mummy,' she protested.

'I know, love, but there are different ways of feeling pain. I think that after we've seen her you think about her a lot and about some of the other residents there. Am I right?'

'Yes,' she said quietly.

'That's normal. I do too. But what I don't want to happen – and neither does Neave – is that you remember your mummy like she is now. We want you to remember her as she was before she became ill.' I appreciated that even then Amanda had struggled to cope and her parenting had been grossly lacking, but she and Melody had had a loving relationship. Better that Melody had that image of her mother – regardless of how inadequate she may have been – rather than the current one.

'What, like when Mum and me used to do a runner in the middle of the night from the places we stayed, so we didn't have to pay the rent?' Melody suggested. 'It was fun climbing out of the window.'

'Yes, if you like,' I said dubiously.

'Or when Mummy and me used to cuddle up close in bed with our clothes on to keep warm? I liked to feel her arms around me.'

'Yes, it's nice to remember a cuddle.'

'Or when we used to hide from the social worker and pretend we were out. I got the hiccups once so loudly Mummy had to put her hand over my mouth so I wouldn't give us away. We were laughing so much. Or the time she pinched a pair of shoes for me so I could go to school. I never used them because we had to move again and they got left behind.'

I smiled sadly. How different Melody's recollections of her time with her mother were compared to those of the average child. But they were Melody's memories, personal to her, and an improvement on how her mother was now. Back then she'd been feisty, able to communicate and make decisions for herself and Melody, even though they'd been the wrong ones. Now Amanda was a mere shadow of her former self, as though her personality had been hollowed out. Trapped in an expressionless existence and totally reliant on the care-home staff. It was much better that Melody remembered her mother laughing as they hid from their social worker.

With Melody's case going to the adoption panel next month and the final court hearing approaching, Nina French, the Guardian ad Litem, telephoned to say she needed to see Melody again. This time she gave me plenty of notice of her visit and appeared well informed and up to date. Sort of – for as I let her into the hall, she said, 'So is Melody looking forward to meeting her new mummy?'

'She's not to be told yet,' I said, glancing towards the living room and hoping Melody hadn't heard.

'Not the details, but I understand that Neave has talked to her generally about adoption. She should have done by this stage.'

'Yes, but that was months ago. It hasn't been mentioned since and Neave asked me not to say anything just yet.'

'OK, I'll talk in general terms then, although at Melody's age the judge will want to know what the child's wishes are.'

I showed Nina into the living room where Melody, used to having visits from professionals connected with her case, was now sitting on the sofa waiting patiently. Nina said hello and I asked her if she wanted me to stay in the room. She said I could, so I sat on the sofa next to Melody while Nina took one of the easy-chairs opposite us. She began by asking Melody about school, what she liked, her favourite subjects, her friends and so forth. Melody told her more or less what she'd told her review and Neave when she'd visited. Nina then talked to her about living with me and finally said she'd visited her mother in Oak Lane House.

'When?' Melody asked.

'Two weeks ago.'

'Why?'

'I needed to see your mother so I could include her in my report to the judge for the final court hearing. Has Neave told you about that?'

Melody looked at her carefully. 'Did Mummy know who you were?'

'I told her, but I don't suppose she understood or remembered, do you?'

'She doesn't remember much any more,' Melody admitted sadly.

'I know. It must be very difficult for you to see her like that,' Nina said. I knew where this was leading, although Melody didn't reply.

'I would find it difficult if she was my mother,' Nina said.

'Miss May's dad was the same,' Melody replied.

Nina looked puzzled. 'Miss May is the teaching assistant who helps Melody,' I said. 'Her father had dementia and was in the same care home. You met Miss May at Melody's first review.'

'Oh yes.' She returned her gaze to Melody. 'So you understand that your mummy has to stay in the care home where she can be looked after?'

'Yes,' Melody said.

'When children can't live with their own mummy and daddy they sometimes have to come into foster care – like you did,' Nina continued, slowly getting to the point. 'Then some children in foster care are found new forever parents who adopt them. They become their permanent family. I think Neave has talked to you about this?'

Melody nodded.

'How do you feel about having a new forever family?'

Melody shrugged. 'Don't mind.'

'Do you think it's something you might like?'

Melody shrugged again. I thought it was probably asking a lot of a child to make a commitment or say much when talking in abstracts. Melody didn't know Dana or what to expect in terms of living with her. Once the introductions had begun and Melody had met Dana and seen her new home, it should become much clearer and easier. In my experience the child is then far more accepting and enthusiastic and their move to permanency usually runs smoothly.

'Neave and Cathy will talk to you more about all of this over the coming weeks,' Nina said. 'But you're happy for me to tell the judge that you'd like to be adopted?'

Melody nodded.

Nina was with us for about an hour and then made a point of saying goodbye to Melody and wishing her well for the future. This would be the last time we saw Nina, as the Guardian ad Litem's role usually ends with the final court hearing.

The following day Dana telephoned me to arrange her visit and we decided on next Wednesday at around midday. I suggested Wednesday as Melody would be staying later at school for sports club, so I'd have an extra hour. Melody wouldn't know of Dana's visit or anything about her until the match was approved by the panel and introductions could begin. If the match wasn't approved – which can happen, although it's not often – then Melody would be none the wiser.

On Thursday evening Melody and I baked cupcakes as usual and on Friday I visited Amanda alone. From now on I would be going alone for two consecutive weeks, as Melody would be seeing her mother every third week. How long I'd be able to keep this up I didn't know. It would depend on my future commitments, for the return journey of two hours, plus at least an hour with Amanda, meant that a good chunk of the day was taken up.

As it happened I was relieved that Melody wasn't with me that Friday, for Amanda didn't manage to get to the toilet in time and messed herself in the lounge. This was upsetting and degrading enough, but when a care assistant tried to take Amanda to the bathroom to clean her and change her into fresh clothes she became aggressive and pushed him away. It took three care assistants to persuade her into the bathroom. I waited in the lounge and when she returned, washed and clean, the first thing she did was to pull down her slacks and try to take off the incontinence pants they'd put on her. A care assistant came to my aid and we told Amanda a number of times the pants had to stay on. Not only did I admire the patience, care and understanding of the staff, but I knew that Amanda's condition had worsened and taken another step in robbing her of the last vestiges of her dignity. It was heartrending.

CHAPTER TWENTY-FOUR

TRUE HEROES

I was apprehensive about meeting Dana, but I knew it was important that we got along, for once the panel had passed the match and introductions began, we'd be seeing each other most days. I also had some concerns about what, if anything, I should say to her about her daughter, Katie, who'd died. If I was meeting someone who'd been recently bereaved then I'd offer my condolences and say how sorry I was, but Dana's daughter had passed twelve years ago. Would she want reminding of that sorrowful time now she'd moved on with her life and was hoping to adopt Melody? Yet to say nothing seemed cold and callous. I was in a dilemma, but as it turned I needn't have worried, for Dana mentioned her daughter shortly after she arrived.

Dana was gently spoken, with an open warm smile – I couldn't help but like her. 'Thank you for making the time to see me,' she said as she came into the hall. 'I know how busy you foster carers are.'

As I showed her into the living room (which I had tidied) she remarked, 'What a lovely house, so cosy. I can't wait to have children's clutter in my house again. You know I lost my daughter Katie twelve years ago?'

'Yes, I did, I'm so sorry.'

'Thank you. But you mustn't ever think that Melody will be second best. As I told Neave and Gaynor from the family-finding team, I will never forget Katie, but I have plenty of room in my heart for Melody too.'

A lovely lady, and after that the conversation just flowed. I made us coffee and toasted teacakes and we sat in the living room where I told Dana all she wanted to know about Melody. Although she'd been given Melody's basic details and background information when she'd first applied to adopt her, she was now eager to know about her time with me. I went back to the beginning when she'd first arrived and had been described as feral, having lived rough with her mother and not attended school. I talked of the huge progress she'd made – and continued to make – both in her education and her self-worth. However, I added that while Melody was a joy to look after, like all children she still needed boundaries sometimes. Dana came across as being gentle and placid and was clearly so delighted and looking forward to being a mother again that I thought she might forget she'd have to be firm sometimes.

I also talked to Dana about Amanda and how quickly her illness had progressed and the effect it would be having on Melody, even though she didn't say much about it. Dana confirmed she'd continue CAMHS in her area and was antic-ipating bringing Melody to see her mother every month for as long as it was appropriate. She mentioned that she'd begun her career in safeguarding adults before changing to child protection, so she had experience of the course Amanda's disease was likely to take. I thought she was in a good position to support Melody through it.

'I'm planning on still visiting Amanda once Melody has left,' I said, 'but I don't know how often.' I didn't mention that I was already going alone on the weeks Melody didn't visit her.

We continued talking and suddenly it was 2 p.m. I asked Dana if she'd like some lunch, but she refused, saying she'd have to leave soon. I made us another coffee and then showed her Melody's bedroom. 'Melody loves her room and keeps it tidy,' I said. 'When she came to me it was the first time she'd had a room of her own.

Dana nodded. 'The conditions some children live in are beyond belief,' she said. 'Some of the things I've seen keep me awake at night.'

'I can imagine.'

By the time Dana left I was convinced this was a match made in heaven, and that Dana and Melody were exactly what each other needed and would be very happy. I was bursting to tell Melody, but that would have to wait until the panel had sat and the introductions could begin.

September gave way to October and autumn set in. A chilly north-easterly wind whipped up, bringing down conkers, acorns and the leaves from the trees. Gone were the long, lazy days of summer and the nights drew in, so we were switching on the lights in the house before 7 p.m. Jill paid me her usual monthly visit, but I didn't hear any more from Neave, so I assumed she'd be in contact after the adoption had gone to panel when she'd want to visit to explain to Melody what was going to happen.

I had concerns about taking Melody to see her mother again after my last visit when Amanda had been both incontinent and aggressive. I tried to prepare Melody by telling her that, as it was three weeks since she'd last seen her mother, she might notice a difference in her.

'You mean she may be worse?' she asked.

'Yes. I don't know for sure, but it's something we need to be prepared for.'

'I hope she's not dead,' Melody said with a child's forthrightness.

'No, I would have been told,' I replied as honestly.

As I drove to the care home I fed the children's CD into the player and Melody ate the sandwiches I'd made. It was still daylight when we arrived at five o'clock, but it wouldn't be long before winter drew in and we'd be arriving in the dark again. As I opened Melody's car door the wind tried to snatch it out of my hand and tugged at my coat. The flat open countryside stretching to the hills beyond, so idyllic in summer, now left us exposed and at the mercy of the elements. Melody tucked her hand into mine and, heads down against the wind, we crossed the car park to the main entrance.

Relieved to be in the warmth of the porch, we signed the Visitors' Book and I pressed the bell to be admitted. Only Mrs Bennett appeared and my heart sank.

'Where's her husband?' Melody asked, voicing my concerns.

'Perhaps he's using the bathroom,' I suggested. But we'd never seen one without the other before.

A care assistant appeared, gently moved Mrs Bennett out of the way and let us in.

'Where's Mr Bennett?' Melody asked her.

'He's passed away, pet,' the care assistant replied matter-of-factly as she closed the door.

Melody looked as though she might cry and I swallowed hard. Anyone working with patients with life-limiting illnesses must have to adjust to death becoming a regular occurrence in order to do their job, but for us it was raw. Mr Bennett had become as much a part of our visit as Mr Wilson had been calling out that he had a plane to catch. We'd got to know them and others, and we felt their passing. However, Mrs Bennett seemed oblivious to the fact that her husband of fifty years was no longer at her side. Now the door was closed she went through the ritual again of trying the handle and pointing to the lock as she'd always done. I supposed her dementia protected her from the pain of losing her husband, and maybe she'd never realize he'd gone.

Melody was quiet as we walked down the corridor towards the lounge; even when we passed Mr Andrews making his 'boo-boo' noise she didn't comment or smile as she usually did. We found Amanda asleep in one of the chairs in the lounge, head relaxed to one side. The occupational therapist wasn't present. As Melody and I crossed the lounge I said hello to the care assistants we'd got to know, and then Melody gently woke her mother. Amanda came to with a start, looked at Melody and then closed her eyes again. The chairs either side of her were occupied, so I pulled over a couple of chairs from the table.

'Mummy, it's me, Melody,' she said, touching her arm. 'I've made you some cakes.'

Amanda opened her eyes again and Melody took the lid off the box, but Amanda only glanced at them un-interestedly.

'Would you like one?' Melody tried, taking a cake from the box.

Amanda's hand suddenly shot out and she roughly pushed the box away. Melody looked hurt at the rejection. It was the first time Amanda had refused a cake, and in such an abrupt manner.

'Maybe she'll have one later,' I suggested. Melody put the box away.

We sat with Amanda as she gazed absently into space as many of the other residents were doing. 'Shall we go to your room?' Melody asked after a while. She preferred being in her mother's room to the lounge, especially if the occupational therapist wasn't present to make something.

Amanda looked at Melody — not so much *at* her but *through* her — and made no attempt to move. We continued to sit beside her while Amanda returned her gaze to some distant point across the room. Then abruptly she stood and began to cross the lounge. We followed her, but instead of turning right out of the door towards her room, she turned left.

'Where are we going?' Melody asked.

Amanda kept walking.

We followed her to the end of the corridor and down another corridor on the left where she began opening various doors, peering in, and closing them again as if looking for someone or something. A care assistant approached us on her way to answer a call bell. 'Are you all right?'

'I'm not sure,' I said. 'Does Amanda still know where her room is?'

'Amanda, are you looking for your room?' she asked her.

Amanda looked at her with the same blank expression.

'Try her,' she said to us. 'You know where her room is?'

'Yes.' She left us to tend to the other patient.

'Amanda, your room is this way,' I said, touching her arm. She gazed at me absent-mindedly. 'This way,' I said and, taking her arm, began along the corridor. Melody linked her other arm and together we walked three abreast along the corridors to her room. But even inside she didn't show any sign of recognition and remained distant and unresponsive. Melody offered her a cake again, but she turned her back and walked away across the room.

'Put them in the cabinet and she can have them when we've gone,' I suggested. But when Melody opened the bedside cabinet she found two cakes left in the last box.

'You didn't eat all the cakes I made you!' Melody exclaimed, hurt.

Amanda looked at her blankly.

'I expect she forgot they were there,' I said. 'I think maybe leave the new box where she can see it on the table or her bookshelf. We'll throw those old cakes away.'

As I put the old box in my bag, Melody set the fresh box of cakes on Amanda's shelf, pointing out to her mother where she'd left them. Amanda didn't give them a second glance. I replenished the fruit bowl, which was empty, and also replaced the plant, which had died. I'd replaced it a couple of times during my visits, as it didn't always get watered. Clearly Amanda wouldn't know a plant needed watering, and the staff were too busy caring for the patients.

Presently Melody took out the photograph album, but Amanda wasn't interested. Even when she sat on the bed beside Melody she didn't look at any of the photos as she had done in the past. It seemed Amanda was barely relating to her surroundings and recognized virtually nothing. Abruptly she stood and left the room, and we followed her back to the lounge. The chair she'd been sitting in was now occupied by another resident – quite a frail elderly lady who I'd seen before. Without warning, Amanda grabbed the woman's arm and pulled her roughly from the chair. A care assistant quickly intervened and Amanda tried to push him away. He calmly but firmly steered her to another chair. I saw the look of horror and confusion on Melody's face and decided it was time to leave. As I'd warned Melody, her mother had deteriorated – I'd noticed a difference even from the week before. Amanda the person had gone and Melody summed it up so touchingly as we returned to the car.

'That's not my mummy. Where has Mummy gone?'

'I know, love. Try to remember the person you knew.'

Driving home, we had another heart to heart, although there was little I could say beyond what I'd already told her.

The following week I couldn't visit Amanda, as my week was full, including a three-day foster-carer training course on challenging behaviour and promoting positive outcomes. I telephoned the care home to see how Amanda was and a member of staff told me she'd had lunch and was asleep in the lounge. The next week I saw her again without Melody and she seemed about the same – detached, uninterested, no longer able to remember where her room was and a shadow of the person she had been. Many of the other residents behaved similarly, sleeping in chairs and being woken to be taken for their meals or to the bathroom to be changed. Amanda appeared to have accepted she needed incontinence pants and there'd been no repetition of her trying to take them off. I often thought the quality of her life, and that of the other residents, was nil, and I had to concentrate on the positive – that they were being well looked after. Seeing them made me appreciate my own parents even more and I gave them an extra hug when I next saw them.

With Melody attending CAMHS after school on Tuesday and sports club on Wednesday, then cake-baking on Thursday (which often included Lizzie) and swimming on Saturday, plus homework, the weeks flew by. At the start of November the air chilled again and many of the shops began displaying Christmas gifts. One card shop even started playing Christmas music.

I heard from Neave that the match had been passed by the panel and the final court hearing had taken place and gone according to plan. She then telephoned with details of the adoption planning meeting, where we would get together to plan the timetable of introduction and Melody's move to her adoptive mother. In preparation for this, Neave had previously sent me a form to complete and return – a questionnaire about Melody that gave a portrait of her character. I wasn't to say anything to Melody, as Neave said she'd tell her at the start of the process. However, I told my children that the adoption was proceeding so that they could prepare themselves for Melody leaving us. They obviously had mixed feelings too.

The day before the planning meeting, Dana telephoned. I hadn't spoken to her since she'd visited me and her voice was so slight that for a moment I thought she was going to tell me something awful, like she didn't want to go ahead, which had happened before. But she said in a shaky voice, 'It's all go then. I'm so nervous. All these months of working towards adopting and now I am.'

'You'll be fine,' I said. 'Melody is going to love you.' I swallowed hard.

'Oh Cathy, I'm being so insensitive. I should know better, being a social worker. How are you and your family feeling?'

'Were doing all right. Obviously we'll miss Melody, but it helps knowing she is going to a really good home.'

'That's kind of you. I know social workers don't always remember to tell the foster carer, so I'll say it – you and your family did a fantastic job turning Melody around. It could so easily have been different.'

'Thank you. I appreciate that.'

We said goodbye and I replaced the handset, tears in my eyes, but with a warm glow of satisfaction from Dana's kind words. She was right: certainly the social workers I'd dealt with (apart from Jill) hardly ever remembered to say thank you, and while praise and thanks aren't something foster carers expect, it's nice to hear. I did feel that I'd 'turned Melody around', as Dana had put it, and yes, the outcome could have been very different, but part of that was due to Melody and her acceptance and willingness to lose her anger and move on with her life. She and the other children I've fostered are true heroes.

CHAPTER TWENTY-FIVE

INTRODUCTIONS

The following day at 1 p.m., Neave and her team manager Tony, Dana and her social worker Gaynor from the family-finding team, Jill and I all sat around the table in a meeting room at the social services offices, ready for the adoption planning meeting. In contrast to some of the meetings I'd attended in respect of children I'd fostered, the atmosphere was light and joyous. Tony was chairing the meeting and we began by introducing ourselves. Then Neave spoke first, referring to and outlining the placement plan she'd drawn up, which we'd all receive a copy of after the meeting. This document was a carefully structured timetable that, over two weeks, would allow Melody and Dana to get to know each other and bond. As Neave went through it, Jill made some notes, Tony took minutes, and Dana and I entered the dates and times in our diaries. I knew from experience what to expect and had kept these two weeks free. The pages of my diary quickly filled.

Neave would be starting the process that afternoon when she visited Melody after school to tell her about her adoptive mother and also go through the photograph album Dana had specially prepared for her, and had brought to the meeting. It showed pictures of Dana, her home and extended family and was Melody's to keep. The next day Dana would visit us for an hour and meet Melody for the first time. She would return the next day and stay for longer, including dinner. The following day Dana would visit us again and take Melody out for dinner, then return and spend time with her – playing and helping with her homework, and putting her to bed. So the introduction would continue, though not every day; it's so emotionally intensive that 'days off' had been built in when Dana would just phone Melody, and they had space to reflect and consolidate. Midway through the process we would meet and look at how the introduction was going and if there were any problems, when the pace could be slowed to longer than two weeks if necessary. Because Dana lived over a hundred miles away, she had booked into a local hotel.

I'd brought some recent photographs of Melody with me as was expected and passed them to Dana. She would have been given a photo of Melody when she'd first applied to adopt her, but that was often the only photo the prospective adopter had prior to the start of the introduction. She would have also received an updated copy of Melody's profile, and of course Dana had had the benefit of seeing Melody's home with me, which most adopters hadn't at this point.

Usually the second week of the introduction for a child Melody's age takes place at the adoptive parent's home, with the child and carer visiting for longer each day, building to two separate overnight stays and then the move. However, because Dana lived so far away this wasn't practical, so Neave had restructured the plan slightly. At the start of the second week Melody would have time off school and I would take her to Dana's, spend some time with her there until she felt comfortable and then leave her to stay the night and collect her the next day. This would happen twice before the move, so I'd need to book into a hotel near where Dana lived. At the end of the plan was my visit to Melody approximately a month after the move, when the schools would have broken up for Christmas. Previously Dana had thought that she might then visit us at home when she took Melody to see her mother at the care home as it was in the same direction, but having thought it through and discussed it with Gaynor, it had been decided that returning to our house could be unsettling for Melody, especially after seeing her mother. It was decided that any future meetings between Melody and my family should be on neutral territory – perhaps with us meeting halfway.

At the very end of the meeting, when we were all relaxed and smiling, Gaynor asked how Amanda was and I had to say that she'd deteriorated considerably. 'It's so sad in someone so young,' Gaynor said. 'My mother-in-law has dementia and will need to go into a care home soon.'

I nodded sympathetically and Tony said it was frightening just how many people were developing dementia now and the numbers were on the rise. However, we finished on a more positive note with everyone looking forward to starting the introductions and the beginning of Melody's new life with Dana. After the meeting, Dana was going to check in to her hotel, shower, have something to eat and catch up on some paperwork. We said a warm goodbye and I left the meeting first and drove straight to Melody's school with that bittersweet feeling of happiness and loss. Yes, Melody was making a fresh start in life, but in doing so she was leaving us. It's a feeling foster carers never completely come to terms with, regardless of how long they have been fostering.

Melody knew that I'd gone to a meeting at the social services – she often asked me what I was doing during the day, which I think was a legacy from having to worry about her mother and what she was doing or not doing. When she came out of school I said that Neave was coming to see us at four o'clock, so we said a quick goodbye to Miss May and left.

'Not her again,' Melody groaned as we crossed the playground. 'What does she want now?' It wasn't that Melody didn't like Neave – she did, or at least she was more accepting of her now – but a visit from any professional after school meant her evening was disrupted, when she just wanted to relax and watch some television.

However, it was important that Melody was in a positive frame of mind to receive the news Neave was bringing and, while I couldn't tell her, I could get close. 'I think Neave has got some good news for you,' I said as Melody climbed into the car.

'What?' she asked, disgruntled.

'She wants to be the one to tell you,' I said with a bright, engaging smile. I checked her seatbelt, closed her car door and went round to the driver's door.

'I bet she's found me that forever family she keeps going on about,' Melody grumbled as I got in. But her expression said otherwise – that she was interested and looking forward to hearing what Neave had to say.

'We'll have to wait and see,' I said, adding to the sense of expectation.

Melody didn't mention it again on the way home but sat quietly in her seat, gazing out of her side window. However, once home, she went straight to Lucy – the only one in yet.

'Neave's coming and she might be going to tell me she's found me a forever family,' she declared, then watched to see what Lucy's reaction would be. She trusted Lucy's view, because she'd been through similar.

'That's fantastic,' Lucy said without hesitation.

'Is it?' Melody asked. It was natural she'd have doubts at this stage – she hadn't met Dana yet.

'Yes, of course it's good news,' Lucy replied. 'You don't want to stay in care and have visits from social workers and have to go to reviews. You want to be like all the other kids at school and have a proper mummy.' This was coming straight from Lucy's heart. I remembered how relieved she'd been when her adoption had gone through and she was – as she put it – like all the other kids with a proper mummy: me. I kissed her cheek.

'You'll be fine,' Lucy added. 'Neave will have found you a really nice family who will love you and look after you forever.'

I felt my eyes fill, but Melody was smiling.

Ten minutes later when Neave arrived with Dana's photograph album tucked under her arm, Melody was beside me in the hall looking forward to hearing what Neave had to tell her.

I went with them into the living room, fetched Neave the drink of water she'd asked for and then sat in one of the easy-chairs as Neave settled on the sofa beside Melody. With the album on her lap, Neave told Melody about her adoptive mother and then talked her through the photographs, reading out the captions beneath each one, which said a little about the pictures. Melody sat in awe, silent and wide-eyed, taking it all in. At the end Neave closed the album and gave it to Melody.

'It's yours to keep,' she said. 'Mummy made it specially for you.' We would all be calling Dana 'Mummy' from now on; it's normal practice to refer to the parents as Mummy and Daddy right from the start of the introductions as it helps the child and parents bond.

Melody clutched the album to her as Neave continued by outlining the proposed timetable of introduction, beginning with Melody meeting her new mummy the following afternoon and ending with her moving in two weeks' time.

'You don't have to remember all of this,' Neave said. 'Cathy knows what's happening.'

Melody was looking serious and I threw her a reassuring smile.

When Neave had finished she asked Melody if she had any questions and, overwhelmed by all she'd heard, she shook her head. 'Well, if you think of anything, ask Cathy. She'll know or, if not, she can phone me.'

I saw Neave out and Melody wanted to go through her album with me, so we sat together in the living room and spent some time talking about the photographs. Then Melody went off to show Lucy, Adrian and Paula while I made dinner. They were all home now and I knew they could be relied upon to show the same enthusiasm for the photos that I had. They appreciated how important this album was to her.

Melody kept the album with her during dinner, placing it under her chair as she ate. All of this was very positive – the first stage in Melody accepting her adoptive mother. It can be difficult if the child refuses to look at the album or pushes it away, as they are in effect rejecting their forever family. It then takes longer for them to bond, but in my experience they always do accept them in the end, as they have been matched and not just randomly selected. Not all children in care who can't live with their birth families are put forward for adoption, and reasons for this include that they might be too old or have such strong ties with their birth family that they couldn't transfer their affection. Indeed, when Melody had first come into care adoption hadn't been part of the care plan, but it had become appropriate, partly due to her mother's deteriorating condition.

Included in my role as Melody's foster carer was to prepare and support her during her move to permanency, a process that had now begun. Of course Melody may have doubts, especially to begin with, and that evening, although she cherished the album, she also began finding fault with the photographs and sounded us out for our views.

'Do you really like her house?' she asked, showing me the picture of the front of Dana's house.

'Yes, I do,' I said. 'It's got real character.'

'It's very old,' Melody said.

'It's Victorian, a few years older than this house. I like older houses.'

Then I heard her telling Lucy, 'The garden isn't very big.'

'It's not as big as this one, but there's plenty of room for you to play,' Lucy replied positively. 'And you've got a park close by. Read what your mummy has written under that photo.'

'The park is only a short walk away,' Melody read, with Lucy's help.

'Exactly, and what do you see in the photo of the park?'

'Swings and roundabouts and climbing frames,' Melody admitted.

'Fantastic.'

Melody asked similar questions of Paula and Adrian, who gave positive responses.

She was moving to a lovely picturesque part of rural England and Dana had included some shots of the area. Her house was on the edge of a historic market town, which featured in tourist guides. The centre of the town had original cobblestones, a museum, cottages with thatched roofs and a river. In terms of location and scenery, it was impossible to fault.

'I wouldn't mind moving there myself,' Adrian said, which meant a lot to Melody. She'd sought our reassurance – our approval and permission to move on with her life.

One photograph Melody couldn't find any criticism with was of her new bedroom. It was a double-size room, so much larger than her bedroom with me, and had been freshly decorated in pale lemon, with delicate floral curtains, matching duvet, cushions and a beanbag. A whitewood wardrobe, chest of drawers, shelves, table and chair still left plenty of space in the centre of the room to play. A lamp stood on the bedside cabinet and on top of the chest of drawers was a portable television.

'Lucky you,' Paula said. 'I only had my own television this year.' Which of course made Melody swell with pride.

Neave had told Melody she would be meeting her adoptive mother the following day and that if she had any questions about her, to ask me. She didn't have many questions during the evening, but come bedtime when I was hoping for a quiet sit down she had plenty. 'How tall is she?' 'Does she smoke or drink?' 'What time will I have to go to bed?' As I answered Melody's questions I told her I'd met her mother twice and that I really liked her and I knew Melody would too. Melody listened intently as I extolled Dana's virtues and then at the end she said in a deadpan voice, 'She sounds very nice, but I'm not sure about her being a social worker.'

I had to smile. 'That's her job. More importantly, she is going to be an excellent mother to you, not your social worker.'

Neave had told Melody that Dana had another child who'd sadly died, but Melody didn't mention her to us that evening and we didn't bring up the subject. Doubtless at some point she and Dana would have a conversation about Katie, and I knew that Dana would handle it sensitively and easily as she had with me.

Unsurprisingly Melody took a long while to go to sleep and kept thinking of new questions. I had to resettle her a number of times. Her last question was, 'Will Father Christmas know where to visit me after I've moved?'

'Yes, love, definitely.'

'Are you sure?'

'Yes, I promise. I know your mummy and I know how much she is looking forward to celebrating Christmas with you. He will visit your new home for sure.'

Finally Melody snuggled down to sleep.

Like many children from poor backgrounds who come into care, Melody hadn't ever had a proper Christmas. She'd never known the joy of decorating the house and Christmas tree, or hanging up a pillowcase on Christmas Eve and being too excited to sleep, safe in the knowledge it would be full of presents in the morning. Christmas for her and Amanda had been another day of trying to keep warm and find something to eat. Melody had told me that last Christmas they 'got lucky' as a local café owner who didn't celebrate Christmas had opened and given them something to eat for free, which for me summed up the charity of Christmas.

It had been a busy day, so not long after Melody finally fell asleep I went to bed, and I thought of Amanda. The next couple of weeks would be very busy and I doubted I'd have time to visit her. I'd also need to ask my parents to stay with my family while I was away settling Melody with Dana. I knew Adrian, Paula and Lucy would be delighted to have their Nana and Grandpa stay.

The following day Melody was eager to go to school to tell Miss May her news, but after much deliberation decided not to take her photograph album in case it got lost. Neave would have contacted the school to advise them that Melody would be leaving and that prior to that she would need some days off to visit her adoptive mother and stay overnight. I didn't see Miss May at the start of school, but at the end she came into the playground with Melody and said quietly to me, 'Good luck for this afternoon. I hope it all goes well when she meets her new mummy.'

'Thank you, I'm sure it will.'

'I've told Melody we'll miss her when she leaves but that she's very lucky to have this chance of a new life.'

Miss May was such a treasure and instinctively knew the right thing to say. I made a mental note to buy her and Miss Langford, Melody's teacher, a leaving card and gift.

Once home that afternoon, there was enough time for a hot drink before Dana arrived. Paula and Lucy were in and knew they should just carry on as normal. I'd found before with introductions (and contact) that it was better if everyone behaved as normal while allowing the child and their parents some time together. If the house was too quiet, with everyone on their best behaviour, it felt unnatural and awkward. So when the doorbell rang at exactly 4 p.m. Paula was busy telling off the cat who'd bedded down on her best jersey, leaving cat hairs all over it, and Adrian and Lucy were in their rooms, competing to see who could play their music the loudest.

'Can you turn it down a bit, please?' I shouted up before answering the front door. They didn't hear me. 'Welcome,' I said to Dana over the cacophony of sound. 'Do come in.' Melody was standing beside me.

'Thanks, Cathy. And you must be Melody. Nice to meet you.'

Melody took a step back and looked her adoptive mother up and down.

'Do I look like my photos?' Dana asked easily, slipping off her coat.

'Yes, you do,' Melody replied.

'Well, that's a good start then,' Dana said with a big smile. 'You look just like your photo.'

As I hung Dana's coat on the hall stand, Paula came by with the lint roller in one hand and her jumper in the other, on her way upstairs. I introduced her to Dana and asked her to tell Adrian and Lucy to turn their music down a bit.

We went through to the living room and the music above quietened. The photograph album Dana had given us was on the sofa – Melody had brought it down earlier in preparation, and she now picked it up and sat on the sofa. Dana joined her.

'We've looked at the album a lot,' I told Dana. 'Melody has a few questions about the people in some of the photos that I couldn't answer.'

'Let's have a look together then,' Dana said. The album would be a good focal point and encourage conversation.

Melody flicked to the first photograph she had a question about.

'Who are all those people?' she said, referring to a posed photo of a large family gathering.

'Yes, there are a lot of people there,' Dana laughed a little nervously. 'There wasn't space to write all their names, but I thought it would be nice for you to see all my family. It was taken at my cousin's wedding last year. There's my sister – your aunt – and her children.' She told Melody their names. 'Your cousins go to the same school you will be going to. You'll meet them all when you visit me.'

She went through naming the others in the photo and then Melody turned the page. 'Are those your parents?' she asked. Dana had written 'Nana and Grandpa' beneath.

'Yes, your nana and grandpa. They are so looking forward to meeting you.'

'I haven't had a nana and grandpa of my own before. I share Adrian, Lucy and Paula's here.'

Dana smiled. 'You'll have to share my parents with your cousins, but don't worry, they have plenty of love to go round.'

'Like Cathy's parents,' Melody said, which I thought was lovely.

As they continued going through the album, with Dana answering Melody's questions and adding a little more information to each picture, I saw Melody slowly move closer to her adoptive mother, then relax against her, resting her head on her shoulder. The physical contact was another good sign that Melody was willing to accept her. They came to the end of the album and Dana closed it and slipped her arm around Melody's waist.

'I'm so pleased you like the photos,' she said, drawing Melody close. 'I spent a lot of time deciding what to include. I've got plenty more photos at home and we can look at those when you come to visit me next week.'

Melody nodded and then, raising her head, asked, 'Would you like to see a photo of my mummy?'

I watched Dana for her reaction.

'Yes, of course,' she said easily. 'I'd love to see a picture of your birth mummy. We will visit her once you've moved in.'

I saw the look of gratitude and relief on Melody's face and felt sure it would be OK. In acknowledging and accepting her birth mother, Dana had allowed Melody to embrace her new life without feeling guilty about her past.

CHAPTER TWENTY-SIX

OVERTIRED AND EMOTIONAL

Dana stayed for an hour as timetabled, and that evening when I wrote up my log notes I included details of her visit, which were all very positive. Melody must have given Miss May a very good account of Dana's visit too, for at the end of school the following day Miss May gave me the thumbs-up sign, which I returned with a smile. She didn't come over to talk, as she knew we had to get away quickly again.

Dana arrived promptly at 4 p.m. and spent time with Melody, helping with her homework and playing various board games; she also stayed for dinner. The next day Dana took Melody out to eat and then spent the rest of the evening with us, when she was largely responsible for Melody – running her bath and seeing her into bed. I was gradually handing over Melody's care to her, which would continue the bonding process so Melody's confidence in her adoptive mother grew. By the end of the week Melody was calling Dana 'Mummy' naturally and referring to Amanda as her 'birth mummy' – also very positive.

Because there was a lot going on for Melody and she was seeing her adoptive mother most evenings, she didn't attend

CAMHS or the after-school sports club that week; neither did she see Lizzie, although on Thursday evening we did bake cakes, as it was one of the evenings Dana just telephoned and didn't see Melody. Her LAC review, scheduled for November, was postponed until after the move, but at the end of the first week those of us involved in Melody's adoption met as planned to take stock and assess how it was going. It was only a short meeting, as there weren't any issues, and Jill and Neave had telephoned regularly for updates so knew everything was going well and according to plan. Dana left that evening to return home, and phoned Melody as arranged on Saturday. On Sunday my parents arrived in the morning to stay the night, and I left in the car with Melody to continue the introductions at what would soon be her new home with Dana. As is usual when a child moves to permanency, I took some of her belongings with us in the car to leave there. Having their possessions with them engenders a feeling of being 'at home' in the child, and practically all Melody's belongings – accumulated since coming into care – were more than one carload.

Melody was very excited and chatty at the start of the journey, but then as we entered the area where Dana lived she fell quiet. 'Are you OK?' I asked, glancing at her in the rear-view mirror. She was gazing through her side window, deep in thought.

'Those hills over there look like the ones near the care home where my other mummy lives,' she said.

'They are similar,' I agreed, 'although the care home is in the opposite direction, not near here.' I glanced at her again. 'Were you thinking about her?'

'Yes.'

'That's all right. I hope they were nice thoughts.'

'I was thinking she won't know I've got a new mummy, because she doesn't know anything any more.'

'No, love, but if she did I'm sure she'd be happy and would want what's best for you.' I wondered if Melody was feeling a little guilty about being happy in her new life. 'Mummies want what's best for their children,' I emphasized. 'I'm a mummy and I know that.' Melody nodded and seemed to accept my reassurance.

As we entered the market town where Dana lived, Melody recognized it from the photographs and sat upright in her seat. 'There's the church with the tall steeple,' she said, pointing and getting excited again. 'And that's where they have the market.' It was Sunday, so no market was being held today and only a few of the shops were open. I drove slowly through the centre, which was as picturesque as in the photographs. Quaint, full of character, spotlessly clean – and, despite it being winter, troughs of flowers and evergreen shrubs decorated the main high street and market square. Dana had told me to follow the road round through the centre and her house, number 45 with a red door, would be further up on our left. 'Watch out for a red door and the number 45,' I told Melody.

'There it is!' she shouted, recognizing it from the photo in the album.

'Well spotted.'

I pulled over and parked behind Dana's car in a resident's bay. She'd said that most of the area close to the centre had controlled parking, so she'd give me a visitor's permit when I arrived. Her house, like the others in the street, was a Victorian terrace with original sash windows and the doors opening straight onto the pavement. While they didn't have front gardens, most of them – including Dana's – had window boxes full of winter pansies, continuing the charm of the town square.

As soon as I let Melody out of the car she was at the red front door, pressing the bell. Her previous pensiveness had gone and she was now eager to see Dana again, and her new home for the first time.

The door opened immediately. 'Well, hello!' Dana exclaimed, with a big, welcoming smile. 'Come on in.' Melody gave her a hug, which was nice, then Dana handed me the parking permit. 'Put it on the dashboard so it can be seen,' she said.

I did so while they waited just inside the hall.

'Come through,' Dana said as I returned, and she showed us into the one main room, which ran from the front of the house to the back. It was just as we'd seen it in the photographs. The end we were now in looked out over the street and was used as a living room, with a sofa, easy-chair and a black leather pouffe that doubled as another seat. It was full of character; the original fireplace and wooden mantelpiece had been retained, although the fire was no longer in use and the grate contained a lovely arrangement of dried flowers. Beside the coffee table was a pine wooden toy box overflowing with new games and puzzles; a teddy bear peeped out.

'Is that mine?' Melody asked, her eyes rounding.

'Yes. Take a look,' Dana said. 'We'll play a game later.'

The atmosphere in the house was very warm and cosy. 'You've got a lovely home,' I told Dana.

'Thank you. I've been here for five years now. I moved in after my divorce – I needed a fresh start.'

I nodded and my gaze went to the many framed photographs on the wall above the sofa. One was of a young girl who I thought might be Katie.

'Would you like to look around first and then I'll make us a drink?' Dana asked Melody.

She was immediately on her feet. 'Can I see my room?'

'Yes, of course, but we'll start down here first.'

Dana led the way to the other end of the room, which was the dining area and again familiar from the photographs. A pine table and four chairs with floral seat cushions stood by the French windows, which looked out to the patio and garden beyond.

'There's the bird feeder,' Melody said. As we looked, a couple of small garden birds flew down to feed.

'I sit here with the doors open in summer to eat,' Dana told Melody. 'It's lovely on a warm evening.' I could picture it. Idyllic.

'Can I feed the birds?' Melody asked.

'Yes, when the feeder is empty I'll show you how to refill it.'

We watched the birds feed for a while longer and then Dana showed us into the kitchen – again, it was as we'd seen in the pictures.

'Can I help you cook,' Melody asked, 'like I help Cathy?'

'Yes. I'm always happy to have help cooking,' Dana laughed. We then followed her up the stripped-pine staircase, our feet clipping on the wooden steps, to the bedrooms. First we went into Melody's room and she was delighted. 'It's so big,' she said. 'Just like in the photo.'

'Yes, you're a lucky girl,' I said.

'Do you knock before you come into my room, like Cathy does?'

'Yes, if you'd like me to,' Dana said.

Melody looked out of her bedroom window to the garden beyond, and then opened and closed a few drawers and the wardrobe doors – all were empty at present.

'We'll put the belongings you've brought with you today in here later,' Dana told Melody.

Melody spent a bit more time looking round and then asked, 'Where do you sleep?'

'This way, I'll show you.'

We crossed the landing and looked in Dana's bedroom, which was at the front of the house, then she showed us the small box room, which was used mainly for storage, and finally the bathroom. 'Can you see your towel and flannel?' Dana asked Melody.

Melody spotted them straight away. 'They've got my name on!' she exclaimed, rushing over. Dana had had a set of towels embroidered with 'Melody'.

'How lovely,' I said. It was, but impractical for us, I thought, when we had children arriving and leaving, sometimes in quick succession.

Melody loved her personalized towel set and asked if she could have a bath.

'Yes, at bedtime,' Dana said, pleased they were a success.

So far so good, I thought, watching Melody. We returned downstairs, where Dana made us drinks and also produced a plate of cling-film-wrapped sandwiches from the fridge and set them on the table. As we ate we watched the small birds fly down, take a few seeds and then fly off again. It was fascinating. There were many more different varieties of garden birds here compared to at my home. Once we'd finished, I helped Dana clear the table while Melody went to explore the contents of the toy box again. 'I'll leave soon,' I said to Dana. 'Melody seems pretty settled.'

'That's fine. I might take her out for a while later. I'll just see how it goes.'

We returned to the living room where Melody was now studying the photographs on the wall. 'I know some of those people,' she said, pointing and meaning she recognized them from the photograph album. That's why the photograph album is such an important part of the introductory process when moving a child to permanency – the familiarity kindles a feeling of 'knowing' their new family and home.

'Do you recognize that couple?' Dana said, pointing.

'Yes, your parents, Nana and Grandpa,' Melody said, pleased she knew.

'Well done. And here is my sister and her family – your aunt, uncle and cousins.'

'Who's that?' Melody asked, pointing to the picture of the child I'd noticed earlier.

'That's Katie, my other daughter who passed away,' Dana said easily. I thought it was very sensitive of her to refer to Katie as her 'other' daughter.

'It's a lovely photo,' I said.

'It was one of the last ones we took before she became very ill.'

Melody looked worried. 'I won't be ill here, will I?' she asked Dana, with a child's directness.

'No, love, you won't,' Dana replied. 'Katie was born with something wrong with her heart and the doctors couldn't mend it. You are fit and healthy and I will make sure you stay that way.'

'Good. My mummy in the care home has something wrong with her that the doctors can't put right.'

'I know, sweet,' Dana said. 'It's very sad when that happens, isn't it?'

Melody turned from the photo to look at her and in their gaze I saw something unique that I hadn't been able to give her – an understanding, an empathy, a bond formed because they both knew what it was to gradually lose a loved one through illness.

I stayed for another ten minutes, then, assured that Melody was fine to leave, I said I would go to my hotel now and see them tomorrow. The three of us unloaded my car and Dana said they'd unpack Melody's bags as soon as I'd gone, so she had her belongings around her. I kissed them both goodbye, returned to my car and drove to the hotel. Within reason, the social services reimburse foster carers for any expenses they incur in moving a child to permanency.

It was a strange feeling entering that impersonal hotel room alone. I couldn't remember ever being in a hotel room by myself and I didn't feel comfortable with it. My family was at home being looked after by my parents, Melody was settling in with her adoptive mother and here I was alone for the night. I'm a family person and although I like solitude sometimes, I also like to know that someone will be coming home soon. As I unpacked my overnight bag my thoughts went to Dana, who'd moved house five years ago after her divorce and having lost her daughter. How many days had she spent alone? It would have taken a lot for her to get back on her feet, but she'd done it. Her home was clearly a happy one and I was sure Melody would be happy there too.

It was mid-afternoon and I decided to explore the small town centre where I found a cornershop open on a Sunday and brought a newspaper and something to take back to the hotel to eat later. I wandered down some of the side streets where I discovered some thatched cottages with their plaques showing they'd been built in 1760. When I returned to my hotel room I phoned home, spoke to everyone and then settled down with the Sunday paper. Later I watched some television, resisted the urge to phone home again and then showered and had an early night.

I slept fitfully, and the following morning, once washed and dressed, I went down to the dining room for breakfast. I checked out and passed the morning by exploring more of the town. It was busier now on Monday with the shops open. I came across a couple of craft shops aimed at tourists and I bought my parents a small thank-you gift for helping out, then returned to Dana's at 12.30 to collect Melody. She didn't want to leave and while this was a good sign, Dana knew as I did that we had to stay to the timetable.

'Come on,' I encouraged, 'what about the rest of your belongings? They are still at my house.'

'You can bring them,' Melody replied a little grumpily. 'While I stay here.'

'No, love, I'm pleased you want to stay here, but we have to follow the timetable and do what Neave decided.'

'Not going,' she said. Folding her arms across her chest, she scowled, reminiscent of when she'd first arrived at my house.

'You're coming here again on Wednesday,' Dana said. 'That's only two sleeps.' Melody didn't look convinced. 'And I'm phoning you tonight – or better still, why don't you phone me? Do you know how to use a telephone?' It was a good piece of child psychology – giving Melody the challenge and responsibility for making the phone call.

'I'll phone you,' Melody said. She lowered her arms and stopped scowling.

'Great. Good choice,' I said.

Melody hugged Dana goodbye and we left. She had another moan in the car about leaving, but then began looking forward to telling Paula, Lucy and Adrian about her new home, as well as Miss May and Lizzie the following day at school. My parents would have left now, having seen Adrian, Paula and Lucy off to school, and would return on Wednesday for the second overnight. I fed in the CD of popular children's songs and concentrated on the traffic on the motorway.

Once home, Melody looked a bit bemused. At this point in the introductions the child has a foot in each home, which can be confusing for them, but I knew from experience that these timetables worked, so at the end of the introductory period the child is ready to leave and start their new life without feeling rushed or rejected.

I waited until Melody had settled with some toys in the living room before I telephoned Jill and Neave to update them. I told them both that the first overnight had gone really well. I also invited them to the small leaving party I was having for Melody on Friday at 5 p.m. It's usual for the foster carer to give the child a leaving party and a present and card when they move to permanency. Jill could make it, but Neave couldn't. She'd be seeing Melody again anyway at Dana's after the move. Gaynor telephoned for an update and I invited her. I would also invite my parents, Miss May, Miss Langford, and Lizzie and her family. Although Dana had said they would keep in touch, marking Melody's leaving with a party was a pleasant way for us to say goodbye. It would also confirm for Melody that her stay with us had ended and she was going to start her new life with her adoptive mother.

On Wednesday, after Paula, Adrian and Lucy had left for school, I loaded my car again and set off with Melody for her second overnight stay. My parents would arrive later that afternoon and stay the night. Melody was delighted to be there again and, now familiar with the house, went straight to the toy box in the living room to play. I accepted the coffee Dana offered and stayed for an hour, then left to check into my hotel. After that I spent the afternoon in the local museum just off the town centre, had something to eat in a café and then returned to my hotel room where I phoned home. Mum answered.

'Your father and I are relaxing in the living room with nothing to do,' she laughed. 'Adrian, Lucy and Paula are in the kitchen insisting they make us dinner.'

'Excellent, I am impressed.' Like many young people, my children came into their own when their mother wasn't around, although I'd never have left them alone all night. While I considered them responsible for their ages, if something untoward happened they wouldn't have the experience or maturity to deal with it.

I told Mum not to disturb them, to give them my love and I'd see them tomorrow.

On Thursday morning when I collected Melody I briefly met Dana's sister, who'd popped in to meet Melody. I instantly recognized her from the photo in Melody's album. She was a lovely lady who would be helping Dana out when she returned to work at the end of her adoption leave. I formed the impression they were very close sisters. In the car going home Melody said she liked her aunt and would meet her cousins and her new nana and grandpa on Sunday – after she'd moved in.

Friday was Melody's last day at school and understandably she went in feeling a bit sad at having to say goodbye. However, later, when she came out at the end of the day, she was very excited. Miss May and Miss Langford were with her and had clearly been making her last day memorable. Melody had a large good-luck card signed by all the children in her class, and a present of a beautifully illustrated book. I thanked them both for all they'd done for Melody and as we said goodbye I saw Miss Langford's eyes fill. She couldn't come to Melody's leaving party, so this was goodbye, but Miss May and Lizzie and her mother could come, so we'd see them again later.

I'd prepared most of the buffet tea for Melody's leaving party during the day, as well as packing the rest of her belongings ready for the following morning. Once home I set the table with a fancy cloth, paper plates and soft drinks, then just before five o'clock put out the plates of buffet food. It wasn't long before the doorbell began ringing and by 5.15 the house was buzzing. A dozen of us, chatting and laughing, had gathered together to wish Melody well for the future. All our guests had brought her a gift and card – we'd give her ours the following morning when she left. Melody had a fantastic time and was the centre of attention all evening. Then of course, when everyone had gone and the party was over, overtired and emotional, she burst into tears.

'I don't want to leave you all,' she sobbed.

I took her in my arms. 'You'll be fine in the morning, love, after a good night's sleep. Come on, up you go and I'll read you a bedtime story from your new book.'

'You will come and visit me, won't you?'

'Yes, of course I will.'

CHAPTER TWENTY-SEVEN

LUCKY TO HAVE HER

The following morning Melody was up early and looking forward to Dana's arrival at 10.30. Adrian, Paula and Lucy were up and dressed too so they could see her off. After a noisy breakfast with everyone talking at once, we brought down the last of Melody's luggage and stacked it ready in the hall. Lucy and Paula then played with Melody until at exactly 10.30 a.m. the doorbell rang. Melody fell silent as she came with me to answer the door.

'All ready, love?' Dana asked her, smiling.

Melody gave a small, sad nod.

Dana was aware that, despite a really positive introductory period, parting from us might be difficult for Melody and we needed to keep the goodbye short. She came in and I offered her a coffee, but she said she had bottles of water in the car and that they could stop off for something to eat and drink on the way home if Melody wanted to. We then began loading her car. Toscha came out to see what was going on. Melody stroked her and said she'd miss her, which was sweet and very different from when she'd first arrived and accused her of having fleas. With all Melody's luggage in the car, it was time for us to say goodbye. No matter how sure I am that the child's new home is right for them, seeing them off is always sad, not only for me, but for my children too.

The girls and I took it in turns to hug and kiss Melody goodbye, while Adrian gave her a high five. 'Good luck in your new school,' he said. 'Be good.'

'I will,' she returned.

Adrian then waited in the hall while the girls and I went with Melody and Dana to the car. Dana checked Melody's seatbelt was fastened, said goodbye to us and then got into the driver's seat and lowered Melody's window.

'Take care, love,' I said, giving her one last kiss through the open window.

'See you in a month,' Dana said from the front. 'I'll phone to arrange.'

'Yes, good,' I replied. 'Take care, both of you.' As Dana started the car, I looked at Melody and thought how she'd changed during the time she'd been with us. She'd arrived angry, with a reputation for very challenging behaviour, and was used to being in charge. Somewhere along the line, having been relieved of the burden of looking after her mother, she'd become a child again. A lovely child with hopes and dreams, who now knew how to play, make friends and fit in. Certainly she'd come a long way, and my biggest hope was that her past wouldn't ruin her future.

'Bye,' Melody said quietly as the car began to pull away.

'Bye,' we called.

We stayed on the pavement waving until they were out of sight and then slowly returned indoors. Instantly it was obvious that someone was missing from our home. When my children were younger and a child left I used to take them on an outing to give them something else to think about. Now I suggested we went out for dinner that evening.

'Yes ...'

'OK ...'

'Later ...' were their unenthusiastic responses.

The first few days after a child has left are the worst, and going into their empty bedroom is always difficult. I decided to do that straight away. It was a shell of a room without Melody and her belongings. I concentrated on changing the bedding and then I gave the room a good clean, not because it was dirty or I wanted to rid it of any trace of Melody, but because I knew it probably wouldn't be empty for long. Sadly, at that very moment, a family somewhere would be in crisis or a child was being abused, resulting in them coming into care.

On a happier note, just as I'd finished in Melody's room, Mum telephoned to see how the move had gone. I told her and thanked her and Dad again for helping out, for truly I couldn't have managed without them. When I said that we were planning to eat out later she suggested that she and Dad could meet us halfway and we could have a late lunch together, which I knew would please my children. We arranged to meet at a pub restaurant we knew at 3 p.m. and Mum said she'd book us a table. When I told Adrian, Lucy and Paula their response was very different to before.

'Great.'

'Fantastic.'

'I'll get changed now.'

Thank goodness for loving grandparents!

* * *

Sunday morning was strange without Melody. Usually it was just me and her downstairs first thing. Adrian left to play football, and with the girls having a lie-in I wrote up my log notes – the final entry for Melody. Once dressed, I cooked a batch of cupcakes, the warm smell of baking drifting around the house. Paula came down to investigate. 'Hmm, that smells good, but it's not Thursday,' she said. Baking cakes on a Thursday had become something of a ritual.

'No, I know, but we all like these cakes and I can make them any time now, can't I?'

'Yes,' she agreed. 'Let me know when they're ready.'

'I will.'

But I had another motive for making these cakes today. Having not seen Amanda for over two weeks, I was intending to visit her the following day. I'd never told my family I had been going to see her; it wasn't a secret, it just never came up. Also, if I told them then, I knew that after each visit they'd ask how she was and what could I say? Deteriorating? A bit worse? There wasn't anything positive to tell them, and while Melody, the poor child, had to cope and come to terms with her mother's decline, thankfully my children didn't.

On Monday morning I telephoned Neave and Jill and told them the move had gone well. Obviously they were both pleased. Neave said she'd tell Gaynor, and Jill said they'd had a referral over the weekend for a child who may need a foster-care placement and she'd keep me posted. I had an early sandwich lunch at 12 and then set off for Oak Lane House with a carrier bag containing the box of cakes, some grapes and another small potted plant. As I drove my thoughts went to Melody and how she was getting on – her first day in her new school. It was bound to be a bit strange to begin with as it is for any child going to a new school, making new friends and finding their way around the building. Lizzie's mother and Dana had swapped telephone numbers at Melody's leaving party so the girls could keep in touch, but I knew that Dana was planning on letting Melody settle in first before she phoned so it didn't unsettle Melody. For the same reason, we wouldn't see Melody for a month and Dana was going to wait a couple of weeks before she took Melody to see Amanda.

How long I'd be able to continue to visit Amanda I didn't know; it would depend largely on my fostering commitments – a new child would mean a new routine. But today I had a good journey and an hour later I was parking outside the care home. Taking the carrier bag from the passenger seat, I got out and breathed in the fresh, cold November air. I let myself in the outer doors, signed the Visitors' Book and then pressed the bell to be admitted. Nothing much had changed and Mrs Bennett appeared with her handbag looped over her arm, ready to go out. I smiled at her through the glass, but there was no recognition. A care assistant I knew from my previous visits appeared but didn't return my smile. Indeed, she seemed anxious that I was there.

'Didn't you know?' she said as she quickly let me in and closed the door.

'Know what?' I asked, turning cold.

'You've come to visit Amanda?'

'Yes.'

'She's in hospital.'

'No, I didn't know.'

'I'm sorry you've had a wasted trip.'

'When did this happen?'

'Last week. You should have been told.' But there was no reason why I should have been told, as I wasn't a relative.

'Does her daughter know?' I asked.

'Her family and social worker would have been informed.'

'Which hospital is she in?'

'I think it's the City Hospital. If you wait here a moment, I'll check in the office.'

'Thank you.'

Worried, I wondered what was the matter with Amanda that required her being in hospital. Mrs Bennett stayed by the door, hoping it might open again. The care assistant reappeared; she hadn't been gone long. 'I'm sorry,' she said, a little embarrassed. 'I've just spoken to my manager and I can't give you details of the hospital because of patient confidentiality. Only close relatives can have that information.'

'I understand,' I said. 'Thank you anyway.'

With another apology she let me out and I returned to my car. I didn't start the engine but sat gazing through the windscreen. I hadn't asked the care assistant what was the matter with Amanda, as I knew patient confidentiality would have forbidden her telling me that too. I thought it was odd that Dana hadn't said anything to me about Amanda being ill, or was it? She didn't know I still visited Amanda and I could see why she hadn't told Melody partway through the introductory period in case it unsettled her. Amanda's social worker would have presumably passed on the information to Neave, but again there was no reason for her to have told me. I sat for a few moments longer. The care assistant had said she thought Amanda was in the City Hospital. I made the decision to drive there now and hope someone on reception would be able to tell me which ward Amanda was in – if indeed she was there at all.

It took me ten minutes to drive to the neighbouring town and then I followed the signs to the City Hospital. It was 1.30 by the time I'd parked, fed the meter and placed the ticket on the windscreen. I didn't know the hospital at all; parts of it were new and there was still building work going on. I went through the glass revolving door of the main entrance and to the reception desk, behind which sat two elderly gentlemen. Many reception desks in NHS hospitals are staffed by volunteers, and they do an excellent job. It was busy. I waited my turn and then asked which ward Amanda was in, giving her full name. The man attending to me began looking through a long printout. 'When was she admitted?' he asked, so I started to think that maybe she wasn't there.

'Last week. Sorry, I don't know the exact day.'

He continued through the list. 'Here it is,' he said at last, pleased. 'She's in Beech Ward.'

'Thank you so much.'

'Straight down this corridor to the end,' he said. 'Then take the lift or stairs to the second floor. Visiting is from two o'clock, but they might let you in early.'

I thanked him again and began along the main corridor as he'd directed. With fifteen minutes before the start of visiting time, I stopped off at the hospital shop and bought a packet of juice, which I drank sitting on one of the benches just outside the shop. Dropping the empty carton into the bin provided, I continued up the stairs to the second floor, then followed the signs to Beech Ward. Sanitizing my hands from the dispenser, I went in. The ward corridor stretched ahead of me and then curved round out of view. I had no idea which bed Amanda was in, so I went to the nurses' station and asked there.

'Side room three,' the nurse replied. 'On your left, about halfway down.'

Thanking her, I went in the direction she'd pointed, passing four bedded wards as I went. Then on my left were the side rooms, 1, 2 and 3. I looked through the glass panel of the door marked 3 but could only see that someone was in bed, nothing more. Another hand sanitizer was beside the door, and having again rubbed a little of the foam into my hands, I knocked on the door and went in. For a moment I thought I'd come into the wrong room.

I've found before when visiting friends or family in hospital that they often look very different. Propped up on a mound of white pillows, hair flattened from lying in bed and in their nightwear rather than day clothes, they often appear more poorly then they feel. But nothing could have prepared me for Amanda's decline. Lying flat on her back with her arms straight at her sides, her eyes were closed and she lay perfectly still. Her skin was deathly white, and her face was sunken beyond recognition. Over the top of her hospital gown her collar and neck bones jutted out. She'd always been very thin, but now she was emaciated. I gingerly went over and sat on the chair beside the bed. There'd been a huge change in her in just over two weeks and I dreaded to think what was the matter with her. It must be very serious; she looked awful.

She had a drip dispensing fluid attached to her arm and a urine drainage bag hung from the side of the bed. I sat for some moments watching her as her chest lightly rose and fell – it was the only sign she was alive. I didn't know if she was in a deep sleep, unconscious or sedated. I was reluctant to wake her, for she wouldn't know who I was. She hadn't recognized me (or Melody) for some time. Not sure what to do for the best, I continued to sit beside her and then took the box of cakes and grapes from the bag and set them on the bedside cabinet. She clearly wasn't up to eating them now, but hopefully when she felt better she would be. I left the potted plant in my carrier bag, as I knew that NHS hospitals didn't allow flowers and plants on the ward for fear of them bringing in disease or triggering allergies. I wondered if Amanda had any of her belongings with her from the care home and I opened her bedside cabinet. It contained a pair of slacks, a jumper and shoes – presumably the clothes she'd been wearing when she'd been admitted to hospital – but that was all. Perhaps her washbag was in the bathroom. I quietly closed the cabinet door.

Another five minutes or so passed as Amanda slept on. The window was open a fraction and through it came the distant sounds of building works from another part of the site. Suddenly the door opened and a nurse came in, making me start. She seemed surprised to see anyone here. 'Oh, sorry, I didn't know Amanda had a visitor,' she said. 'I really need to change her. Could I ask you to wait outside for a few minutes?'

'I was going soon anyway,' I said. I stood and she wheeled in a treatment trolley. There didn't seem a lot of point in waiting. 'What's the matter with Amanda?' I asked as she pushed the trolley to the bed.

'You'll need to ask the ward sister or her doctor,' she replied.

I thanked her and came out. I didn't go to find the ward sister or a doctor, as I knew the same patient confidentially would apply as it had at the care home – with only close relatives being given information on the patient. I returned to my car. Clearly Amanda was very poorly and I wondered if Dana knew just how ill she was. I guessed from the nurse's reaction to my being there, and the fact that Amanda was wearing a hospital gown and my cakes and fruit were the only items that had been brought in, that she hadn't had many visitors, if any at all. It upset me to think of her lying there in that impersonal hospital gown. They are usually only used for emergency admissions before relatives have the chance to bring in the patient's own nightwear, washbag and any personal items they might need. I wondered when Dana was thinking of bringing Melody and I decided to phone her later.

It was 3.30 when I arrived home and Dana would be collecting Melody from school now. At the end of her first day in her new school they'd have plenty to talk about, so I decided to wait until Melody was likely to be in bed before phoning. At nine o'clock, with my family in other parts of the house, showering, reading and listening to music, I sat in the living room with Toscha beside me and keyed in Dana's number.

'Hello?' she answered quietly.

'Dana, it's Cathy.'

'Oh, hi. I didn't expect to hear from you yet.'

'No, I'm sorry to disturb you, but I wanted to ask you about Amanda. I visited her today.'

'That was nice of you. I was planning to take Melody in a couple of weeks.'

'Yes, I thought that's what you said, but I wondered if you knew how ill she really was. She seemed very poorly to me.'

'Oh dear. I am sorry to hear that. So her dementia has progressed rapidly?'

'I don't know. She slept the whole time I was there. Do you know what's the matter with her?'

I heard Dana's hesitation before she said, 'Sorry, Cathy, I don't understand. I thought you knew Amanda had dementia.'

'Yes. I meant the reason for her being in hospital.'

'She's in hospital?'

'Didn't you know?'

'No, no one's thought to tell me.'

'I'm so sorry. The assistant I spoke to at the care home said you'd been informed, or rather she said Amanda's family would have been informed, so I assumed that meant Melody and you.'

I heard her sigh. 'No, we weren't told, but we certainly should have been. Can you imagine if I'd taken Melody to the care home to find her mother was ill in hospital? What a shock that would have been for her! Sometimes our [the social services'] information sharing isn't what it should be.' I couldn't disagree. 'Do you know what's the matter with Amanda?' Dana now asked me.

'No, but she's very pale and has lost a lot of weight. She's on a drip. I stayed for about twenty minutes and she didn't wake at all, not even when the nurse came in to change her.'

'I can't phone anyone tonight, it's too late, but as soon as I've taken Melody to school tomorrow morning I'll find out what's going on.'

'Will you tell me, please? I know I'm not family, but I feel I've got to know Amanda quite well.'

'Yes, of course. I'll phone you as soon as I've found out anything.'

'Thank you. How was Melody's first day at her new school?'

'Good. Although I was quite emotional taking her in. I never thought I'd be seeing my child into school. I'm so lucky to have her.'

'Melody is very lucky to have you too,' I said.

It was mid-afternoon the following day before Dana returned my call. It came just after Jill had telephoned about a child the social services might be bringing into care and for whom they'd need an experienced foster carer.

'It's not good news,' Dana said, her voice flat. 'Amanda has terminal cancer.'

CHAPTER TWENTY-EIGHT

FAMILY

I cried after Dana's call, and again later that night when I was alone in bed. Not only for Amanda, who'd had a difficult and unrewarding life, but also for Melody, who instead of embracing her new life with her adoptive mother would shortly be mourning the death of her birth mother. Dana had said that Amanda had stopped eating at the care home and had been taken to the hospital for tests, but the cancer had spread. She was already very frail, and the doctors had given her weeks rather than months to live. It was a huge shock. Of some consolation was that Melody had Dana, otherwise she would have been an orphan. Also, a part of me felt that perhaps passing quickly from cancer was preferable to a lingering and dehumanizing death from dementia. But it was only a small consolation. How dearly I wished Amanda's life could have been different.

Dana didn't yet know if and how often she should take Melody to see Amanda. She was going to discuss it with Neave, who was still involved until the adoption went through. Jill phoned and said that the child I'd been put on standby to take had gone to live with a relative instead, so I wasn't needed for now. I took the opportunity to visit Amanda again that week. I didn't take any food – there was no point, as she wasn't eating – but I did take a little Christmas angel I'd seen while out shopping. With Christmas only four weeks away, the shops were full of festive goods and indeed I had started my Christmas shopping. The angel was about three inches tall and made from porcelain, with a long, white silky dress and delicate wings. She had a beautiful smile on her face, peaceful and serene, and I felt that if angels were real then they would surely be like her.

Amanda was the same as at my first visit on Monday, the only movement the slight rise and fall of her chest. I placed the angel on her bedside cabinet so she was watching over her. A greetings card now stood open on the cabinet, and on the front of the card was printed, *Thinking of You*. Inside someone had written, 'Love, Beth'. I didn't know who Beth was, but I thought it was nice that someone else had visited Amanda or at least sent her a card. I stayed for about half an hour, then kissed Amanda's forehead and came away. Later, I telephoned Dana and told her I'd visited Amanda and there was no change. Dana said she was planning on taking Melody to see her on Saturday afternoon and was trying to prepare her for seeing her mother so ill.

Late Saturday evening, Dana telephoned and said Melody was in bed now but had been very upset at seeing her mother, although Dana had tried to get her to focus on how peaceful she was now. We agreed it was a lot for a child to cope with. Dana said they'd seen my angel on the bedside cabinet and she'd told Melody it was from me. Melody had said, 'Mummy and Cathy were good friends,' which choked me up. Dana said she'd take Melody again the following weekend, but only if she asked to go, as it had been so upsetting for her. I said I was planning to visit Amanda again on Tuesday, assuming a child hadn't arrived as an emergency in the interim.

It wasn't to be.

Around midday on Monday, Dana telephoned to say that Amanda had passed away in her sleep in the early hours of Sunday morning. This was sooner than the doctors had predicted but Amanda's heart, already weak from years of drug abuse, had given up and just stopped beating. Melody was at school, so Dana would have to tell her when she collected her that afternoon. I said I was so very sorry, thanked her for telling me and asked her to let me know if there was anything I could do. I put down the phone and cried.

It was a sad day and I found myself tearing up regularly. Foster carers don't just look after the child; they often get to know their family and bond with them. I thought of Amanda and felt Melody's loss. That evening when I told my children Amanda had passed they felt Melody's loss too although they'd never met Amanda. No amount of training can prepare carers for times like this. Fostering affects the whole family in ways you don't always anticipate. When I told my parents of Amanda's passing they were sorry.

At 10 p.m. that Monday, the phone rang and my first thought was that it was my fostering agency with a child that needed an emergency placement. However, it was Dana. 'Sorry it's late, Cathy. Are you still up?'

'Yes.'

'Melody wanted to talk to you. Is that all right?'

'Yes, of course.'

'She's been very brave. She thinks talking to you might help her, as you knew Amanda.'

303

'Yes, put her on.' I took a deep breath. I needed to hold it together for Melody's sake.

'Hello, love,' I said as she picked up the phone.

'My mummy's died,' she said, her voice slight.

'I know, love, I'm so sorry. You'll miss her dreadfully. I feel sad too.'

'She liked you. She told me at contact when she could still talk that she liked you. I'm glad you were friends.'

'So am I, love.' I swallowed hard.

'I know she got angry with you sometimes, but she was like that with everyone. She didn't mean it. She was pleased you were looking after me. She said if I had to go into care, she was glad it was with you.'

'That's good.' My eyes filled. 'She's at peace now.'

'Cathy, do you think she's with the angels, even though she wasn't a good mummy?' My heart clenched and I stifled a sob.

'Yes. Definitely. She did her best to look after you. She loved you. Don't blame her for what happened. Try to remember the good times.'

'Yes. That's what my new mummy says,' and she passed the phone back to Dana.

It was a few moments before I could speak. I didn't feel I'd been much help, but it seemed that Melody just wanted to talk to someone who'd known her mother, which was understandable. I told Dana that if she or Melody wanted to talk they could telephone me whatever the time, for it occurred to me that this was a lot for Dana to cope with too, so soon after Melody had moved in. I also asked her to let me know when the funeral was, as I wanted to go.

* * *

I spoke to Dana a few times during the next two weeks. Amanda's cremation, arranged by the local council, was set for 2 p.m. on the 17th of December, at a small crematorium about a twenty-minute drive from my house. I learned from Dana that Amanda's other children, all adopted as infants and now adults, had been contacted and informed that Amanda was terminally ill and then again that she'd passed. One of them, Beth, had been planning on making contact with her birth mother prior to her death, fifteen years after being adopted, when she'd got the call to say she was in hospital. She'd visited her and had left the card I'd seen and would be at her funeral. Dana didn't know who else would be there.

By the 17th of December our house, like many others, was decorated ready for Christmas, although I'm sure the lights shone less brightly on the morning of Amanda's funeral. I was fostering a nine-year-old boy and, aware I was unlikely to be back from the funeral in time to collect him from school, I'd asked another carer if she could collect him and look after him until I returned. She was happy to do so – carers often help each other out, and doubtless I would return the favour at some point.

It was a crisp, cold morning with a wintry sun low in the sky. I took my lad to school, returned home, made a few phone calls and then changed into a black skirt, top and jacket and set off in the car. The high street was festively decorated. Dana had told me theirs was too. I could imagine it looked very pretty. She'd told me she had been planning to wait until after the funeral to decorate their house, but Melody had wanted to do it earlier. It would be Melody's first proper Christmas, as she'd come to me in January, and I knew how much she was looking forward to it. They were travelling to the crematorium that morning and would return home after the service. It had been decided at the adoption planning meeting that my children and I would visit them over the Christmas holidays, but I doubted that would happen now.

I arrived in the small crematorium car park with fifteen minutes to spare. About six other cars were there, including Dana's, but no one was in them. The doors to the chapel were open, so I assumed the mourners were going in as they arrived. I didn't know what format the service would take other than it was a cremation. I walked in through the vestibule and one of the crematorium staff handed me a white order-of-service sheet. Amanda's name was printed on the front and beneath that her date of birth and death. I went down the centre aisle and slid into an empty pew. Amanda's wooden coffin was in place on the elevated plinth at the front. About a dozen or so mourners were already here – more than I'd anticipated. I saw Dana and Melody, chief mourners, sitting in the very front pew, and in the pew to my left was the manager of the care home. She recognized me, nodded and smiled. Melody turned and saw me and whispered something to Dana who motioned for me to come forward to join them as head mourners and next of kin. I was touched.

'Thanks for coming,' Dana said quietly as I slid in next to Melody. 'Nice to see a familiar face.'

Melody snuggled between us but didn't say anything. The poor kid must have been completely overwhelmed. 'Paula, Lucy and Adrian send their love,' I told her quietly.

During the next few minutes, other mourners arrived and I wondered who they were. Then the music faded and the reverend went to the front of the chapel to start the service.

The congregation fell silent and everyone looked to him. He began by saying that we were here to celebrate the life and mourn the passing of Amanda, and that while he hadn't had the privilege of knowing her personally, he had spoken to those who had looked after her at the care home where she spent the last six months of her life. He gave her date of birth and said that Amanda hadn't had an easy life but was at peace now and that God welcomed everyone to his flock. As we stood for the first hymn, Melody slid her hand into mine and I gave it a little reassuring squeeze. She was already holding Dana's hand and she continued to hold our hands throughout the service. She was very brave; to be honest, I don't think she fully understood what was going on. What child of her age would? It was the first funeral she'd been to. All she knew was that her mother was dead and this was a final goodbye. It was only when the reverend spoke the committal – 'To everything there is a season ... a time to be born and a time to die ...' – and the velvet curtains began to close around Amanda's coffin that Melody realized the finality of what was happening.

'Is Mummy going now?' she quietly asked Dana.

'Yes, love.'

And her tears fell.

Dana put her arm around her and held her close as the curtains drew together and the coffin was no longer in view. Organ music began softly in the background again, and presently the mourners stood and left the chapel. I sat with Melody and Dana until our tears subsided.

'You've done very well,' she told Melody, wiping her eyes.

'Very,' I agreed, wiping mine.

We stood and slowly left.

As often happens after a funeral, most of the mourners were gathered outside in small groups and talking quietly. Again I wondered who all these people were. The manager of the care home came over and said how sorry she was for Melody's loss, but she had to leave now, as she was needed at work. I thanked her for all she'd done for Amanda. It wasn't really my role, but there was no one else to thank her. She told Melody the occupational therapist sent her best wishes and was sorry to hear of her mother's passing, which was very thoughtful. I supposed the staff at the care home would miss Amanda as they had Mr Wilson and Mr Bennett and the other residents who'd passed. As she left, a young man I guessed to be in his twenties came over with a middle-aged couple.

'Are you Melody?' he asked. Melody gave a small nod. 'I'm Jamie, one of your brothers.' He offered his hand for shaking.

Dana recovered first. 'Hello, lovely to meet you, Jamie. I'm Dana, Melody's adoptive mother, and this is Cathy. She fostered Melody before she came to me.'

'Great to meet you, Jamie,' I said, and we shook hands.

'These are my parents,' he said, and introduced the couple with him – his adoptive parents. Melody was staring at Jamie, completely overwhelmed.

'I'm sorry about your loss, darling,' Jamie's mother said to Melody. 'You knew your birth mother. Jamie can't remember her, he just has a photograph of her, but he wanted to come to her funeral to pay his respects.'

'That's nice,' Dana said. 'I didn't know Amanda, but Cathy did.'

'I used to take Melody to see her at the care home,' I told

Jamie and his parents. 'The last time I saw Amanda, in hospital, she was sleeping and very peaceful.'

'That's good to know,' Jamie said. 'Thank you.' He seemed a lovely lad. Clearly his parents had done a good job, but of course he and the other siblings had been spared the turmoil of Melody's early years.

'Have you met Beth and the others?' he now asked us.

'No,' Dana said. 'Are all Melody's brothers and sisters here?'

'Yes. Some of us have been in touch before, but we've never all been together like this. It's amazing.' Jamie looked around and signalled to the others to come over. The previously sombre mood of the funeral began to lift.

'We're going to make sure we stay in touch,' Jamie's mother said.

'Absolutely,' Dana agreed, and delved into her handbag for a pen and paper.

'Here's Beth,' Jamie said as a young woman in her twenties came over together with her parents.

'My little sister?' she said to Melody. 'Hi!' And kissed Melody's cheek. For the first time that day Melody smiled, so did I.

'And this is Kim and Tom.'

Before long all of Melody's extended family – half-siblings and their parents; in fact, virtually everyone who'd been at the service – had gathered in a circle around us and were swapping telephone numbers. Melody was smiling, but she also looked a bit bewildered. As the youngest, she was enjoying all the attention. As we talked I learned that none of the other siblings had any memory of Amanda, but they all had at least one photograph of her.

After a while I decide it was time for me to leave. I had a child to collect and this had turned into a family occasion, so I said goodbye and slipped away. The hum of conversation followed me to my car. I got in and sat looking through the windscreen at the family gathering outside the chapel, all talking happily. Tears filled my eyes, but not from sadness. It had taken over twenty years and Amanda's funeral to bring her children together. I knew if she was looking down how pleased she'd be to see them reunited at last. Rest in peace, Amanda, your children are happy and well cared for. There is nothing for you to worry about now.

For the latest on Melody and the other children in my books, please visit www.cathyglass.co.uk.

SUGGESTED TOPICS FOR
READING-GROUP DISCUSSION

At the start of the book, when Cathy is told the reasons for bringing Melody into care, she says she has 'heard it all before'. Why do you think that drug and alcohol dependency, resulting in a child being neglected, is so prevalent now?

Despite Melody's anger and 'feral' behaviour, she quickly settles with Cathy and becomes an integrated member of her family. How is this achieved?

What indications are there early on in the book that Amanda has been relying heavily on her daughter? As the story unfolds, what do we learn of their interdependent roles?

Cathy makes a point of meeting the staff at Melody's school soon after she arrives. Why do you think this is important?

Amanda vents her anger at Cathy at contact. Why? And what, if anything, could the Family Centre staff have done to defuse the situation?

Discuss the possible short- and long-term effects of a parent not attending contact.

From readers' comments on Cathy's website and social media, many readers feel they are there with Cathy and her family as part of the story. Discuss how the narrative achieves this?

Discuss the role of a LAC (Looked After Child) review. Would you make any changes to improve them?

After Amanda is sectioned under the Mental Health Act, Cathy pushes for Melody to have contact with her again. Was she right to do so? Are there any indications later in the book that she might have regretted it? How beneficial was contact at the care home for Melody and her mother?

When contact is reduced in preparation for Melody's move to her adoptive mother, Cathy continues to see Amanda. What are her reasons?

Discuss the timetable of introduction for the move. Would you change anything?

When Melody has reservations about a 'forever family', Lucy, speaking from her heart, reassures her and says, 'You want to be like all the other kids at school.' What insight does Lucy offer?

Cathy says Melody and Dana are a match 'made in heaven'. What can they both bring to their relationship?

Cathy Glass

—

One remarkable woman, more
than **150** foster children cared for.

Cathy Glass has been a foster carer for
twenty-five years, during which time she has
looked after more than 150 children, as well
as raising three children of her own. She was
awarded a degree in education and psychology
as a mature student, and writes under a
pseudonym. To find out more about Cathy
and her story visit **www.cathyglass.co.uk**.

Finding Stevie

Fourteen-year-old Stevie is exploring his gender identity

Like many young people, he spends time online, but Cathy is shocked when she learns his terrible secret.

Where Has Mummy Gone?

When Melody is taken into care, she fears her mother won't cope alone

It is only when Melody's mother vanishes that what has really been going on at home comes to light.

A Long Way from Home

Abandoned in an orphanage, Anna's future looks bleak until she is adopted

Anna's new parents love her, so why does she end up in foster care?

Cruel to be Kind

Max is shockingly overweight and struggles to make friends

Cathy faces a challenge to help this unhappy boy.

Nobody's Son

Born in prison and brought up in care, Alex has only ever known rejection

He is longing for a family of his own, but again the system fails him.

Can I Let You Go?

Faye is 24, pregnant and has learning difficulties as a result of her mother's alcoholism

Can Cathy help Faye learn enough to parent her child?

The Silent Cry

A mother battling depression. A family in denial

Cathy is desperate to help before something terrible happens.

Girl Alone

An angry, traumatized young girl on a path to self-destruction

Can Cathy discover the truth behind Joss's dangerous behaviour before it's too late?

Saving Danny

Danny's parents can no longer cope with his challenging behaviour

Calling on all her expertise, Cathy discovers a frightened little boy who just wants to be loved.

The Child Bride

A girl blamed and abused for
dishonouring her community

Cathy discovers the
devastating truth.

Daddy's Little Princess

A sweet-natured girl with
a complicated past

Cathy picks up the pieces after
events take a dramatic turn.

Will You Love Me?

A broken child desperate
for a loving home

The true story of Cathy's
adopted daughter Lucy.

Please Don't Take My Baby

Seventeen-year-old Jade is
pregnant, homeless and alone

Cathy has room in her heart
for two.

Another Forgotten Child

Eight-year-old Aimee was on the child-protection register at birth

Cathy is determined to give her the happy home she deserves.

A Baby's Cry

A newborn, only hours old, taken into care

Cathy protects tiny Harrison from the potentially fatal secrets that surround his existence.

The Night the Angels Came

A little boy on the brink of bereavement

Cathy and her family make sure Michael is never alone.

Mummy Told Me Not to Tell

A troubled boy sworn to secrecy

After his dark past has been revealed, Cathy helps Reece to rebuild his life.

I Miss Mummy

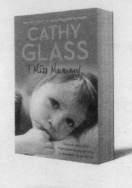

Four-year-old Alice doesn't understand why she's in care

Cathy fights for her to have the happy home she deserves.

The Saddest Girl in the World

A haunted child who refuses to speak

Do Donna's scars run too deep for Cathy to help?

Cut

Dawn is desperate to be loved

Abused and abandoned, this vulnerable child pushes Cathy and her family to their limits.

Hidden

The boy with no past

Can Cathy help Tayo to feel like he belongs again?

Damaged

A forgotten child

Cathy is Jodie's last hope. For the first time, this abused young girl has found someone she can trust.

Run, Mummy, Run

The gripping story of a woman caught in a horrific cycle of abuse, and the desperate measures she must take to escape.

My Dad's a Policeman

The dramatic short story about a young boy's desperate bid to keep his family together.

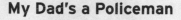

The Girl in the Mirror

Trying to piece together her past, Mandy uncovers a dreadful family secret that has been blanked from her memory for years.

About Writing
and How to Publish

A clear, concise, practical
guide on writing and the best
ways to get published.

Happy Mealtimes
for Kids

A guide to healthy eating
with simple recipes that
children love.

Happy Adults

A practical guide to achieving lasting
happiness, contentment and success.
The essential manual for getting
the best out of life.

Happy Kids

A clear and concise guide to
raising confident, well-behaved
and happy children.

Be amazed
Be moved
Be inspired

———

If you loved this book
why not join Cathy on
facebook and **twitter** ?

Cathy will share updates on the children
from her books and on those she's currently
fostering – plus, you'll be the first to know
as soon as her new books hit the shops!

Join her now

f /cathy.glass.180

t @CathyGlassUK